FISH
— of the —
ROCKIES
Including Best Fishing Sites

Michael G. Sullivan
David L. Propst
William R. Gould
with contributions from
Amanda Joynt & Krista Kagume

Lone Pine Publishing

The Publisher: Lone Pine Publishing
10145 – 81 Avenue
Edmonton, AB T6E 1W9 Canada

1808 B Street NW, Suite 140
Auburn, WA, USA 98001

Website: www.lonepinepublishing.com

Library and Archives Canada Cataloguing in Publication

Sullivan, Michael G. (Michael Gary), 1958-   Fish of the Rockies : including best fishing sites / Michael G. Sullivan, David L. Propst, William R. Gould ; with contributions from Amanda Joynt & Krista Kagume.

Includes bibliographical references and index. ISBN 978-1-55105-396-7

    1. Fishes--Rocky Mountains. 2. Fishes--Rocky Mountains-- Identification. 3. Fish watching--Rocky Mountains--Guidebooks. 4. Fishing--Rocky Mountains--Guidebooks. 5. Rocky Mountains-- Guidebooks. I. Propst, David L. II. Joynt, Amanda, 1977- III. Kagume, Krista IV. Gould, William R., 1931- V. Title.

SH462.S92 2009   597.0978   C2009-901221-9

Editorial Director: Nancy Foulds
Project Editors: Gary Whyte, Nicholle Carriére, Genevieve Boyer, Wendy Pirk, Krista
    Kagume, Sheila Quinlan
Production Manager: Gene Longson
Design and Layout: Volker Bodegom, Rob Tao
Maps: Volker Bodegom
Cover Design: Gerry Dotto

Illustration and Photo Credits: All photography and illustration credits are on page 4, which is a continuation of this copyright page.

We acknowledge the financial support of the Government of Canada through the Book Publishing Industry Development Program (BPIDP) for our publishing activities.

PC: 16

CONTENTS

ACKNOWLEDGEMENTS

We would like to thank Harry Vermillion, Colorado Division of Wildlife, Wildlife Research Centre for the use of range map information from the Aquatic Data Management System. Further thanks go to Bill Elmblad, Jim Melby, Greg Polisky and James Romero of the Colorado Department of Wildlife, Fisheries Department. Thanks also to D. Miller and D. Weitzel of the Wyoming Fish and Game Department; and Richard Wallace, Professor Emeritus, University of Idaho for information on range maps and life history. Also, a thank you is extended to Bill Horton, State Fisheries Manager of the Idaho Department of Fish and Game for his assistance with our Idaho fishing sites information.

Krista would like to dedicate this book to Toby and to future generations of fishermen.

To the many people who have helped us produce this book, thank you. Finally, a special thank you to all who help protect our water systems and the fish that live in them.

ILLUSTRATION & PHOTO CREDITS

Illustration Credits
George Penetrante 43, 47, 49, 51, 53, 55, 57, 59, 61, 71, 77, 81, 83, 85, 89, 93, 95, 101, 103, 105, 107, 117, 119, 139, 141, 143, 149, 153, 155, 157, 163, 165, 167, 171, 177, 181, 191, 192, 193a&b, 194, 195. Ian Sheldon 11abc&d, 12ab&c, 13abc&d, 17, 19, 36, 37a&b, 38ab&c, 39, 41, 45, 63, 65, 67, 69, 73, 75, 79, 87, 91, 97, 99, 109, 111, 113, 115, 121, 123, 125, 127, 129, 131, 133, 135, 137, 145, 147, 151, 159, 161, 169, 173, 175, 176, 180, 182a, 183, 185, 187, 188a&b. New York State Department of Environmental Conservation 178, 179, 182b.

Photography Credits
The photographs in this book are reproduced with the generous permission of their copyright holders. Allan Bibby 32. Craig Johnson 4, 30, 31. JupiterImages 22, 23a&b, 24, 25, 26. Ian Sheldon 10, 20.

Sturgeons

White Sturgeon
page 40

Minnows

Chiselmouth
page 42

Lake Chub
page 44

Red Shiner
page 46

Common Carp
page 48

Utah Chub
page 50

Leatherside Chub
page 52

Humpback Chub
page 54

Bonytail
page 56

Rio Grande Chub
page 58

Roundtail Chub
page 60

Brassy Minnow
page 62

Peamouth
page 64

Fathead Minnow
page 66

Minnows

Flathead Chub
page 68

Colorado Pikeminnow
page 70

Northern Pikeminnow
page 72

Longnose Dace
page 74

Speckled Dace
page 76

Redside Shiner
page 78

Creek Chub
page 80

Suckers

River Carpsucker
page 82

Utah Sucker
page 84

Longnose Sucker
page 86

Bridgelip Sucker
page 88

White Sucker
page 90

Bluehead Sucker
page 92

Flannelmouth Sucker
page 94

Suckers

Largescale Sucker
page 96

Mountain Sucker
page 98

Rio Grande Sucker
page 100

Razorback Sucker
page 102

Catfishes & Pikes

Black Bullhead
page 104

Channel Catfish
page 106

Stonecat
page 108

Northern Pike
page 110

Trouts

Coho Salmon
page 112

Kokanee/Sockeye Salmon
page 114

Chinook Salmon
page 116

Cutthroat Trout
page 118

Trouts

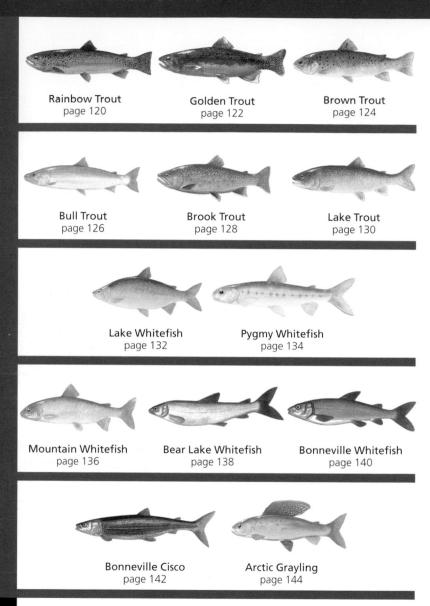

Rainbow Trout
page 120

Golden Trout
page 122

Brown Trout
page 124

Bull Trout
page 126

Brook Trout
page 128

Lake Trout
page 130

Lake Whitefish
page 132

Pygmy Whitefish
page 134

Mountain Whitefish
page 136

Bear Lake Whitefish
page 138

Bonneville Whitefish
page 140

Bonneville Cisco
page 142

Arctic Grayling
page 144

Cods & Livebearers

Burbot
page 146

Western Mosquitofish
page 148

Sticklebacks

Brook Stickleback
page 150

Sculpins

Prickly Sculpin
page 152

Mottled Sculpin
page 154

Paiute Sculpin
page 156

Slimy Sculpin
page 158

Shorthead Sculpin
page 160

Bear Lake Sculpin
page 162

Wood River Sculpin
page 164

Torrent Sculpin
page 166

Spoonhead Sculpin
page 168

Sunfishes

Green Sunfish
page 170

Perches

Yellow Perch
page 172

Walleye
page 174

INTRODUCTION

A White Sucker rests camouflaged in its lakeside habitat.

Whether you find yourself boating on a turquoise cirque lake in Canada or hiking next to a sparkling stream in the southern United States, the rugged peaks and colorful formations of the Rocky Mountains will likely draw your attention upward. Surrounded by this majestic mountain landscape, the amazing things that await your discovery in the underwater realm may easily be forgotten. But the cold slap of a fish's body re-entering the water can suddenly snatch your eyesight away from the towering mountains, and the lingering ripples remind you that Mother Nature does not stop at the water's surface. We rarely think about the aquatic world, yet there is a meaningful connection between us and the fishes. Many of us were introduced to fishes with a small net and pail in our hands, catching "minnows" to watch them swim confused around their new world until we released them back to the wild. Watching a fish gliding through a backyard pond or aquarium is easily mesmerizing, but watching a fish in its natural environment is often even more intriguing.

This book is for anyone who appreciates fishes and wants to learn more about them. Anglers, boaters and nature enthusiasts will appreciate having this book in their collection. The introduction discusses fish biology, describes some of the challenges facing fishes in the mountains, and shows you how to identify fishes. This book includes familiar sport fish, of course, but goes beyond them to introduce you to the not-so-well-known fishes that are also part of the underwater Rocky Mountain world and their remarkable biology and life history. We let you know some of the best places to fish and also introduce you to other ways of appreciating these fascinating animals. The species accounts that follow describe in detail the lives of 68 species found in the Rocky Mountains, and 53 other notable species are included in the appendix.

IDENTIFYING FISHES

One of the first things you will want to do after spotting a fish is determine what species it is. Knowing the species of a fish opens the door to information about its food preferences, spawning habits and general biology. You may make some exciting discoveries. If you think you have found a species outside the range that is shown in this book, get some pictures of it or draw a quick sketch if you can.

Plenty of confusion surrounds the use of the words "fish" and "fishes." If more than one species of fish is being discussed, scientists use the term "fishes." If more than one individual of the same species is the topic, for example, two Burbot, they say "two fish."

Biologists will be interested to hear of your find, and they will want to be able to verify your identification. Some species, such as White Sturgeon, are rarely found in waters of the Rocky Mountains today, though they once migrated from the Pacific Ocean all the way to the West Slopes.

With the many species that occur in the Rocky Mountains and foothills, determining the species of the fish you hold in your hand may not be an easy task. Humpback Chub and Chiselmouth are pretty distinctive, but identifying a minnow or a sculpin species can be very difficult. Hybrids, between trout species especially, can also make determining the identity of a fish challenging. In most cases, it is possible to accurately determine the species with careful consideration of the physical features discussed here. A description of the families included in this book can be found on page 36. Described below are many of the features that can be found on a fish, but note that not every fish will have all of the features mentioned.

One of the first things to look at is a fish's mouth. Fishes with a **terminal mouth** have upper and lower jaws meeting at the tip of the snout. By contrast, when the upper and lower jaws meet behind the snout, the fish has a **subterminal mouth**. A mouth that is either terminal or subterminal can also be **oblique**, meaning that when looked at in a side view, the mouth angles down from the snout rather than extending horizontally. Fishes that feed on organisms found on the bottom of water bodies sometimes have a **fleshy, ventral mouth**. Both their upper and lower lips are placed on the underside of the head. Sometimes you will see structures that look like whiskers around the fish's mouth. These structures are called **barbels**; they act as "feelers" for fishes that live in darkened or silty water, and they also have a gustatory function. During the spawning

barbel

Terminal mouth of Burbot

Oblique mouth of Mooneye

Subterminal mouth of Longnose Dace

Fleshy, ventral mouth of Longnose Sucker

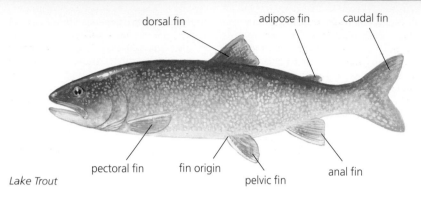

dorsal fin   adipose fin   caudal fin

pectoral fin   fin origin   anal fin

pelvic fin

Lake Trout

season, some members of the trout family, such as Brook Trout and Bull Trout, develop a **kype**, meaning that the upper and lower jaws are enlarged and hooked. This feature often develops in conjunction with increasingly brilliant coloration.

The placement and structure of a fish's fins are two of the most important traits in species identification. The **pectoral fins** are the fins closest to the mouth, and they can be on the side or underside of the fish. **Pelvic fins** are usually just beneath and behind the pectoral fins. Along the fish's back, you will find the **dorsal fin**; some fishes such as perches have two dorsal fins. The **anal fin** is found on the ventral side of the fish, between the pelvic fins and the tail. The fin at the end of the tail is called the **caudal fin**. The end of the caudal fin can be forked or straight, or even asymmetrical, as with the White Sturgeon. The **adipose fin** can be found on members of the trout, bullhead catfish and trout-perch families. It is a small, fleshy, rayless fin that is located opposite the anal fin. **Rays** are the long structures that support most fin membranes. They can be hard and spiky (called **spines**) or soft and branching (called **soft rays**). Sometimes the number, length or type of rays on a fin is used to identify a fish species or sex.

The **lateral line** extends medially along both sides of the fish from the gill covers (**opercula**) to the tail fin. Young fishes in the trout family may develop dark, vertical blotches, or **parr marks**, along the lateral line. Parr marks usually disappear as the fish matures, but on some species, parr marks are retained, albeit faintly, for several years.

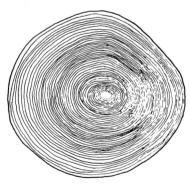

Cycloid scale

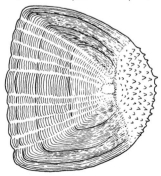

Ctenoid scale

A fish never stops growing; its growth just slows down once it becomes an adult. The number of scales a fish is born with does not change. The scales grow with the fish, developing "growth rings" like a tree.

Two types of scales can be found on the skin of mountain fishes. Most fishes have **cycloid scales**, which are relatively smooth and circular. **Ctenoid scales** are found on more evolutionarily advanced fishes, such as perches. These scales have small spines and make the fish feel rough to the touch. Some of the mountain fishes don't have scales. All of the sculpins, as well as the Stonecat and the Pacific Lamprey, lack scales. The White Sturgeon has what some scientists would call modified scales: two rows of bony plates called **scutes** run along its body to create an armor that no other mountain fish can match.

THE LIVES OF FISHES
LIFE STAGES

Fishes go through a number of stages before they become adults. When they hatch from their eggs, they become **proto-larvae** but still depend on their yolk sacs for nutrition. Once they have absorbed their yolk sacs, the **meso-larval stage** begins, and they are developed enough to capture food on their own.

There are two main strategies to producing young fishes: some species produce relatively few young with a good chance of survival because their habitat is stable and they receive parental care; others produce large numbers of eggs with less chance of survival because of variable habitats and no parental care. Species such as trout follow the first strategy; the few eggs they produce are proportionally large in relation to adult body size (most of the extra bulk is yolk). Larvae of these species tend to have well-developed eyes and mouths and are able to swim efficiently at the beginning of the larval stage. They also have well-developed digestive systems that can extract up to 80 percent of the energy available in their food. Larvae of other species such as suckers, which follow the second strategy, have poorly developed eyes and mouths and swim less efficiently. Despite these shortcomings, they must eat more food because their digestive systems are poorly developed; they can extract only some 20 to 30 percent of the energy from their food. However, because so many young are produced, some individuals are bound to be in the right places at the right times and will successfully grow to maturity.

BULL TROUT	WALLEYE
larva	larva

11.5 mm	4.5 mm
juvenile	juvenile

| 75 mm | 100 mm |

A comparison of the average sizes of Bull Trout and Walleye as just-hatched larvae and as juveniles at the end of their first summer.

The incubation period for each species depends on many factors. Physiologically, fishes that release few eggs have a longer development period than species that release many eggs. To determine the incubation time of a species, fish biologists will raise eggs in the lab at a constant temperature. The number of days it takes the eggs to hatch multiplied by the degrees Celsius of the water is the number of "degree days" for that species. For example, if the eggs in the lab were raised at 20° C and they hatched in five days, then the number of degree days would be 100. With this result, fish biologists can determine how long it will take the eggs to hatch in any water temperature. If the same species of eggs in the wild were in water with a temperature of 10° C, it would take 10 days for them to hatch. This concept explains why there can be such great variation in the length of the incubation period within a species, especially considering the huge variations in latitude and elevation within the Rocky Mountain range.

As with incubation, the length of the larval period varies among species and depends on temperature, but also on food availability and quality. The young are considered **juveniles** when they are basically identical to adults except that their reproductive organs aren't yet mature. Once fishes are capable of breeding, they are considered **adults**. In the species accounts, we focus on the biology of adult fishes because the biology of each stage can be very different. Fishes may eat different food and be found in different habitats at each stage, and it is beyond the scope of this

Because members of the trout family are important to humans, their reproduction has been well studied, and special terminology has developed. These fishes build gravel nests, called **redds***, in which they release their eggs. Young fishes are called* **alevins** *before they have fully absorbed their yolk sacs and are called* **fry** *afterward. Alevins that emerge before their egg sacs disappear are called* **button-up fry***. A juvenile with a series of bars on its sides is called a* **parr** *(the marks are called parr marks).*

book to include information for all life stages. Unless we specifically refer to larvae or juveniles, you can assume that we are discussing the biology of adults.

ACTIVITY PATTERNS

Feeding, followed closely by avoiding being another fish's meal, is a fish's highest priority, and fishes have a variety of anatomical and behavioral feeding adaptations. For example, suckers and sculpins, which are bottom-feeders, have both jaws located on the underside of their bodies. In comparison, species that feed on insects at the surface of the water, such as ciscoes, have their jaws located at the tips of their snouts, and their lower jaws may be longer than their upper jaws. Fishes also have different feeding habits—some carnivores ambush their prey, some are chasers and some create suction to draw animals into their mouths. Fishes may be nocturnal feeders, relying on the cover of darkness to hide from predators, or they may be crepuscular, feeding at dawn or dusk.

Fishes need rest, just like people do. They do not have eyelids, so they cannot close their eyes, but they enter a sleeplike period of deep relaxation in which very few stimuli will disrupt them (they can even be unaware of a diver's presence unless touched). Not surprisingly, most fishes find a place to hide while they are resting.

In winter, the lives of fishes change very little. The water under the ice is between 32° and 40° F (0° and 4° C), and most of the fishes found in the Rockies are so tolerant of cold that such temperatures in winter affect them very little. It is amazing to think that in the mountains, these cold-blooded animals can spawn and be most active at low temperatures, when other ectotherms, such as snakes and amphibians, are motionless lumps. The challenge for mountain fishes at the end of winter can be surviving low-oxygen conditions. When a water body freezes over, the water is effectively sealed off from the atmosphere, and the amount of oxygen present in the water must maintain fishes and other aquatic animals until ice breakup in spring. Plants do not photosynthesize in winter because ice and snow cover blocks out most of the light, although sometimes there is a thin film of algae just under the ice. When oxygen levels are extremely low in late winter, some species, such as the Northern Pike, remain motionless just below the ice, taking advantage of the small amount of oxygen produced by the algae.

Winterkill, caused by lack of oxygen, is most common when a hot summer is followed by an early, snowy winter. In some mountain lakes in the northern Rockies, the shallow water promotes warming over summer, which in turn provides a good environment for algae blooms. The decomposition of algae uses up oxygen. When the lack of photosynthesis in winter is combined with a lot of algae decomposition, all the oxygen can get used up quickly, and fishes may suffocate—in effect, fishes can drown. Most of the time, winterkill is only partial, meaning that a few fishes will survive in special spots of higher oxygen. These surviving fishes can then quickly repopulate the lake. Sometimes, complete winterkills occur. Then the lake depends on fishes swimming up or down creeks to repopulate the system.

Although winterkill is not usually a concern in the lakes of the southern Rocky Mountains, **low nutrient levels** are. Alpine lakes are fed by glaciers and melting snow, which carry few nutrients in their melt waters. As well, because the vegetation at high altitudes is so sparse, woody debris or falling leaves add little organic matter to the water. With few biological inputs, the alpine waters remain low in nutrients, support only a few fish species and make spawning and rearing juveniles difficult.

SPAWNING

The spawning season is an intense time for fishes, often involving extraordinary risks. Some males become very eye-catching in their bright colors, not only to the females that they are trying to impress, but also to predators. The production of eggs and **milt** (the fish equivalent to semen) can require a lot of energy, and fishes that are spawning or searching for mates are often less wary. For salmon, spawning is soon followed by death. Many other mountain species spawn every year or every few years, while the very long-lived White Sturgeon spawns only once every 4 to 11 years.

Fishes have a variety of spawning adaptations, and all methods are designed to keep the eggs healthy and surrounded by clean, oxygen-rich water. Some eggs are semi-buoyant, so that they remain suspended in the water column and do not fall into the bottom of a silty river, and other eggs are adhesive so that they can attach to vegetation or rock surfaces above the suffocating silt of lake and river bottoms. Wave-swept beaches and fast, turbulent water below beaver dams and rapids are other favorite silt-free and oxygen-rich spawning sites. Some species build nests. Nests may be made simply when fishes brush away gravel and silt with their tails, as with trouts. Other species, such as the Brook Stickleback, have intricate nesting behaviors.

Whether a species builds nests or doesn't, the eggs may be taken care of after spawning, usually by the male. He defends the eggs from predators and may also fan them with his tail to make sure they receive enough oxygen or clean them off periodically with his mouth so they don't get coated with silt. Other species abandon their eggs after releasing them.

In a number of species, particularly trouts, males defend territories during the breeding season, and females mate with them within these territories. Larger males are able to bully smaller males out of the best territories, and small males may even be left without any breeding territory. Many small males, such as Coho Salmon "jacks," find ways to continue their lineage by lying in wait and darting out as the female is releasing her eggs. They often

Fishes are the largest group of vertebrates, with about 25,000 living species. They have an incredible diversity of adaptations, from arctic fishes that don't freeze because of antifreeze proteins in their blood to lungfishes that can remain dormant for up to four years in response to drought. Some fishes are capable of producing electricity and light; others can leave the water and glide and fly.

have the opportunity to release milt before territorial males are aware of their presence. Deception in the mating season is not limited to males. A female may wander into a male's territory and grab a free meal of another female's fresh eggs while the male attempts to court her.

In the United States, LeHardy Rapids or Fishing Bridge in Yellowstone National Park, Wyoming, are excellent places to watch spawning Cutthroat Trout. Throughout June and July, a National Park Service ranger is often on duty to explain the spectacular event and answer questions as fish enthusiasts watch the Yellowstone River migration. In the Canadian Rockies, a great place to go is Bill Griffiths Creek near Canmore, Alberta. In November, Brown Trout from the Bow River congregate there, within easy viewing distance of streamside trails.

ADAPTATIONS TO LIFE IN WATER
MOVEMENT
Water is 800 times denser than air, so it is not surprising that many fishes have long, smooth, streamlined bodies that generally taper at the head and tail. Strong muscles along the length of the fish's body, especially in the tail, provide it with the power to propel itself in water. The caudal fin helps to give the tail strokes more power, and the single and paired fins along the fish's body help it with balance and steering. In addition, as anyone who has handled a fish would know, fishes' bodies are covered in mucus. Mucus reduces friction from movement in the water, waterproofs the fish and helps protect the fish from parasites and disease. Human skin is only semi-waterproof. We know our skin is not waterproof because after spending too long in water our skin shrivels like a prune. This peculiarity is caused by tiny amounts of water leaking in and swelling up our skin. Maybe if humans had a good mucous covering, we wouldn't get prune-skin when we swim.

Just as atmospheric pressure is greater at sea level than it is at the top of a mountain, water pressure increases with increasing depth. Many fish species have adaptations to maintain neutral buoyancy in the water so

that they don't have to expend too much energy to stay at a particular depth. These fishes have a **swim bladder**, which is a flexible, gas-filled organ. Species that inhabit relatively shallow water have a duct that connects the swim bladder to the gut, and they swallow air at the surface to fill the swim bladder. Species that frequent deeper water have a different mechanism whereby gas from the blood enters and exits the swim bladder at a structure called the **gas gland**. When a fish descends in the water column, the increased pressure on the fish from the water surrounding it causes the gas in the bladder to compress. More gas diffuses into the swim bladder, keeping the fish buoyant. Conversely, when the fish moves upward in the water column, the decreased pressure on the fish causes the gas to expand, and excess gas diffuses out of the swim bladder back into the blood. The gas is then used by the body or removed from the blood at the gills. When fishes are swimming, they change depth slowly enough that the gas bladder has time to pressurize, but if some species of deepwater fishes, especially spiny-rayed fishes such as Walleye and Yellow Perch, are pulled up too fast by anglers, the bladder can grow to a lethal size and compress the kidney or rupture itself. Soft-rayed fishes such as trouts and whitefishes have a special connection between the swim bladder and their mouths to allow for rapid pressure changes and are not as severely affected as their spiny-finned relatives.

BREATHING
Another challenge facing these aquatic animals is that water contains only 10 parts per million or less of oxygen compared to about 200,000 parts per million in air. As a result, fishes have evolved a highly efficient way of absorbing oxygen. They are able to remove about 80 percent of the oxygen in water, whereas humans remove only 10 to 20 percent of the oxygen in air. A fish takes water in through its mouth and closes its throat to push the water out through its **gills**. Inside each gill is a network of very thin-walled capillaries. In the capillaries, blood flows in the opposite direction of the water. As a

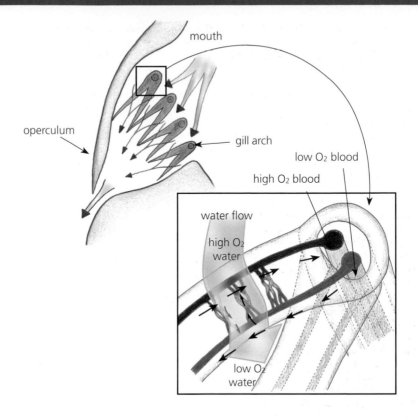

mouth

operculum

gill arch

low O₂ blood

high O₂ blood

water flow

high O₂ water

low O₂ water

result, the water always comes into contact with blood that has lower oxygen concentration than the water. Molecules always move from an area of high concentration to an area of low concentration, so the oxygen moves from the water to the blood. The carbon dioxide that is left over from respiration passes from the blood, where it is in high concentration, to the water. A bony gill cover, the **operculum**, protects the gills on the exterior of the fish, and long, thin, fleshy **gill rakers** block out particles drawn in with the water that may harm the delicate gill tissue. In some species, the gill rakers are also used for filter-feeding. Fish-lovers must be very careful to avoid harming a fish's gills. Fish hooks or a misplaced finger can easily damage these delicate and critical organs, leaving the poor fish hemorrhaging or with impaired breathing.

THE SENSES

The animal kingdom is divided into **vertebrates** (animals with a spinal column) and **invertebrates** (animals without a spinal column). Like us, fishes are vertebrates. Overall, their sensory systems are similar to ours, but in some ways, they are very different.

Because the eyes of fishes bulge out of their heads and because of the way that the lens is positioned in the eyes, they are able to focus close up when they are looking forward and far away when they look out to the side. Fishes have the luxury of both binocular depth perception, which helps them to know exactly how far away a prey item or obstacle in front of them is, and the ability to watch for predators on both sides of their bodies at once. Most fishes can see in color, although the Goldeye that lives in very silty rivers of central North America trades color vision for excellent low light vision and can see only in black and white. The range of colors that fishes see depends on the depth of the water they are in. Red wavelengths are absorbed close to the surface of the water, while ultraviolet light can penetrate as far down as 330 ft (100 m) in a clear, calm lake. Fishes that inhabit very deep water or very silty water must rely more on their other senses to find food and detect predators. The Stonecat makes its home in the murky waters of the Madison and Missouri rivers in Montana and must feel around with its barbels to make up for the poor visibility in its watery home.

Fishes sense taste in much the same way that humans do, but the location of their taste buds is not limited to their mouths. Taste buds can also be located on "lips," barbels, fins and even skin. Fishes smell with the **nares** located at the tips of their snouts and can often determine on which side of their bodies a substance is more concentrated. In addition to helping fishes find prey, the sense of smell is important for detecting **pheromones** (hormones released into the environment that produce a response in individuals of the same species), which are particularly important in the spawning season. Sense of smell is also thought to direct fishes during spawning migrations.

Water is an excellent conductor of sound. You may have noticed when you put your head underwater that sounds seem different—sound vibrations travel farther and faster in water. As vibrations move through the water, they move the water back and forth, and the body of a fish naturally moves with the water. Three ear stones, called **otoliths**, in the fish's inner ear sense these movements in a similar way that our ear ossicles sense the sound that is channeled to our eardrums. High frequency sounds, however, are not easily picked up by movements of the body because water is displaced less by high frequencies. Fishes with swim bladders can detect high frequencies better than fishes without swim bladders because the air in the swim bladder pulsates in response to sound. These pulsations vibrate the body tissues of the fish, and the vibrations are picked up by the inner ear. The closer the swim bladder is positioned to the inner ear, the better the fish can hear high-frequency sounds. Some

fishes, such as minnows and catfishes, have evolved a chain of small bones called **Weberian ossicles**, which efficiently transmit vibrations from the swim bladder to the inner ear.

Fishes sense temperature changes and physical touch through their skin. In addition, cells called **neuromasts** enable them to sense water movements. Neuromasts can be found anywhere on the surface of a fish, but many of them are found along the lateral line. The ability to sense water movements can help a fish detect the movements of predators or prey, and it can also help the fish avoid obstacles and maintain schooling behavior in poorly lit situations.

THE UNDERWATER WORLD

Although water seems to be a uniform medium, the world that fishes inhabit is anything but simple. Oxygen content and water temperature can vary greatly among different habitats. Some water bodies are very clear and allow a lot of light penetration, whereas others are very silty. The strength of water currents varies. In addition, the bottom of a water body may be rocky, sandy or silty, and shallow areas may or may not be well vegetated. Boulders, fallen trees and vegetation along the shore and on the bottom offer fishes many places from which to ambush prey or hide from predators.

One of the variables that affects fishes the most in summer is temperature. Fishes are ectothermic (cold-blooded) animals, which means that their body temperature varies with the temperature fluctuations of their environment. While the body temperature of a human is approximately 98.6° F (37° C) no matter what the outside temperature is, the body temperature of a fish is exactly the same as its environment whether ambient temperature is 65° F (18° C) or 40° F (4° C).

The activity level of a fish generally increases with water temperature, although water that is too warm can cause a fish to slow down. A fish is healthiest and can usually swim most efficiently within its preferred temperature range. In mountains, fishes are classified into coldwater, coolwater and warmwater species. Many of the trout species and most of the fishes native to the

Rocky Mountains are **coldwater fishes**. Introduced sport fish, such as sunfishes and perch, are commonly found in human-altered habitats or on the fringes of the mountains and are considered **warmwater fishes**. A few species such as Walleye are considered **coolwater fishes** because they fall somewhere in between and tolerate both cold and warm environments.

LAKES

During summer, the water in a lake settles into layers, with the warmest, most oxygen-rich water at the surface and the colder, most oxygen-poor water at the bottom. In many lakes, coolwater species inhabit the surface of a lake, and coldwater species are found along the bottom. Warmwater sport fishes are usually introduced to human-altered waters such as impoundments or reservoirs from which native fish have been displaced or eliminated. Because there are exceptions to every rule, coldwater and warmwater species occasionally mix in a few rare "two-story" lakes or reservoirs along the fringes of the Front Range. For example, in the Pueblo Reservoir in Colorado, coldwater trout species thrive in the deep, lower levels, while warmwater fish are found in the upper levels and shallows.

The natural lakes of the mountains and foothills are often deep and V-shaped, with steep shorelines. These cold waters are generally low in nutrients. High alpine lakes may be so cold and unproductive that they support

Many fishes have dark-colored backs that grade to light-colored undersides. This coloration is called **countershading**. *When viewed from above, the dark color helps the fish blend into the darkness of the water below it. Similarly, the pale underside blends in well with the lighter water above the fish when it is seen from below.*

only one or two fish species. A number of reservoirs have been formed along the rivers of the Rocky Mountains. Dams constructed for flood control, irrigation and hydropower flood the upstream riparian habitat, creating large, deep reservoirs that also often support very few fish species because they are low in nutrients.

Within any lake, there are **littoral** (shoreline), **pelagic** (open-water) and **benthic** (bottom) areas. Most rooted vegetation is found along the shoreline, although some shallow lakes have rooted vegetation throughout. Fish species that spawn in lakes usually move to shorelines to breed because the water is warm and oxygen-rich and because vegetation provides cover for the eggs and juvenile fishes. Also, large predators are less likely to frequent the shallows because of their size. Many small fishes, such as members of the minnow family, are often found in the littoral area. Away from the shoreline, the pelagic area of a lake is home to fishes that feed on plankton and to

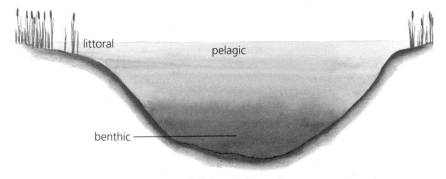

The three major habitats for fishes within a water body.

the predators of plankton feeders. **Plankton** is the term given to microscopic organisms that live in water. The benthic area is home to species that feed on **detritus** (dead plant and animal matter) and, of course, the predators of detritus feeders.

As summer moves into fall, temperature changes encourage mixing of the water in a lake. The layers dissolve, and the temperature and oxygen content become uniform. Water is heaviest at 40° F (4° C), so in winter, when ice covers the lake, the 40° F (4° C) water sinks to the bottom of the lake, and the colder water sits on top. In spring, the water mixes again, producing uniform temperature and oxygen content before summer stratification begins.

RIVERS

In rivers, oxygen content and temperature don't vary much in relation to depth, but they do vary as the water gets farther from its source. Headwater rivers are usually fast-flowing, coldwater streams, and because of the rapids and rocky shallows splashing and mixing the water, they are generally oxygen-rich. Their bottoms are usually rocky and often low in nutrients. These headwaters unite to form larger rivers, which are joined by tributaries and become still larger, and on and on until the largest river finally meets the ocean. The gradient of rivers often decreases as the rivers move out of higher areas onto flatter land, and as a result, water movement becomes slower. As rivers move away from their sources and get larger, the water generally gets warmer, and nutrient availability increases, so plant growth is generally more abundant. Larger rivers tend to have a higher silt load and, as a result, can get very murky.

Rivers are less affected by the seasons than lakes are. Many of the larger rivers freeze over in winter, but the water under the ice keeps flowing. Parts of mountain streams may even stay open throughout the year, providing sources of much-needed oxygen and great viewing sites for hardy fishwatchers.

Cold climate is the single most important feature of fish habitat in high elevation waters. Seven months of ice cover and relatively cool summers means that fish grow very slowly compared to most other places in North America. Some Lake Trout in high alpine lakes are only about 12 in (30 cm) long after 20 years.

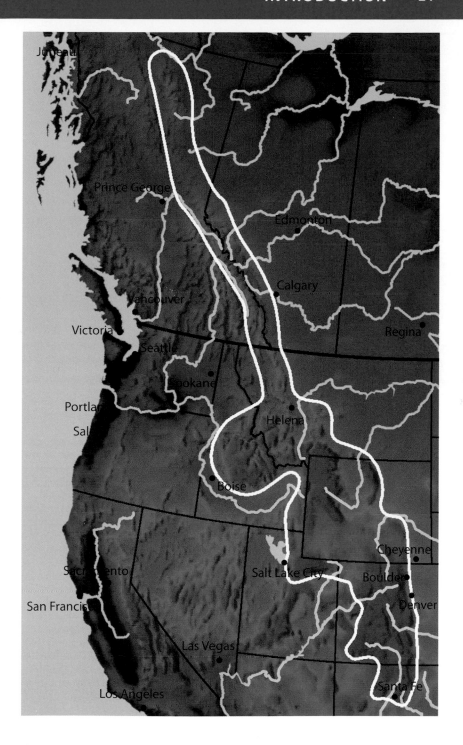

Golden Trout and Cutthroat Trout are found in the Alpine Zone.

HABITAT OF
THE ROCKY MOUNTAINS

The peaks of the Rocky Mountains are some of the highest in the world, and they call out to climbers who dare to attempt to conquer them. Some of the most extensive alpine areas and the highest peaks in the Rockies are found south of Wyoming, with 54 summits in this area over 14,000 ft (4250 m). Although these southern peaks are generally higher than the Canadian Rockies, the southern mountains are typically shorter from base to summit because the valley bottoms are high to begin with.

The Rocky Mountains contain different environments, known as "biological zones" or "life zones." Biological zones are the product of unique combinations of geology, climate, elevation, latitude, slope direction (aspect) and slope angle. The following section lists these zones and some of the fishes and other wildlife that you may expect to find in them.

ALPINE (TUNDRA) ZONE

The alpine zone comprises the bare rocks, glaciers, tundra and alpine meadows above treeline. This cold, windswept environment may have snow-free areas early in spring and even through most of winter, but the alpine can lay blanketed with drifts for most or all of summer. In this cold environment, air temperature is just high enough to permit vegetative growth. At treeline, the ground thaws only long enough for trees to gain their yearly supply of soil moisture and minerals, and summer growth barely replaces needles and twigs killed over winter. Fewer species of plants and animals survive in the alpine than in other ecoregions, and the waters are not very productive. Fish in high alpine lakes grow slowly and remain small because there is a slim choice of food organisms. Golden Trout and Cutthroat Trout are found in glacier-fed cirque lakes, but these fish may remain small and stunted throughout their lives.

SUBALPINE ZONE

This zone exists from treeline down to the upper edge of the montane zone and consists of dense clumps of evergreens and wildflower meadows. The subalpine is what most people envision when they think of the Rocky Mountains. Stunning waterfalls, rocky cliffs dotted with mountain goats and golden eagles soaring against an impressive backdrop of towering mountain peaks are a few of the spectacular images this ecoregion offers. At these elevations and higher, headwater streams begin their downward course in an alternating series of riffles and pools. In the turbulent riffles, caddisfly and midge nymphs hide under the rocks or in the bottom rubble, and periodic algae blooms cover the rocks with a slippery coating. Pools serve as settling and decomposition sites for organic materials and production sites for carbon dioxide. Surrounded by riparian vegetation that provides essential shade and organic material, these riffles and pools serve as spawning and rearing grounds for Bull, Rainbow and Cutthroat trouts.

The Subalpine Zone is home to Bull, Rainbow and Cutthroat trouts.

As elevation decreases, the shrublike trees turn to spruce and fir forests. As streams widen and deepen, the aquatic habitat shifts noticeably. Merging tributaries increase the flow, while the gradient softens and currents slow. Mid-elevation slopes receive the heaviest snow accumulation, leading to highly variable flows and water temperatures, especially during spring runoff. As the streams progress further, water from terrestrial sources, such as snow accumulation and runoff, becomes less important. Species diversity is higher in these midsized streams than in the headwaters. With a wide selection of invertebrates to feed on, the braided areas of subalpine streams make ideal rearing grounds for Mountain Whitefish, trouts and chars. Mountain Suckers and Spoonhead Sculpins forage along tributary bottoms, while Longnose Dace inhabit the mainstream channels.

MONTANE ZONE

This zone consists of the lower slopes and valleys above the foothills. The western slopes are wetter, heavier and shrubbier than the eastern slopes. A wide variety of wildflowers, trees and shrubs are found in the montane. These lush valley corridors provide critical winter habitat for elk, deer and bighorn sheep, and for predators such as wolves and coyotes. In the montane, the wider, slower rivers become slightly warmer, making ideal homes for suckers, sculpins and Burbot. Tributary streams serve as summer feeding areas for Mountain Whitefish, while lower-elevation lakes can support Brook Trout and Lake Chub.

In the montane, heavy effects of human encroachment occur. These effects include roads and freeways, railways, campgrounds, towns, convention centers, golf courses and

The Mountain Zone supports Mountain Whitefish, trouts, suckers and sculpins.

cross-country ski trails. Many conflicts between humans and wildlife have occurred, and predator-prey populations have been separated in some areas. In the United States, the montane meadows are heavily used for agriculture and grazing or have been altered by fire suppression, while the wetlands are affected by irrigation and water diversion. Montane habitat is essential but comprises only a small percentage of the Rockies. The montane is a threatened ecoregion in need of protection and restoration.

FOOTHILLS ZONE

The foothills are a transition from the mountains to the plains and prairies. The first low elevation slopes before the treed montane slopes are considered the foothills. In northern Canada, the transition is not very distinct; the foothills blend into the boreal forest in the east and the Columbian forest in the west. In the United States, the foothills are generally low-elevation scrublands that blend into the prairies. The cool, moist, north-facing slopes and valleys are where shrubs first grow, spreading to south-facing slopes with increased elevation. Trees then begin to appear on the opposite northern slopes and valleys, eventually becoming montane forests. Grasses provide scattered ground cover in these dry communities.

Foothill communities vary drastically from northern Canada to the southern United States. In Canada, where lodgepole pine and trembling aspen dominate the foothill slopes, common species include Brook Trout, Brown Trout, western toads, pileated woodpeckers, woodland caribou, beavers and black bears. Just south of the border, in Idaho and Montana, juniper, sagebrush and chokecherry cover the foothills. Northern Pike and Sauger are stocked in the lakes, and bullsnakes, red-tailed hawks and white-tailed jackrabbits are found in the surrounding meadows. In the southern U.S., the foothills are where many warmwater sport fish have been introduced, including Walleye, crappies and bass. Flora of this arid area include blue gramma grass, aster and flea-bane, and fauna include the Great Basin spadefoot toad, western smooth green-snake and American kestrel.

The species found in the Foothills Zone can vary greatly from northern Canada to the southern U.S.

Brown Trout is one species at home in the Plains and Prairies.

PLAINS AND PRAIRIES

This zone is the only one that is technically not part of the Rocky Mountains. The plains and prairies lie in the rain shadow of the Rockies and blend into the foothills but do not form a definite zone within the mountains. Scattered tracts of grassland can be found almost anywhere in the Rockies south of the Athabasca Valley in Jasper National Park, Alberta. The grasslands provide homes for Brown Trout, northern leopard frogs, prairie dogs, brown-headed cowbirds and badgers.

THE HISTORY OF FISHES IN THE ROCKY MOUNTAINS

Fishes have been present in the Rocky Mountains, on and off, for many millions of years.

Native fishes come from a variety of historical and geographical backgrounds. Over hundreds, thousands and millions of years, the ever-changing climate and geology of the region has lead to a unique mix of native fish species. The geological history of the Rockies is a fascinating and complex story that scientists are still piecing together.

The regions of the mountains were formed at different times and in a variety of ways. The Rockies of Canada and northern Montana were thrust upward 140 million to 145 million years ago. These mountains are relatively young and are composed mainly of sedimentary rock such as limestone and shale. Glaciers sculpted the deep, U-shaped valleys, steep slopes and high peaks.

The Rockies south of northern Montana are geologically very different from the Canadian Rockies. Many of these mountains are volcanic in origin. Those that are not are generally composed of metamorphic and igneous rock such as gneiss and granite, the "basement rock" material that makes up the continental plate and underlies the Canadian Rockies. The effects of glaciation tend to be less dramatic in the U.S. Rockies, and not even a factor south of central Colorado. Wind and water have played a strong role in sculpting the southern mountains, forming spectacular canyons and mesas.

The volcanic activity that has been a major force in the formation of the U.S. Rockies is generally associated with a "hot spot" underneath the continental plate. Today, the hot spot is located under Yellowstone National Park, as revealed by the many geysers and hot springs in that area. Two major volcanic eruptions occurred 2 million and 600,000 years ago (events that make the Mount St. Helens eruption of 1980 look like a small firecracker). Ash deposits from these eruptions and subsequent geological upheavals contributed to the formation of huge ancient lakes, changed the course or direction of waterways and created natural barriers such as waterfalls. These events acted together, mixing or isolating fish populations at different times, leading to adaptation and the evolution of new species, subspecies and variations.

After these large eruptions, several minor eruptions alternated with ice ages. The last ice age occurred 24,000 to 13,000 years ago. During this time, most of the Rocky Mountains from Colorado northward were covered by ice. As a result, the native fishes found in the mountains today are relative newcomers and are generally species with great dispersal capabilities. They traveled to the mountains from three drainage basins that remained ice-free. About two-thirds of the fishes returned to the Rockies from the Missouri-Mississippi drainage basin. The present distribution of the White Sucker is typical of these fishes. Almost all of the remaining fishes, including species with present ranges similar to the Northern Pikeminnow, came from the Columbia drainage basin of the northwestern United States. There was also a small, ice-free region in the Yukon during the last ice age from which a few species such as the Arctic Grayling migrated. Some fishes likely entered by more than one route, making for interesting subpopulations and assemblages, weird disjoint distributions and enough questions to keep generations of ichthyologists happily studying and puzzling over them.

In the last few centuries, humans have contributed to the dispersal of fishes. People have introduced species from all over the world to the mountains, including Brown Trout from Europe and warmwater sunfishes from the central United States. Bait bucket releases and "hitch-hikers," species that are inadvertently included in shipments from hatcheries, have also resulted in invasive populations in some areas of the Rockies. Unfortunately, these unauthorized introductions and other habitat alterations often cause the numbers of native fish to decline. Whatever the reasons for change, human-caused or natural, fishes must continually adapt to their dynamic environment to survive.

CONSERVATION ISSUES

Although archaeologists estimate that people have roamed the Rocky Mountains for 11,000 years, we have only recently begun to really affect the landscape. In the 1800s, the arrival of European explorers, trappers, prospectors and adventurers in the mountains began an era of discovery throughout relatively untouched lands. With the coming of the railways near the end of the century, changes were rapidly set in motion.

Fortunately, a handful of farsighted and enthusiastic individuals campaigned for wilderness protection. In both the United States and Canada, the first national parks were created in the mountains. In 1872, Yellowstone became the first national park in the United States, while the Cave and Basin Hotsprings Park Reserve (later to expand into Banff National Park) in Alberta became Canada's first national park in 1885. These parks were managed primarily "for the benefit and enjoyment of the people," and in the rush to attract visitors, the importance of preserving natural landscapes and protecting wildlife was almost overlooked.

For the fishes, especially in the parks, the influx of tourists meant an increase in angling and competition from introduced species. By the 1880s, fish culture techniques were advanced enough that fish could be brought from anywhere in the country by railway and stocked in the mountain lakes. Later, highways and roads made remote areas even more accessible. Hasty stocking took place in hopes of encouraging the growing numbers of visitors. As the fisheries began to decline, gulls, pelicans and cormorants that had coexisted with the fishes for thousands of years were often blamed. But archival photographs of anglers with strings full of dozens of fish—many more than they could use—attest to the excessive harvests and the real cause of the decline. By the 1950s, rangers and wardens were finding garbage cans full of discarded trout near campgrounds. It soon became clear that angling ethics had to change.

In the northern Rockies of Montana and Canada, the cold climate results in slow growth and late maturity of fishes. Because lakes at high latitudes and altitudes have very low productivity, only a relatively limited number of fishes can be taken sustainably. If the harvest is too big, anglers will first notice that the size of their catch is declining. This stage of overharvest is called **growth overfishing** and is a sign that fishes aren't surviving as long as they once did and trouble is on the horizon. When this pattern is noticed early and the proper measures are taken (usually by simply reducing the harvest), the fish population will quickly recover. If this pattern isn't noticed early or if effective measures aren't taken, the situation will worsen and the fishery may collapse. **Recruitment overfishing** occurs when adult fish numbers have declined to the point where there are too few fish spawning, and not enough young fishes are being born to replace those that are taken by anglers. Anglers are still be able to catch fishes (especially if they know the best spots), but at this stage, the overall quality of the fishery is merely a shadow of its former self.

FISHERIES MANAGEMENT

One function of fisheries biologists is to recognize the signs of overfishing and to prevent fish populations from declining. However, the Rocky Mountains stretch over a large area with few biologists, and other than in the parks, overharvests have usually gone unnoticed or unrecognized. Even when the first signs of overfishing were detected (for example, a decline in the size of fishes), these signs were often considered a desirable response to what were considered in those days to be good management practices. In most of North America, a concept called **Maximum Sustainable Yield** guided fisheries managers throughout much of the 1950s to 1980s. Based on fairly simple mathematics, this concept suggested that the largest harvest of fish of a certain species could be taken when a fish population was reduced to about half of its unexploited level. Although the mathematics were correct, this concept failed to include real-world complexities, such as infrequent monitoring, variable spawning success and the strong reluctance of anglers to reduce their catches when times were bad. Now seen as an unfortunate step in the history of fisheries management, Maximum Sustainable Yield did teach biologists, and others involved in sustaining fish populations, many important lessons about the importance of nature's variability and social factors in fisheries management.

From these hard-earned lessons rose the concept of **Precautionary Management**.

In simple terms, this concept redesigned the mathematics of fisheries management to include all those nasty variables such as uncertainty about spawning success, climate change and unpredictable fishing pressure. Sustainable harvest levels were considerably reduced from the levels in the era of Maximum Sustainable Yield. The new design of fisheries management plans allowed changes to be made quickly and effectively, as nature and harvesting pressure dictated. During the 1990s, the conceptual and practical changes inherent in replacing Maximum Sustainable Yield with Precautionary Management created challenges for fisheries biologists and anglers alike. Computer models became commonplace, with complex mathematics and new concepts. Anglers saw very different fishing rules, usually including severe restrictions of catches.

Just as the Rocky Mountains cover a large and diverse area, management practices and goals vary widely from region to region. A useful way of envisioning these goals is to imagine a scale. At one end of the scale is the pure social goal of providing a fishery. At the opposite end is the pure conservation goal of restoring the natural state of the ecosystem. Most management practices fall somewhere in between, depending on the region, the specific habitat and the requirements of the fishes that live there, and on social and political pressures.

When the primary goal is to provide angling opportunities, fish are stocked on a "put and take" basis, meaning that they are not expected to spawn. The numbers of fish stocked reflect angling pressure. The size of these hatchery-raised fish may range from small juveniles to adults that are eating-sized. In areas of the United States where there is a concern of whirling disease or other parasites, only juvenile fish are used. Some habitats, such as reservoirs or impoundments, destroy the native ecosystem, and native fishes cannot survive, either because they are not adapted to the new environment or because they are outcompeted or preyed upon by introduced species. These water bodies may be stocked exclusively with non-native fishes such as warmwater sunfishes or Walleye that are better adapted to the altered temperatures, morphological characteristics or sediment loads of the new environment.

At the opposite end of the scale, some regions are managed for conservation-oriented goals and focus on establishing healthy, self-sustaining populations of native fish within their historical range. Well-known examples include the recovery plans for Bull Trout and native subspecies of Cutthroat Trout on the East Slopes, as well as Colorado Pikeminnow, Bonytail, Razorback Sucker and Humpback Chub in the Colorado River drainage basin. The recovery efforts for these threatened and endangered species may include protecting the current stocks from further losses, restoring or enhancing essential habitats for each life stage, educating anglers and restricting or regulating recreational fishing.

HABITAT CONSERVATION

Fish are considered indicator species, meaning that they act as signals of the biological condition of the watershed—how clean or polluted the water is. By monitoring which fishes and how many are present, as well their overall health, biologists can become aware of pollution or habitat degradation in its early stages. The species accounts in this book go into more detail about conservation issues pertinent to fish in specific areas, but all fishes are vulnerable to habitat alteration and loss. Although there are many conservation threats, habitat fragmentation and increased sediment loads are two major threats that fish species face throughout the Rocky Mountains.

Fragmentation occurs when humans construct barriers that fish cannot move through. Dams constructed for hydroelectricity or water retention act as barriers, as do hanging culverts. For anadromous fishes such as salmon, Pacific Lamprey, White Sturgeon or American Eel, these barriers prevent access to upstream spawning grounds and cause serious declines in population numbers. Other fishes, such as the Rio Grande Silvery Minnow, no longer have access to the deepwater pools sought out in times of drought or low flow. When fishes are cut off from historic migration routes, the resulting smaller, isolated populations are more susceptible to inbreeding, loss of genetic diversity and disease.

Increased sediment clouding the water can spell disaster. Many of the fishes found in the Rockies are dependent on clear streams. Removal of riparian vegetation, road building, streamside livestock grazing and clear-cuts can all result in erosion and excessive silt. This increase in sedimentation can degrade spawning and nursery areas, as well as smother fish eggs, depriving the embryos of the oxygen needed to survive. Also, when the sediment load of the water changes, the organisms living there change as well. Because microscopic plankton, algae and invertebrates are the basis of the aquatic food chain, their occurrence determines which fishes are found where. Just like other wildlife, fishes have specific food requirements and preferences that change throughout their life stages.

Finding a balance that protects native fishes and their habitat as well as satisfies the diverse values and needs of a growing human population provides many challenges. Although the fishes are a silent majority, there are many concerned people working to educate the public and industry on their behalf. Cottagers are being taught the importance of shoreline plants in creating fish spawning and nursery habitat and are turning down opportunities to build unnatural and expensive artificial beaches or concrete shorelines. Forestry and petrochemical companies know about the problems caused by culverts becoming impassable waterfalls that prevent fish migrations, and about roads eroding into fish spawning beds. Although these problems still occur, our society is rapidly learning how to leave a lighter footprint and include a healthy environment as part of an economic bottom line.

WHAT CAN FISH-LOVERS DO TO HELP FISHES?

Become informed and take an interest in your local waters and fishes. What species live in that storm-water pond? Did fishes ever swim up this ditch? Was that beaver pond ever fish habitat? By simply looking at the world around you and asking fishy questions, you'll become aware of possible threats to our finned friends. If fishes are in that storm-water pond, does the runoff from your street have nasty chemicals that might harm them? If so, why not start a "Yellow Fish Road" campaign. Paint yellow fish silhouettes on the sewer covers to let people know that the sewer drains into a fish's home. They may think twice before draining the car's used oil or putting pesticides on their lawn if they know where the runoff is going. Perhaps fishes once swam up a local ditch (before it was a ditch) to get to a great spawning marsh. Ask old-timers in your community if they ever saw such a thing. Maybe it can become fish habitat once again if that hanging culvert is replaced or if a connection is remade to the big river. Lobby your local politicians or local biologists to make these improvements to your neighborhood environment. If you see a problem, act. Bulldozers on shorelines, weird colors in river waters and sand dumped on somebody's "beach" can all be signs of fish habitat destruction. Federal, provincial and state governments have powerful laws, with enforcement staff and biologists specifically assigned to protect fish habitat. You can help by being a habitat watcher, as well as a fish-lover. Learn and teach. Help others become aware of the presence of fishes, their special needs and their value as touchstones of nature.

ADMIRING FISHES

Fishwatching is not yet a popular sport. Sad, but true. Fishes, hidden from easy viewing in their underwater world, just don't have the mass appeal of big-eyed deer fawns and majestic bull elk. Nonetheless, there are many ways of admiring fishes that can be enjoyed by people of all ages. Appreciating fishes in their natural habitat just involves modifying basic fishing techniques to include a broader range of species and approaching fishing from another "angle."

NEW "ANGLES" TO FISHING

Some fishwatchers believe that fly rods are to observing fishes what binoculars are to bird-watching. Certainly, angling is the most common, and likely the most effective, way to see a fish. All fishes must eat; therefore, with enough skill, all fishes should be catchable. Anyone can catch Black Bullhead, Small-mouth Bass and trouts, but consider the challenge of catching a Longnose Dace or being able to consistently hook a tough-mouthed Brook Stickleback. For most of the smaller species, use tiny flies (18s and smaller are the norm), trying to match the common plankton you see on the lake or river bottom. Super-light tippets and two-weight fly rods are standard equipment if your quarry is shiners, sculpins, daces and chubs. The joy in

A young fish-lover holding a Northern Pike.

Walleye spawning in a small stream.

catching one of these tiny jewels is not in their sporting qualities (no one brags about the great fight from a Lake Chub), but in the simple reward of having persistence and skill pay off. More robust angling gear is useful on larger rivers, when a small baited hook lying on the bottom will perhaps reward you with one of several colorful suckers, a sparkling Flathead Chub or a wriggly Burbot (besides the usual sport fishes). When angling, be prepared to handle fishes. Have a plastic dishpan of water ready to harmlessly hold the fish, keep longnose pliers or forceps handy for quick unhooking and be nice to the fish. Hold it gently, with wet hands, but not for long. How long can you keep a fish out of water? A good rule of thumb is to hold your breath. When you have to breathe, the fish probably wants to breathe also. Let it go, into the dishpan if you want a photo or a better look, then quickly back into the lake when you're finished.

Netting is also a good technique for observing fishes. Aquarium dip nets are fine, but to maximize capture efficiency, you'll need to duct-tape a longer willow stick to the handle. On warm summer days, is there anything as fun as splashing around and chasing minnows in the shallows? If your reputation is too stolid and mature for such frivolous sport, borrow a neighbor's kids and blame the nonsense on them. ("Oh…well…you see, I was just teaching these children about aquatic ecosystem function, I wasn't having a water fight.")

More high-tech than dip nets are seine nets. You can purchase a short "minnow net" from most angling stores. Local laws usually allow anglers to catch minnows for bait, so you can take advantage of this loophole and use a seine net to capture the more elusive fishes. Two people are needed to seine fishes, each person holding one end of the net. Slowly walk along the shallows with the net trailing between you in a shallow U-shape. After a short stroll (15–65 ft, or 5–20 m, is typical), gently pull the net up onto a smooth shoreline and see the treasures scooped up in the base of the net. As with angling, be prepared to handle fishes before you start seining. A plastic tub or a bucket of water should be ready. Admire your catches, then release them back into their home. You may be tempted to keep a few beautiful specimens for your home aquarium. Please don't. Horror stories of unwanted fish introductions are too common in the fish world. People take fish home, often a long way from the capture site. After some time, they decide to release the fish into a local lake or river, which often is not the fish's natural habitat. The result is an introduced species and a potential ecological disaster. Most places have laws against moving live fishes for precisely this reason. Even if your jurisdiction doesn't have such a law, it is just being a good natural-world citizen to leave animals in their natural habitat.

Admiring fishes doesn't have to involve angling or using nets to catch them. It can be as simple as peering over a bridge railing or as complex as stalking up to a pool in camouflage gear with a pair 9x32 polarized binoculars. Water reflects light, so viewing can be tricky, but polarized sunglasses are a great help. Pick your location. Looking down helps (stand on a bridge, a high river-bank or on a dock), as does having the sun at your back. Fishwatching is a great hobby that is best practiced on calm, sunny days. Cloudy days are not great, and neither are windy or rainy days.

The spawning season is a good time for "hands-off" observation. When it gets dark, rocky shallows come alive with spawning suckers. Fountain-like spray sometimes results from the large amount of thrashing about during spawning. Gently lift up any garbage that may be floating on a lakeshore; perhaps a Fathead Minnow has used it for a nesting site. If so, don't stay too long because the male Fathead is sure to be very worried about his brood.

The spawning season is also an excellent time to visit a fish hatchery. There are several hatcheries in each mountain province and

A set of binoculars modified for fishwatching (left); the separate parts (right).

state that provide great information and opportunities to get up close and personal with fishes destined for the wild. Some hatcheries, such as the Dexter National Fish Hatchery in New Mexico or the Kootenay Trout Hatchery in British Columbia, raise some endangered species that you would otherwise have little chance of seeing. Most hatcheries are open seven days a week year-round for self-guided tours and also provide interpretive tours by appointment. The Bow Habitat Station in Calgary, Alberta, is an excellent example of a hatchery that has combined environmental education with fish culture. A good number of hatcheries are located near shallow spawning streams, so fishers can see their favorite species lingering in the natural environment.

Binoculars are helpful for seeing the details on a fish, but they have to be modified for observing fishes by adding a polarized filter. Reverse porro-prism binoculars have the two eyepiece lenses farther apart than the two objective lenses and are the best choice for fishwatching. Fit a single polarizing filter for a large camera lens over each objective lens using a rubber sunshade to hold the filter and a couple of elastic bands to hold the filter/sunshade over the binocular lens. By looking at the water through the binoculars and turning the filter, you can find the "sweet spot" and eliminate most of the glare. Suddenly, the fish will be close, clear and beautiful, and you'll be the one who is forever hooked. Fancy modifications include a close-up lens attached to the polarizing filter for close-up focusing on nearby minnows.

Fish photography is a natural extension of admiring fishes, but it is actually one of the most difficult types of nature photography. The natural cryptic coloration of most fishes, as well as watery shimmer and glare, make clear photos almost impossible to achieve. Bringing a fish out of the water helps somewhat, but the fins flop down, the fish looks like it is gasping, and shiny scales and wet skin give photographers a nightmare of exposure trouble. If you can, create a small glass aquarium with small holes on the narrow sides; then insert hoses to create a current. Add clean sand and pebbles to mimic the fish's natural environment. In this setting, a fish will behave naturally but will not be able to go far, increasing the chance of a good photo. When you do try fish photos (and you should try), expect to take lots of shots using a variety of exposures and angles. If you're lucky, one or two pictures will turn out, and they'll be gems.

Underwater fish viewing and photography by snorkeling or scuba diving are popular in the tropical oceans but are less suited to cold and sometimes sediment-laden mountain waters. A few spots have good visibility for divers, but these tend to be the coldest (and often the most fishless) lakes around. Ask around at local dive shops for hot tips. Snorkeling along shallow weed beds or near sunken boats on summer days may produce a few close-up views of Yellow Perch or a motionless Burbot, but the big vistas of underwater reefs teeming with fishes that you see on TV shows from Hawaii just don't happen in the Rockies.

Remote underwater video cameras are a new technology that holds promise for fish observation. A small waterproof camera is lowered below your boat (or through an ice-fishing hole), with a video cable running up to a small television monitor. These cameras have special low-light abilities and can produce totally cool scenes of gray, ghostly fishes cruising through a murky world. Most high-end sport fishing stores carry a few models.

Although fishes throughout the mountains face the challenges of habitat change or loss as well as overharvesting, the degree of these problems varies depending on the region. In general, habitat issues are a more pressing problem in the southern Rockies because the larger human population makes heavier demands on the environment. In the northern Rockies, there are fewer people drawing on the resources, but colder temperatures and fewer ice-free days result in low lake productivity.

ETHICS

As true nature-lovers, fishers should always adopt a "lighter footprint" approach to the sport. Be careful when handling fishes, inform yourself and follow all local fishing regulations. Don't disturb spawning fishes or fishes that are already stressed by unusually hot weather or low water. Even light walkers can love special areas to death, so take care to stay on streamside trails and avoid stirring up unnecessary silt and mud. Be friendly to other fish-lovers by smiling and by happily avoiding a fly fisher's pool or a streambank angler's beach. The sport of fishing has traditional ethics designed to avoid conflicts, such as leaving a pool after hooking a fish, fishing from the head to the tail of a run and exiting and reeling in lines if someone else hooks up. Fish admirers should be no different and should display tolerance and formal politeness and, generally, be paradigms of nature-lover virtues (and splash around in the shallows a lot).

ABOUT THE SPECIES ACCOUNTS

This book gives detailed accounts of 68 species of fishes that are well established in the Rocky Mountains. An extra 53 species are included in the appendix. The appendix species are unusual fishes, either introduced to very restricted spots or just peeking into the edges of the Rockies from their home ranges in other areas, with the exception of a few species that have had their names changed since the printing of that book.

Each account includes the following information.

"Does it hurt a fish when it is hooked?" is a question usually posed to fish biologists. Generally, the answer is yes, hence the thrashing about on the hook. However, most of the stress from a catch and release results from being held out of the water. Some fishes may die from being hooked, but if care is taken in removing the hook and handling the fish, the likelihood of death is lessened.

ID: wherever possible, we have mentioned only external characteristics so that you can identify a fish without disturbing it too much. However, some fishes cannot be told apart only by external characteristics. For example, you may have to stick your finger in a fish's mouth to feel for the presence of teeth in the base of the throat.

SIZE MEASUREMENTS: we have included average measurements for the Rocky Mountain region and maximum measurements recorded in North America for adult fishes. Only length measurements are included for many species, but weight measurements are also included for some of the larger species. Because the Rocky Mountains extend over a wide range of latitudes and altitudes, fishes in the cold waters of the northern Rockies or high alpine lakes may be smaller than average, while the opposite may be true for fishes found in the warmer, southern waters or at lower altitudes.

HABITAT: the habitats we have listed describe where the species is most commonly found outside the spawning season. Depending on water temperature and oxygen concentration, however, fishes may turn up in unexpected places.

SPAWNING: spawning time and habitat, courtship behavior and rituals, time until hatching, age at maturity and lifespan are discussed in this section. The information that we are able to include varies depending on the species; for some species, a lot of information is available, and for others, very little. Keep in mind that spawning dates and hatching times are a function of water temperature and can vary greatly with the latitude and altitude of the water body.

FEEDING: in this section, we mention the kinds of things that adult fishes eat and the way they forage. The diet and foraging styles of larval and juvenile fishes are often different than those of adults and are only included when space limitations allow.

RANGE MAPS: the range map for each species represents its overall range in the Rocky Mountains in an average year. A species is generally restricted to its preferred habitat within the highlighted range. These maps do not show small pockets within the range where a species may actually be absent or how the range may change from year to year. For some federally endangered species, we have also included the historical range.

"Why do fish jump?" is a question often posed to biologists. The answer may be different for some species than it is for others. Insectivorous fishes may overestimate their velocity when they reach for a floating bug, propelling themselves farther out of the water than necessary. Smaller fishes may jump to avoid the jaws of a hungry predator. Sometimes, it appears that fishes just jump for joy. Why else would a trout or pike leap from its deepwater world, or a spawning sucker twirl from the water?

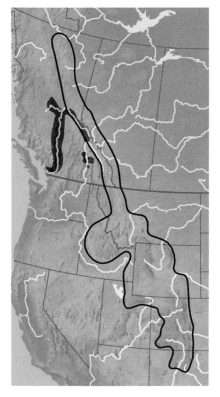

identifies how much a species is at risk of endangerment, based on its rarity and threats to the species and its habitat. For federal listings, we refer to the *Threatened and Endangered Species System* (TESS) put out by the United States Fish and Wildlife Service and on information from the Committee on the Status of Endangered Wildlife in Canada (COSEWIC) listing. Provincial government and State Fish and Game Department listings are also included when applicable.

OTHER NAMES: any species of fish may be known by many different names, depending on who is talking about it. The name that we use throughout the text is the name that has been accepted as the North American standard by scientists. Names change over time, though, and nicknames also form. In this section, we list other names that people may use when talking about the species.

STATUS: definitions of all status descriptions are included in the glossary starting on page 215. Two different descriptions are given for status. The first (abundant, common, uncommon or rare) describes broadly how common the fish is in the mountains. The second is based on government listings and

SIMILAR SPECIES: easily confused species are discussed here briefly. We point out the most relevant field marks, reducing the subtle differences between species to easily identifiable traits. You may find it useful to consult this section when finalizing your identification.

DID YOU KNOW? Finally, here we dig a little deeper to find an interesting bit of trivia that most people do not know about the fish.

THE FAMILIES

Knowing about the families of the fishes of the Rockies will help you with their identification. The families of appendix species are not described, because those species are often rare and are usually distinctive.

Please see the Fishwatching section in the introduction for an overview of the best ways to view fishes. You should be able to keep a fish in water as you examine most of the features mentioned. To view a few characteristics you may need to take the fish out of water, but remember that a fish should not be out of water for any longer than you are comfortable holding your breath. Please also keep in mind that it is illegal to confine a fish that is at risk.

STURGEON FAMILY

These relics of the dinosaur age are widespread throughout the Northern Hemisphere. Their scaleless bodies are covered with five rows of bony armor that have successfully protected them from predation for about 100 million years. Their pointed, needle-like snouts with whisker-like barbels and their asymmetrical tails are also distinctive. One of the most impressive features of this family is the large size and long lifespan that individuals can reach—North American species can reach lengths of over 4 m (13 ft) and can live to over 150 years old. Only the White Sturgeon is found in the Rockies.

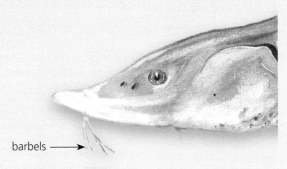

barbels ———▶

MINNOW FAMILY

This family is the largest fish family, with over 2000 species worldwide. Twenty-one species are present in the waters of the Rocky Mountains. Minnows eat algae and zooplankton and, in turn, are food for many piscivorous animals. They are known for their small size (but not all minnows are small: some pikeminnows can grow to at least 1 m [3 ft] in length), and small individuals of any species are often mistakenly called "minnows." Minnows have Weberian ossicles—four modified vertebrae that connect the air bladder to the inner ear—which provide them with better hearing than many fishes. They also have teeth on the last gill arches in the throat instead of on their jaws. In addition, injured individuals release alarm substances that let other fishes in the school know that there is danger ahead.

SUCKER FAMILY

Known as the vacuums of the fish world, suckers can survive in many different environments, as long as there is food to eat in the muck at the bottom of a water body. Both lips of their fleshy mouths are positioned on the underside of their bodies. These fishes are good for fishwatching, because their daytime spawning runs often boast thousands of individuals. Many piscivorous animals depend on these spawning runs for food in spring and early summer. Suckers are closely related to minnows. Like minnows, they have Weberian ossicles, have teeth on their last gill arch and release alarm substances. However, they are generally larger than minnows and have different mouths.

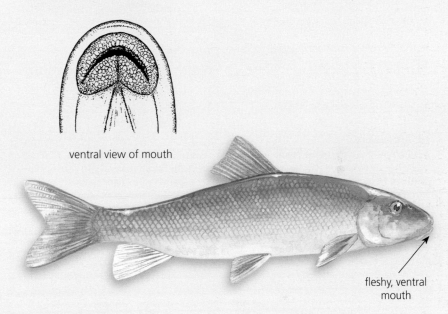

ventral view of mouth

fleshy, ventral mouth

BULLHEAD CATFISH FAMILY

Bullhead catfishes (also known as madtom catfishes) rarely use their sense of sight when feeding (in fact, three species in this family are blind!). Instead, they rely on the eight barbels around their mouths to sense prey hiding in the mud or murky water. Species in this family were given the name "catfish" because the long barbels around their mouths reminded people of cats' whiskers. Fishes in this family can communicate with sound that is produced with their swim bladders or their pelvic fins. They generally use these sounds during courtship and when showing aggression. There are four members of this family in the Rockies.

PIKE FAMILY

All members of the pike family have long, rounded bodies with duck-like snouts. They are found throughout the Northern Hemisphere, where they prey on aquatic animals, including fishes, aquatic birds and amphibians. Their hunting strategy is to lie in wait, hidden by vegetation, until prey swims by. Their sharp jaws grab the prey in the middle and then flip the quarry around so that they can eat it head first. Fishes in this family have teeth not only on their jaws, but also on the roof of their mouths and on their tongues. Only five species make up this family, and the Northern Pike is the only species found in the Rocky Mountains.

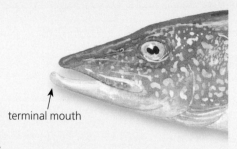

terminal mouth

TROUT FAMILY

Members of this family are commonly referred to as salmonids because the scientific name for the family is Salmonidae. These fishes are generally the most popular sport fishes in the Northern Hemisphere where they are native. They are so popular that many species have been introduced to places outside their natural range by humans. Some have even been successfully introduced to every continent except Antarctica. This family can be broken up into three distinct subfamilies. Members of the whitefish subfamily are just that, silvery or whitish fishes that have large scales and few or no teeth. The grayling subfamily includes the Arctic Grayling, which has a distinctive large and colorful dorsal fin. The trout subfamily, to which the rest of the fishes in this family belong, can be further broken down into chars and true trouts. Chars have no dark spots on their sides and backs. True trouts have dark spots over at least part of their bodies.

red slash

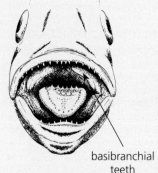

basibranchial teeth

COD FAMILY

The cod family is composed primarily of bottom-dwelling marine fishes, such as Atlantic Cod and Alaska Pollock, which are commercially valuable. The species here in the Rockies, the Burbot, is the only completely freshwater species. Some scientists have suggested that the Burbot belongs in its own family, but so far no conclusive decision has been made. Like its marine relatives, the Burbot is a benthic, coldwater species. However, unlike its relatives, which have three dorsal fins and two anal fins, the Burbot has only two dorsal fins and one anal fin.

LIVEBEARERS FAMILY

Livebearers do just that—bear live young. Some species of these small fish are popular aquarium fish. They are known for their ability to eat mosquito larvae, and one species, the Western Mosquitofish, appears in high enough numbers to merit its own account; a number of other livebearers are described in the Appendix.

STICKLEBACK FAMILY

Spines sprout from the backs of these charismatic little fishes and are also present in the pelvic fins and in front of the anal fin. Sticklebacks are popular with fishwatchers and behavioral scientists because of their involved mating and nesting rituals. Their nests are incredible structures that are glued together by a sticky kidney secretion. The seven species in this family inhabit either saltwater or freshwater habitats or inhabit both at different times in their lives. One species, the Brook Stickleback, is found in the Rockies.

SCULPIN FAMILY

Most species in this large family of bottom-dwelling fishes live within the oceans of the world. Sculpins have arrow-shaped bodies that taper from large, wide heads to skinny tails. They have large, fan-like pectoral fins and long dorsal and anal fins. The pairs of "spines" on their heads discourage predators from eating them—that is, of course, if predators can even find these well-camouflaged fishes in their rocky hiding places. There are about 300 species in this family, 10 of which are found in the rocky lakes and rivers of the Rocky Mountains.

large, wing-like pectoral fins

SUNFISH FAMILY

Members of the sunfish family are prolific freshwater fishes that include the sunfish, crappies, rock bass, and smallmouth and largemouth bass. Some species interbreed, producing fish that can be difficult to identify. Males prepare the nest and guard the eggs. Native to North America, these fish have dorsal fins that are part spiny and part soft. There are nine genera and 34 species in the family, nine of which occur in the Rockies.

PERCH FAMILY

Most of the 155 species in the perch family inhabit lakes and streams in the eastern part of North America. The number of species present generally declines from east to west. Perches are best known for having two dorsal fins, the first supported by sharp spines and the second by flexible rays. Males in this family can be very colorful during the spawning season. Five members of this family occur in the Rockies, and they range in size from the tiny Iowa Darter to the large Walleye.

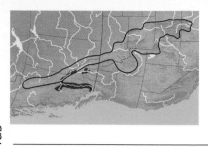

WHITE STURGEON · Acipenser transmontanus

If you are lucky enough to see one of these relics, its armored body and prehistoric disposition will not be easily forgotten. The fossil record suggests that the dinosaur-like appearance of the sturgeon family has changed little over millions of years. Although your chances of seeing a White Sturgeon in the Rocky Mountains are slim, groups are occasionally spotted basking at the surface of large lakes in spring. • The endangered status of this species in western North America is largely owing to overfishing in the early 1900s. In more recent decades, dams and pollution have been factors in the White Sturgeon's decline. Dams have altered stream flows and blocked migration routes, and, unfortunately, this fish is not known to use fish ladders. But because spawning appears to be triggered by peak flows of spring melt water, some recovery efforts include augmenting spring flow rates from dams to induce the spawn. Growth and egg survival are then inhibited by industrial pollutants, which accumulate in the fish's flesh during its long lifespan. However, with releases of juvenile fish from hatcheries and careful cooperation between Canada and the United States, there may be some hope for the future of the White Sturgeon. • Although commonly seen only by sportfishers on popular guided trips for this majestic North American freshwater fish, patient river-watchers will occasionally be rewarded with the unforgettable sight of a broaching White Sturgeon. These giant sturgeon will periodically rocket out of their deep river homes, hang motionless in the air for a split second, then crash back into the depths. If you see a huge splash on one of the large rivers on the western side of the Rockies, keep watching. Leapers often give repeat performances, and you'll have the fishwatching tale of a lifetime.

FEEDING: predacious bottom feeder; uses ventral mouth and barbels to search for aquatic insect larvae, crayfish and fish; young eat mainly midge larvae and mollusks. In British Columbia, some White Sturgeon will convert to a fish diet to take advantage of massive runs of eulachon (also called candlefish). These predatory White Sturgeon may also feed on sculpins, sticklebacks and even sockeye salmon.

SPAWNING: probably May to July with peak melt water flows; move great distances up large rivers to spawn in swift water, close to rapids and over rocks; adults breed less frequently with age, every 4–11 years; female releases up to 4 million eggs in a single spawn (dependent on size of female); small, brown, adhesive eggs hatch in 5–25 days; anadromous fish return to ocean in fall; mature at 15–30 years; male matures before female; may live to over 100 years old.

OTHER NAMES: Pacific Sturgeon, Oregon Sturgeon, Columbia Sturgeon, Sacramento Sturgeon.

DID YOU KNOW? The White Sturgeon is the largest freshwater fish in North America. Sizable, older females

STATUS: endangered in both Canada and the United States; protected by all provincial/state governments in the Rockies.

HABITAT: *Landlocked populations:* large, cool rivers; some are isolated in large lakes. *Anadromous populations:* mainly at sea; spawn inland in large rivers.

can have ovaries that weigh up to 225 lb (100 kg). The sturgeon skeleton is largely made up of cartilage.

ID: pale olive or gray-brown dorsally; white ventrally; opaque to dusky fins; somewhat rounded body; large, broad head; 4 barbels near ventral, tube-like, toothless mouth; covered with rows of light-colored, bony plates; diamond-shaped lateral plates; asymmetrical caudal fin.

SIMILAR SPECIES: none in the Rockies.

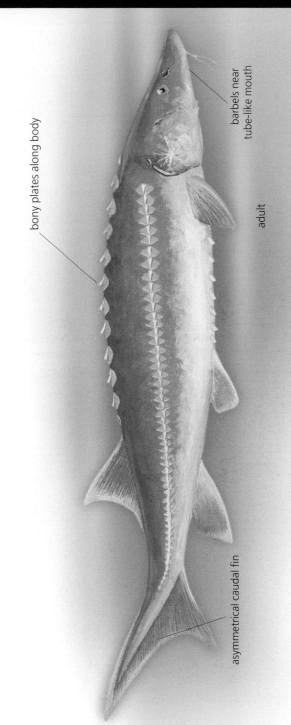

bony plates along body

barbels near
tube-like mouth

adult

asymmetrical caudal fin

LENGTH: *Average:* 7–89 in (18–228 cm). *Maximum:* 20 ft (6.1 m).
WEIGHT: *Average:* 35 lb (16 kg). *Maximum:* 1387 lb (630 kg).

CHISELMOUTH   *Acrocheilus alutaceus*

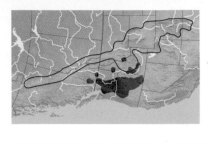

This minnow uses the chisel-like cartilaginous edge on its lower lip to scrape algae off of rocks. The Chiselmouth is one of the few specialized algae feeders found in the Rocky Mountains. The algae this fish eats remains largely undigested, but nutrients are absorbed as the algae passes through the fish's long intestine. • Endemic to the northwestern United States and British Columbia, Chiselmouths are widely scattered within their range. Their spotty distribution suggests that the once continuous range of this temperature-sensitive species was constricted as the climate cooled during an ice age. Chiselmouths are found in relatively warm water bodies, where they often occur with the more common Northern Pikeminnow or Peamouth. These three large minnows may hybridize, especially when low numbers or habitat disturbances stress populations.

FEEDING: feeds near bottom; scrapes algae off rocks.

SPAWNING: late June to early July; spawns in streams; lake populations move a short distance up tributaries; no nest; eggs are buried among gravel or rubble; female produces an average of 6200 eggs; mature at 3–4 years; live up to 6 years.

OTHER NAMES: Hard-mouth, Square-mouth.

DID YOU KNOW? The scientific name *Acrocheilus* means "sharp lip," and alutaceus means "leathery," referring to the Chiselmouth's tough skin.

STATUS: vulnerable in British Columbia; moderately vulnerable in the U.S.

HABITAT: relatively warm water bodies; habitat varies from small creeks to large rivers, backwaters and small to large lakes.

ID: drab coloration; dark brown back; brassy or silver sides; light belly; small, black dots cover body; may have orange markings on pectoral and pelvic fins; elongated body; small, cycloid scales; blunt head; fairly large eyes; rounded snout overhangs mouth; fleshy upper lip; chisel-like cutting edge on lower lip; slender caudal peduncle; distinctly forked caudal fin.

SIMILAR SPECIES: *Redside Shiner* (p. 78): lacks hard jaw plate and protruding snout.

Redside Shiner

fairly large eyes

fleshy uppler lip

distinctly forked caudal fin

adult

LENGTH: *Average:* 6–7 in (15–18 cm). *Maximum:* 10 in (25 cm).

LAKE CHUB
Couesius plumbeus

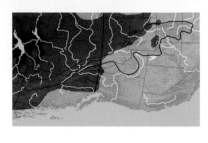

The Lake Chub is one of the most widespread and northerly minnows in North America. Its native range extends from eastern Canada across the continent to Alaska and southward along the Rocky Mountains to Colorado. This generalist is commonly found in lakes, creeks and rivers of the northern Rockies, typically over gravelled bottoms near rocky shores. As lake shallows warm in the heat of summer, the Lake Chub retreats to cooler waters, becoming a good prey species for piscivorous fishes such as Northern Pike and Walleye. • Lake Chubs mature at three to four years old, and few live more than five years. Females grow faster and live longer than males. Lake Chubs are among the larger minnows, commonly exceeding 4 in (10 cm). Individuals over 8 in (20 cm) have been reported. • The Lake Chub was named for Dr. Elliot Coues, an ornithologist who collected the type specimens (*Couesius*), and for its lead coloration (*plumbeus*). • In the beautifully clear lakes of the Canadian Rockies, Lake Chub are one of the easiest fish to watch. Their habit of clustering near docks and along shorelines, especially during warm summer days, allows adults and kids alike to enjoy them. Simply lean over the edge of a dock or footbridge and watch. Polarized sunglasses will help you see through the surface reflections on the water. Try to figure out what choice aquatic morsels they are chasing and which are the dominant fish in the pack. Look for rare all-black Lake Chubs.

FEEDING: feeds in shallows; eats crustaceans, zooplankton, aquatic insects, small fish larvae and algae.

SPAWNING: April to late summer, when water temperature reaches about 50° F (10° C); may migrate to tributaries or stay near a lakeshore; male persistently pursues female over gravelly substrate (if available) and presses her up against a rock; eggs are released in small spurts; about 10,000 eggs per female per spawning season; eggs are scattered with no parental care; hatch in 6–20 days, depending upon water temperature; mature at 3–4 years; live to 5 years.

OTHER NAMES: Creek Chub, Minnow Chub, Northern Chub.

DID YOU KNOW? As glacial relics in Colorado, Lake Chub have always been rare. Until 1989 they were believed to be extirpated, but a population was rediscovered in the St. Vrain River, a South Platte River tributary. Later, Lake Chub were also found in reservoirs along the Cache la Poudre River and in Clear Creek County. These are the southernmost populations of Lake Chub.

STATUS: endangered on the edge of its range in Colorado; common and secure elsewhere.

HABITAT: varied; standing and flowing water bodies; prefers rocky shallows of lakes and gravelly pools in streams; chooses areas with hiding places such as large rocks.

Peamouth

Pearl Dace

small head

small barbels at corner of jaw

adult

forked caudal fin

ID: olive brown back; silver flanks; creamy belly; long, stout body; small head; mouth extends to or slightly past eye; small barbels at corners of upper jaw, sometimes too tiny to see; blunt snout; forked caudal fin. *Spawning male:* slight bit of red at corner of mouth; tubercles on head extend to dorsal fin; black lateral stripe; pelvic and pectoral fins have red base. *Spawning female:* rose color at base of pectoral fin.

SIMILAR SPECIES: *Peamouth* (p. 64): larger; 2 dark stripes on side; dorsal fin does not extend beyond anal fin when pressed flat. *Pearl Dace* (p. 180): barbel not visible at side of mouth; blunter and shorter snout; black lateral stripe above red lateral stripe on spawning male.

LENGTH: *Average:* 2–6 in (5–15 cm). *Maximum:* 8½ in (22 cm).

RED SHINER *Cyprinella lutrensis*

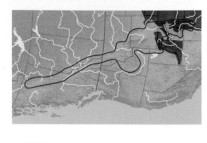

The deep-bodied Red Shiner is tolerant of a broad range of environmental conditions, particularly dissolved oxygen, temperature and salinity, and is known for its ability to outcompete other species. The Red Shiner can tolerate pollution and is often the only species found in seriously degraded habitats. • Native to the central plains, Gulf drainage basins (including the Rio Grande drainage basin) and foothills of the Colorado Front Range, the Red Shiner was introduced to the Colorado River basin in the 1930s. It is now widespread and abundant in the Colorado basin, where it preys upon the young of native fishes and competes aggressively for food and habitat, negatively affecting native endangered, threatened and sensitive fish species. Although the Red Shiner may be found within the Rocky Mountain area, it is more common in lower gradient, warmer streams than in the typical Rocky Mountain stream. • The Red Shiner was previously a member of the genus *Notropis*, which used to be the largest genus of fishes in North America with over 100 species. In 1989, this genus was divided into smaller genera, including *Cyprinella*. *Cyprinella* means "little carp," and *lutrensis* stems from *lutra*, the Latin word for "otter," because the original specimen was collected from Otter Creek, Arkansas. • During their summer spawning season, Red Shiners may be found among smaller cobble and gravel of stream riffles. Brightly colored males dash among crevices, enticing females to spawn. Red Shiners may also be seen along stream margins, patrolling and chasing away other less pugnacious fish.

FEEDING: omnivore; feeds by sight at all water levels; mainly eats small insects, zooplankton, algae and small crustaceans; in backwaters and low-velocity habitats, feeds on small larvae of other species.

SPAWNING: April to September; usually spawns in morning, over clean sand or gravel; sometimes uses abandoned sunfish nests; adhesive eggs sink to bottom and stick to substrate; no parental care; eggs hatch in 4–5 days; mature in 1 year; live up to 3 years. As long as water temperature exceeds 72° F (22° C), an individual female will continue to spawn, potentially producing thousands of eggs in a season. If a spawning season is 4 months or more, individuals spawned early in the season may themselves spawn later that same year.

OTHER NAMES: none.

DID YOU KNOW? Some female shiners transmit sounds while spawning. These species-specific sounds are the equivalent of breeding bird songs and help separate different shiners that are spawning in the same area at the same time. • Because it is so hardy, the Red Shiner is a popular baitfish. Its use as a baitfish has probably contributed to its widespread distribution outside its native range.

STATUS: common; secure.

HABITAT: variety of flowing water habitats, from small creeks to large rivers; most common in backwaters and low-velocity runs. *Summer:* adults may be found spawning in moderate-velocity riffles.

Sand Shiner

Common Shiner

Redside Shiner

ID: olive green back; silver sides; purple to blue bar on side, behind head; white belly; large scales edged with pigment; deep body; small eyes; oblique mouth; down-curved lateral line. *Spawning:* nuptial tubercles. *Spawning male:* blue sheen overall; purple crescent behind head; lower fins and caudal fin turn orange to red.

SIMILAR SPECIES: *Sand Shiner* (p. 182): elongated body; parallel dashes run along lateral line. *Common Shiner* (p. 179): larger, elongated body; larger scales. *Redside Shiner* (p. 78): larger body; blunt nose; large eyes.

blue sheen overall

white belly

orange-red caudal
fin and lower fins

spawning ♂

LENGTH: *Average:* 2 in (5 cm). *Maximum:* 3 in (7.6 cm).

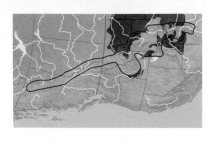

COMMON CARP *Cyprinus carpio*

Those familiar with Greek mythology may associate the Common Carp's scientific name with Cyprus, the home of the love goddess Aphrodite. The reference alludes to the Common Carp's remarkable reproduction capabilities, which have allowed it to thrive throughout much of North America in large and small rivers, shallow lakes, irrigation ditches and even sewage outlets. Although the Common Carp occurs within the Rocky Mountain area, it is found mainly in low-gradient streams, rivers and ponds near the periphery of the region. • Many people harbor strong feelings toward the Common Carp, but usually not feelings of love—this species is probably the most persecuted fish in North America. However, in much of Europe and Asia, the Common Carp is prized as a food and sport fish. Ironically, the Common Carp was introduced to North America in the late 1800s and was promoted by federal and state agencies as a desirable food and game fish. • This prolific fish's high tolerance for environmental adversity, combined with its destructive feeding habits, often adds up to problems for native fish and waterfowl. The Common Carp feeds by uprooting aquatic vegetation or sucking up bottom ooze, which is then expelled back into the water to separate edible items. These habits increase turbidity and destroy spawning, rearing and feeding grounds essential for the survival of native fish and wildlife. • Usually, fishwatchers will see the typical, scaled variety of Common Carp. There are also two other varieties of Common Carp: the exceptionally rare Leather Carp, which has few or no scales, and the Mirror Carp, which has enlarged scales that form three irregular rows. • In lakes and ponds where water is clear, groups of Common Carp may be seen slowly moving about. During storms, swarms of Common Carp feed in the silt-laden mouths of normally dry gullies and arroyos. They can be caught on hook and line or by bow and arrow.

FEEDING: opportunistic omnivore; roots along the bottom for food; mainly eats plants such as algae, wild rice or tree seeds; also consumes mollusks, aquatic insects, annelids or crustaceans that may be attached to vegetation.

SPAWNING: May to August; large numbers gather in weedy areas and exhibit noisy, splashing behavior; break into groups of 2–5 males and up to 3 females; female releases more than 2 million eggs over several weeks; adhesive eggs are scattered randomly and attach to aquatic vegetation; no parental care; eggs hatch in 3–6 days; mature at 2–3 years; live up to 20 years.

OTHER NAMES: Carp, European Carp, German Carp, Scaled Carp, Mirror Carp, Leather Carp, King Carp, Buglemouth Bass.

STATUS: common; secure.

HABITAT: silty, organically rich lakes; warm, weedy areas in moderately shallow water; tolerates turbid waters and low levels of dissolved oxygen.

DID YOU KNOW? When large Common Carp cruise near the surface, their large dorsal fins stick out of the water like shark fins. • By surfacing and gulping air, Common Carp can survive in severely degraded habitats where oxygen levels are so low that other fish cannot survive.

SIMILAR SPECIES: *Goldfish* (p. 178): no barbels; scales have dark edges. *Suckers* (p. 82–103, 184): lack sawtoothed spine and barbels.

ID: variable color; generally olive green or bronze back; yellowish belly; opaque fins; tips of anal and caudal fins may be tinged with red; robust, flattened body with arched back; triangular head; 2 pairs of barbels near toothless mouth; upper jaw extends slightly past lower jaw; sawtoothed spine (modified first ray) on dorsal and anal fins; forked caudal fin.

Goldfish

Suckers

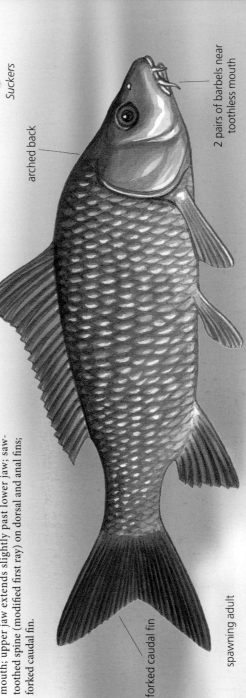

arched back

2 pairs of barbels near toothless mouth

forked caudal fin

spawning adult

LENGTH: *Average:* 15–18 in (38–46 cm). *Maximum:* 40 in (1 m).

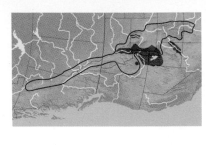

UTAH CHUB   *Gila atraria*

The hardy Utah Chub has adapted well to a myriad of environments. Native to the Bonneville basin and the Snake River above Shoshone Falls in Utah, Idaho and Wyoming, the Utah Chub has been introduced elsewhere through bait bucket releases. This species has become increasingly common in introduced habitats, in part because of the ability of an average-sized female (9–14 in or 23–36 cm) to release an average of 40,000 eggs. Large populations of Utah Chubs compete for food and habitat so intensely that they can reduce the numbers of trouts and other fishes. Several states regard this chub as a nuisance species outside its native range and have made attempts to eradicate it from sportfishing lakes and streams, but Utah Chub populations quickly rebound. • Utah Chubs are an important food for large, piscivorous trouts. Because trout tend to select fish about one-third of their own size, an average-sized (7–10 in or 18–25 cm) Utah Chub makes a perfect snack for a 20 in (50 cm) trout. Chubs avoid the jaws of hungry trout by hiding in dense vegetation, using shallow waters or finding safety in schools. • Utah Chubs grow rapidly their first three or four years of life, attaining 5–6 in (13–15 cm); thereafter, growth slows. In Bear Lake, Utah Chubs as large as 22 in (56 cm) have been reported. • A good place to observe this fish is in the deep, open water and the shallow,

weedy areas of Heart Lake in Yellowstone National Park, Wyoming. In late spring and early summer, look for spawning chubs in the weed beds of the northern and eastern shores.

FEEDING: omnivorous, opportunistic feeder; eats aquatic plants, insects, crustaceans, mollusks and fish.

SPAWNING: late spring or early summer; spawns in shallow water; female is accompanied by several males; yellowish eggs are scattered over various substrates; female releases 5000–84,000 eggs depending on size; no parental care; eggs hatch in 1 week or less; males mature at 2–3 years, females at 3–4 years; most live 5–8 years, some up to 10 years.

OTHER NAMES: Utah Lake Chub, Great Chub, Copperbottom.

DID YOU KNOW? Some researchers suspect that the large Cutthroat Trout of Heart Lake in Yellowstone National Park need to reach above-average sizes in order to outcompete Utah Chubs. • One of the largest problem-fish removal efforts in North America was conducted in Strawberry Reservoir, Utah, to suppress Utah Chub abundance to benefit a popular trout fishery.

STATUS: common; secure.

HABITAT: prefers lakes, ponds and reservoirs but is also found in streams; slow-moving or still water; in flowing water, often among dense vegetation; in open water, often at depths to 75 ft (23 m); thrives in waters as cool as 60–68° F (16–20° C) and as warm as 81–88° F (27–31° C).

ID: variable color; dark olive brown, black or blue back; brassy or silver sides; pale belly; fine, black specks on scales; elongate yet plump body; short, wide head; terminal mouth does not extend to front of eye; origin of dorsal fin is even with origin of pelvic fin. *Spawning:* metallic or brassy color brightens.

SIMILAR SPECIES: other *Gila* species have dorsal fin origins behind pelvic fin origins. *Leatherside Chub* (p. 52): overall silver color; larger scales; reddish tinge on belly. *Colorado Pikeminnow* (p. 70): larger mouth; slender, pike-like body.

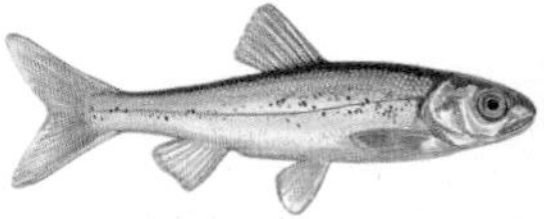

Leatherside Chub

Colorado Pikeminnow

terminal mouth

bright metallic color

origin of dorsal fin even with origin of pelvic fin

spawning adult

LENGTH: *Average:* 7–10 in (18–25 cm). *Maximum:* 22 in (56 cm).

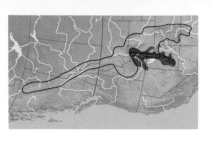

LEATHERSIDE CHUB *Snyderichthys copei*

The Leatherside Chub is native to the small streams of the Bonneville Basin and the Wood, Bear and Upper Snake rivers of Utah, Wyoming and Idaho. This chub is extremely rare, especially in the northern part of its range. Found in deep pools and clear to turbid waters of cold creeks, it prefers areas with a cover of aquatic vegetation or complex shorelines. • So little is known about the Leatherside Chub that lack of knowledge has stymied conservation efforts for this sensitive, and increasingly rare, species. Poor water quality and habitat degradation have led to the decline of this fish, which is regarded as ecologically sensitive. Flow manipulation and elevated sediment loads have had an adverse effect on spawning habitat, which is believed to be a primary reason for the decline of the Leatherside Chub. Leatherside Chub populations are also especially sparse and fragmented where Brown Trout have been introduced. • Because of its rarity, it is unlikely many people will observe this fish. However, pools of cool, clear streams offer the best opportunities.

FEEDING: not studied; probably eats invertebrates like other chubs do.

SPAWNING: little known; probably May to August (based upon collection of males in spawning coloration and gravid females); nothing known of spawning habits; Leatherside Chub in Provo River may spawn at age 2; average number of eggs is about 1800; no parental care; may live up to 8 years.

OTHER NAMES: Leatherside Minnow.

DID YOU KNOW? Although the name "Leatherside" obviously refers to the feel of this fish's body, the exact origin of "Chub" is not known. The word is believed to stem from an old Anglo-Saxon word meaning "head" because most North American and European species have large heads.

STATUS: declining; listed as sensitive in Utah.

HABITAT: quiet pools and riffles; cold creeks or rivers with moderate currents; clear to slightly turbid or muddy waters; prefer shallow, weedy areas.

Utah Chub

SIMILAR SPECIES: *Utah Chub* (p. 50): larger scales; brassy sides; no red on dorsal fin.

ID: slim body is bluish above and silvery below; dorsal fin may have orange-red tinge; small scales give skin leathery texture; pharyngeal (throat) teeth in 1–3 rows.

dorsal fin may have orange-red tinge

slim body

adult

small scales

LENGTH: *Average:* 3–5 in (7.6–13 cm). *Maximum:* 6 in (15 cm).

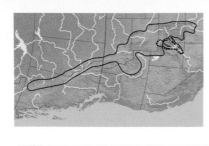

HUMPBACK CHUB *Gila cypha*

Living for centuries in the Colorado River and its major tributaries, the Green, Yampa, Gunnison, and Little Colorado rivers, the Humpback Chub is highly adapted to the fast, turbid waters of canyon-bound river reaches. When water rushes over this chub's flattened head and crashes into the hump at the back of the head, the fish's body is forced down toward the river bottom where currents are weaker. Meanwhile, the keel-like dorsal fin acts as a stabilizer in strong currents. These adaptations allow the fish to swim through the rushing rapids to resting places in calmer eddies. • There are only six known populations of Humpback Chubs remaining, and they are all in white-water canyons. Three populations are found in the foothills of the Rockies in Utah and Colorado: Westwater Canyon, Black Rocks on the Colorado River and Yampa Canyon on the Yampa River. As with other fish endemic to the Colorado River basin, habitat loss and degradation and establishment of non-native fish species are the main causes of the Humpback Chub's decline. Introduced species compete for limited habitats, prey upon native fish and transmit diseases for which native fish have no immunity. Dams have flooded former habitat and altered natural flow regimes. As a consequence, water temperature, turbidity, volume and current speed have changed to the detriment of native fish. • In Colorado, Utah and Wyoming, the Upper Colorado River Recovery Program (a cooperative effort of several state, federal and non-government organizations) directs efforts to recover the Humpback Chub, along with the Bonytail, the Colorado Pikeminnow and the Razorback Sucker, with an ultimate goal of a sufficient number of self-sustaining populations of each so that persistence is assured. • Because of its rarity and restriction to turbulent waters of canyon-bound river reaches, it is unlikely most fishwatchers will ever see a Humpback Chub in the wild. However, individuals may be observed congregating at the mouth of the Little Colorado River during spawning season.

FEEDING: omnivore; eats mostly aquatic invertebrates but will take small fishes and algae.

SPAWNING: April to June, when spring flows are high or receding; spawn in shallow backwaters or over cobble and gravel bars; no nest or parental care; mature at 3–4 years; males may mature 1 year earlier than females; live up to 8 years.

OTHER NAMES: none.

DID YOU KNOW? Humpback Chubs apparently have a strong affinity for canyon-bound reaches; few have been captured outside the six documented areas of concentration. • All chubs have special adaptations for locating food. Chubs that live in turbid water, such as the Humpback Chub, have well-developed taste buds, while those that live in clear water search by sight.

STATUS: rare; on the federal endangered species list; endangered in every state throughout its range.

HABITAT: canyons with deep, fast water; turbid or muddy waters; rocky substrate and boulders.

ID: olive gray back; silver sides; white belly; streamlined body; scales deeply embedded but almost absent except along lateral line; flattened head; small eyes; large, subterminal mouth; pronounced snout; prominent hump behind head; well-developed fins; strongly forked caudal fin. *Spawning male:* reddish "cheeks"; nuptial tubercles on head and paired fins.

SIMILAR SPECIES: *Bonytail* (p. 56) and *Roundtail Chub* (p. 60): hump behind head much smaller or absent; larger eyes; deeper and longer caudal peduncle; anal fin base angle continues into middle of caudal fin.

Bonytail

Roundtail Chub

pronounced snout and small eyes

prominent hump behind head

spawning

strongly forked caudal fin

LENGTH: *Average:* 12 in (30 cm). *Maximum:* 18 in (46 cm).

BONYTAIL *Gila elegans*

The Bonytail is an ancient and extremely rare minnow that is found only in the Colorado River basin. Of all the fishes native to the basin, the Bonytail is the closest to extinction; most of the remaining Bonytails are 40 or more years old. A few may persist in the upper Green River in Utah and a small, but senescent, population persists in Lake Mohave on the mainstem Colorado River. • Historically, this species was common and well adapted to the extreme fluctuations in temperature, turbidity and flow velocity of the Colorado River basin. However, modified flow regimes caused by numerous dams, habitat alteration and loss and introduction of non-native species have all contributed to the near extinction of the Bonytail. Although release of hatchery-raised juveniles has met with limited success, the Bonytail faces mounting conservation challenges, as the increasing human population places even greater demands on limited water supplies. • It is very unlikely that Bonytails will be seen in a natural setting, but spawning aggregations have been observed over gravel-bottomed areas of Lake Mohave.

FEEDING: surface feeder; eats mainly terrestrial insects found floating on the surface; also takes debris, algae, plankton and, occasionally, fishes.

SPAWNING: spring; spawns in shallow pools and eddies over gravel or boulders; several males attend a single female; female releases 5000–21,500 eggs; no nest; adhesive eggs fall between crevices; no parental care; eggs hatch in 4–7 days; mature at 3 years; can live to over 40 years.

OTHER NAMES: Bonytail Chub, Colorado Bonytail.

DID YOU KNOW? The Bonytail's endangered status is not unique among endemic species of the Colorado River basin. In fact, a whopping 60 percent of all native fishes in the southwestern U.S. receive protection and are listed by federal and state governments as endangered, threatened or of special concern.

STATUS: extremely rare; endangered; protected by every state government within its native range.

HABITAT: mainstream areas of large, turbid rivers; near swift water; spend much time in low-velocity pools or backwaters with mud or rock substrate; prefer open areas; habitat may vary in reservoirs and lakes.

ID: dark olive gray back; silver sides; white belly; stream-lined body; small hump on nape; flat head; terminal mouth; narrow caudal peduncle; angle drawn from front to rear of anal fin base continues above caudal fin. *Spawning male:* area around mouth and paired fin bases may turn orange; tuberculate. *Spawning female:* may show spawning color-ation and tubercles, but not as intensely as male.

SIMILAR SPECIES: *Humpback Chub* (p. 54): subterminal mouth; anal fin base angle lines up with upper edge of caudal fin; deeper caudal peduncle; larger nape hump. *Roundtail Chub* (p. 60): stouter body; larger eyes; deeper caudal pedun-cle; anal fin base angle continues into middle of caudal peduncle; no nape hump; less distinct caudal fin.

Humpback Chub

Roundtail Chub

flat head

small hump on nape

spawning

origin of dorsal fin behind
origin of pelvic fin

narrow caudal peduncle

LENGTH: *Average:* 10–15 in (25–38 cm). *Maximum:* 24 in (61 cm).

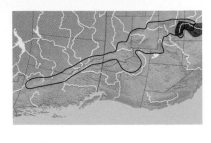

RIO GRANDE CHUB *Gila pandora*

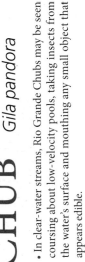

Found in headwater streams of New Mexico and Colorado, the Rio Grande Chub is native to the Rio Grande and Pecos basins but was probably introduced to the Canadian drainage through bait bucket releases. This chub likely gained access to the Pecos River when geological events altered flow patterns and direction of headwater streams during the Pleistocene, about 1.6 million years ago. Even within this relatively small range, these now isolated populations have evolved into slightly different forms. For example, Rio Grande populations usually have one more pelvic fin ray than Pecos drainage populations. • Range fragmentation, water withdrawals for irrigation and drought have contributed to the decline of the Rio Grande Chub. As with many native Rocky Mountain fishes, competitive and predaceous non-native fishes, particularly Brown Trout and Brook Trout, also imperil extant Rio Grande Chub populations. Adequate flow is essential during spring as an environmental cue for spawning and in summer to avoid channel drying. • Unlike many native Rocky Mountain minnows, Rio Grande Chubs can survive in artificial impoundments.

• In clear-water streams, Rio Grande Chubs may be seen coursing about low-velocity pools, taking insects from the water's surface and mouthing any small object that appears edible.

FEEDING: midwater carnivore; eats aquatic plants, juvenile fishes, aquatic insects, crustaceans and other invertebrates.

SPAWNING: March to June during spring snowmelt; require riffles; no nest or parental care; eggs are broadcast over gravel; age of maturity unknown, but females longer than 3.5 in (9 cm) produce eggs.

OTHER NAMES: none.

DID YOU KNOW? The Rio Grande Chub is one of only two members of the genus *Gila* that occurs east of the Continental Divide in the United States. A small population of Rio Grande Chubs persists in the Davis Mountains of west Texas, more than 100 miles from the nearest population in New Mexico.

STATUS: uncommon to rare; species of special concern in Colorado and New Mexico; may be declining.

HABITAT: flowing pools in streams with undercut banks and organic debris; lakes and reservoirs; associated with gravel or rubble substrate and aquatic vegetation.

Other Gila Species

ID: light olive overall; silver side has 2 dusky stripes, with lower stripe extending to anal fin only; moderately deep, compressed body; rounded snout; slightly subterminal mouth; thick caudal peduncle. *Spawning:* red or orange on sides of head; orange on lower sides and paired-fin bases (more pronounced in male); tuberculate.

SIMILAR SPECIES: *Other Gila species:* lack lateral stripes.

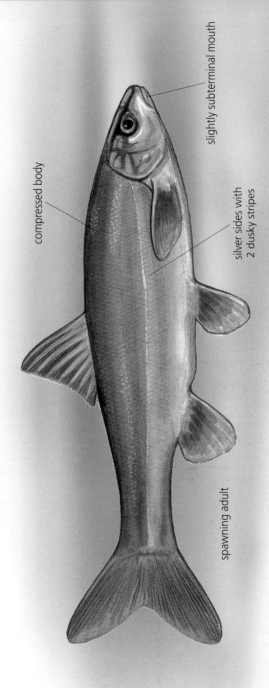

compressed body

slightly subterminal mouth

silver sides with 2 dusky stripes

spawning adult

LENGTH: *Average:* 5–6 in (13–15 cm). *Maximum:* 8 in (20 cm).

ROUNDTAIL CHUB   *Gila robusta*

Like many chubs in North America, the Roundtail Chub is protected by most states in which it occurs. With a native range that once extended throughout the Colorado River basin and southward into Mexico in the Rio Yaqui drainage, this chub is now restricted to mainly the Upper Colorado and San Juan rivers in the southern Rocky Mountains. The Gunnison River, a Colorado River tributary, probably supports the most secure population of Roundtail Chubs; an irrigation diversion dam blocks upstream movement of non-native predators such as channel catfish. Recently, a selective fish passageway was added to the diversion, enabling upstream movement of desirable native fishes and removal of non-native fishes. • Loss of natural flow regimes, water quality degradation, range fragmentation, habitat modification and predation by introduced species are the main reasons for the decline of the Roundtail Chub. Conservation efforts include attempts to suppress abundance of non-native fishes and protection or restoration of native habitat. Augmentation of wild populations with hatchery-reared individuals is an active conservation activity. Roundtail Chubs do not survive in impoundments. • Roundtail, Humpback and Bonytail chubs are closely related, and the latter was once regarded as a subspecies of the Roundtail Chub. Because the three chubs sometimes hybridize and produce fertile offspring, some ichthyologists refer to the three species and their young as the "*Gila robusta* super-species."

FEEDING: opportunistic omnivore; eats aquatic and terrestrial insects, aquatic plants and detritus; larger adults may eat fishes.

SPAWNING: late May to early July; spawns in riffles upstream of pools; female is attended by 3–5 males; pasty white, adhesive eggs sink between spaces in gravel or cobble; number of eggs varies with size; no parental care; males mature at 2 years, females at 3 years; live up to 10 years or possibly longer.

OTHER NAMES: none.

DID YOU KNOW? The many members of the minnow family are loosely divided into shiners, chubs and daces. Shiners are silvery overall, chubs are less shiny and have stout bodies, and daces are small and fine-scaled.

STATUS: rare; endangered in New Mexico; threatened in Utah; species of special concern in Colorado.

HABITAT: large rivers; runs and pools with cover such as boulders or undercut banks; near swift water; prefers sand and gravel substrates.

ID: olive to slate gray; occasionally silvery, mottling on back and sides; creamy or white underside; stout body; small scales; mouth extends to front of eye; origin of dorsal fin behind origin of pelvic fin; deeply forked caudal fin. *Spawning male:* bright orange or red underside and ventral fin bases; dense nuptial tubercles cover body and fins (only on head of spawning female).

SIMILAR SPECIES: *Humpback Chub* (p. 54) and *Bonytail* (p. 56): very slender caudal peduncle; more compressed body; hump on nape; anal fin base angle continues above caudal fin.

Humpback Chub

Bonytail

stout body

origin of dorsal fin behind origin of pelvic fin

spawning ♂

deeply forked caudal fin

LENGTH: *Average:* about 12 in (30 cm). *Maximum:* 17 in (43 cm).

BRASSY MINNOW　*Hybognathus hankinsoni*

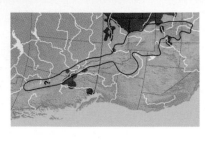

The Brassy Minnow's spotty occurrence west of the Continental Divide is a subject of deliberation for ichthyologists. How the Brassy Minnow ended up in British Columbia is a mystery because this fish is normally found in the central plains. Because populations are scattered throughout the province, some experts believe that the fish is native to British Columbia. Throughout the rest of the Rocky Mountains, there have been other disjunct populations introduced through bait bucket releases. • Wherever they are found, Brassy Minnows tend to be abundant but extremely unpredictable. These fish have a puzzling habit of becoming temporarily absent from areas where they were once known to be common. Although Brassy Minnows are secure throughout much of their native range, they are considered to be at risk in British Columbia, and the few isolated and scattered populations in Alberta are likely in the same predicament. Colorado lists the species as threatened. Pollutants and possibly trout predation affect their survival.

FEEDING: mainly eats zooplankton, phytoplankton and other algae; occasionally eats plant material and aquatic insects or invertebrates found in bottom ooze.

SPAWNING: late May to July; spawns in shallow, weedy areas of lakes, streams or flooded marshes; adhesive eggs are scattered and stick to aquatic vegetation; female releases 150–600 eggs; eggs hatch in 7–10 days; mature at 1–2 years; live up to 5 years.

OTHER NAMES: Hankinson's Minnow, Grass Minnow.

DID YOU KNOW? Be aware that when you dump harsh chemicals such as antifreeze, paint thinner or oil down household drains or sewage outlets, these pollutants find their way into the water system. Pollutants affect all wildlife, not only sensitive species such as the Brassy Minnow.

STATUS: vulnerable in British Columbia and Colorado; common and secure throughout rest of its range.

HABITAT: cool waters; sluggish, weedy creeks; boggy lakes; shallow bays; small to mid-sized streams; tolerates acidic waters.

ID: olive brown back; brassy or gold sides; creamy belly; usually has dark band along sides; slender body; deepest before dorsal fin; large scales; triangular head; small mouth with upper jaw slightly longer than lower jaw; origin of dorsal fin in front of origin of pelvic fin, tip of dorsal fin is rounded; forked caudal fin. *Spawning male:* bronze color deepens.

SIMILAR SPECIES: none in the Rockies.

small mouth

adult

origin of dorsal fin in front of origin of pelvic fin

brassy or gold sides and creamy belly

forked caudal fin

LENGTH: *Average:* 2½ in (6.4 cm). *Maximum:* 4 in (10 cm).

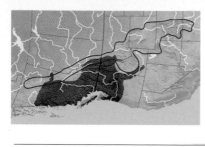

STATUS: common; secure.

HABITAT: lakes and slow-moving areas of rivers or streams; concentrates in weedy shallows; often in schools.

PEAMOUTH *Mylocheilus caurinus*

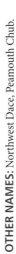

Named for Caurus, the northwest wind, the widespread Peamouth can be found in many northern Pacific Slope drainage basins. The Peamouth is unique among minnows because it can withstand dilute salt water for short lengths of time. This tolerance to brackish water was probably one of the traits that allowed the Peamouth to extend its range to West Coast deltas and Vancouver Island, British Columbia. • Spawning season is a real party for these silvery minnows and provides a great opportunity for fishwatchers to spot these fish. Groups of up to 400 spawners pack into shallow waters, often only 25–100 ft (8–30 m) from another large group. Two or more males will then herd a female right into the shore, where she scatters her gray-green, adhesive eggs. Inshore spawning makes the Peamouth easy pickings for predatory mammals and birds such as mergansers, so by watching Peamouths, you could brush up on your birdwatching skills as well.

FEEDING: eats a variety of insects and their larvae; also planktonic crustaceans, mollusks and occasionally small fishes.

SPAWNING: May and June; groups of fish crowd into shallow water near a shoreline to spawn; two or more males crowd a female into 1–2 in (2.5–5 cm) of water; gray-green, adhesive eggs are broadcast over gravelly substrate; 5000–30,000 eggs are produced per female; males mature at 3 years, females mature at 4 years; live up to 13 years.

OTHER NAMES: Northwest Dace, Peamouth Chub.

DID YOU KNOW? In error, the Peamouth has been called herring or whitefish and has even been served in some hotel restaurants as whitefish.

ID: silvery with dark back; 2 dusky lateral stripes; corners of mouth, "cheeks" and sometimes sides are reddish; slender body; long snout extends past mouth; small barbel on each side of mouth; dorsal fin extends over anal fin when pressed flat. *Spawning:* colorful red lower lip; red lateral line; male has green back; female has dark brown back.

SIMILAR SPECIES: *Northern Pikeminnow* (p. 72): larger mouth; no barbels. *Lake Chub* (p. 44): much smaller adult; dorsal fin origin lies behind pelvic fin origin.

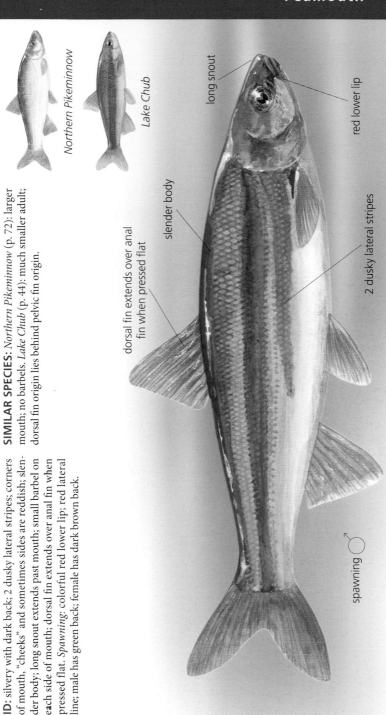

Northern Pikeminnow

Lake Chub

long snout

red lower lip

slender body

dorsal fin extends over anal fin when pressed flat

2 dusky lateral stripes

spawning

LENGTH: *Average:* 4–8 in (10–20 cm). *Maximum:* 14 in (36 cm).

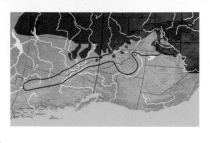

FATHEAD MINNOW
Pimephales promelas

Often described as the jellybean of the fish world, the widespread and abundant Fathead Minnow provides a tasty snack for many piscivorous species. Also described as a "plastic" species because of its ability to adapt to many conditions, the Fathead Minnow can tolerate low oxygen levels, high levels of acidity and alkalinity and silty conditions. Native to the interior United States and Canada, this fish is popular as bait or feed for sport fishes, which has helped expand its range throughout the continent and into several water bodies in the Rockies. • The Fathead Minnow maintains its large population by combining frequent breeding with plenty of parental care by the male. A female does not invest any effort in parenting and visits several males during the spawning season. • The scientific name describes one of the three major characteristics of the male's breeding attire. *Promelas* is Latin for "forward black," referring to the male's dark head. During spawning, his raging hormones promote the development of a fleshy pad on his forehead. Nuptial tubercles sprout from this fleshy pad, reminding most people of their own adolescent pimples. The male Fathead Minnow uses these nuptial tubercles to head-butt unwelcome visitors and to scrub his well-defended nesting site while preparing for a spawning female. • If you wade along in the warm shallows of lakes that do not have great sport fisheries and watch near large rocks, chunks of logs or other shoreline debris, a male Fathead may be seen guarding a batch of eggs stuck to the underside of these microhabitats. Schools of non-breeding juveniles may also scoot out of the wading fishwatcher's way, but if you stand still, these fish will usually return to nibble and tickle bare toes.

FEEDING: generalist diet includes organic detritus, algae, zooplankton, insect larvae and occasionally benthic organisms.

SPAWNING: May through August; spawn in water 8–40 in (20–100 cm) deep and over 60° F (15° C); eggs are released under floating or submerged vegetation (or garbage), sometimes under rock crevices; male defends a small territory and allows more than 1 female to spawn at a time; female spawns again in 2–16 days; male fans well-guarded eggs with his tail to increase oxygen; eggs hatch within 4–6 days; mature in the first year; live up to 3 years.

OTHER NAMES: Bluntnose Minnow, Hornyhead, Blackhead Minnow.

STATUS: widely distributed and often locally abundant; secure.

HABITAT: muddy and stained water pools or ditches; ponds and lakes; streams and slow rivers; silty pools of intermittent streams; tolerate low oxygen levels and warm water.

Lake Chub

DID YOU KNOW? The Fathead Minnow has an extensive North American distribution, and it has also been introduced to parts of Europe. This species is widely used in aquatic toxicological studies.

ID: dark back; yellowish belly; dorsal fin is black near body; thick-bodied; large head; terminal mouth; origin of dorsal fin parallel to or just in front of origin of pelvic fins; first ray of dorsal fin about half-length of second ray; thick caudal peduncle. *Spawning male:* dark head; nuptial tubercles on forehead; dorsal pad; thick lateral line.

SIMILAR SPECIES: *Lake Chub* (p. 44): small barbels on sides of larger mouth; no dorsal pad on spawning male.

dark head

nuptial tubercles

black on dorsal fin

thick caudal peduncle

spawning

LENGTH: *Average:* 1½–3 in (3.8–7.6 cm). *Maximum:* 3½ in (8.9 cm).

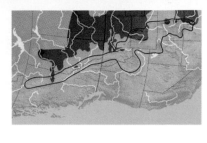

FLATHEAD CHUB   *Platygobio gracilis*

The scientific name of the Flathead Chub describes how the fish's body is specially designed to withstand strong currents. *Platygobio* means "broad minnow," referring to the flattened head of the fish. This feature gives the chub heightened hydrodynamics, pushing it to the bottom where there is more shelter from currents. The second part of the scientific name seems contradictory—*gracilis* describes the slenderness of the fish's body, which allows it to work less against the current. • The Flathead Chub is most commonly found in silty water or in rivers that historically have a heavy silt load. Small barbels that peek out of either side of its mouth aid it in finding aquatic insects within the darkened water. Anglers may find a Flathead Chub hanging on the end of their line if the fly feels similar to an aquatic insect. • The average length of a Flathead Chub is double or triple that of most other minnows in the Rockies. It is one of the longest-living members in its family, and its long lifespan allows it to reach "monstrous" lengths of 12 in (30 cm) or more. • This minnow, although very common in big rivers, is unknown

to most fishers. Anglers occasionally catch a Flathead Chub but usually mistake it for a small whitefish.

FEEDING: uses barbels and sight to feed on aquatic insects, terrestrial insects and insect larvae.

SPAWNING: very little information available; believed to spawn from late June into August in northern portions of its range, but likely earlier in the year in southern portions, in reaction to increased flow and silt load from spring melt; spawns in tributaries of large, silty rivers; semi-buoyant eggs float downstream until hatching; mature at 4 years; live up to 10 years.

OTHER NAMES: Saskatchewan Dace.

DID YOU KNOW? The distribution of the Flathead Chub extends far north, past Inuvik, Northwest Territories, and south in the Mississippi River to Louisiana, making it one of the most latitudinally wide-ranging species in North America.

STATUS: common in much of its range; secure.

HABITAT: silty waters of large rivers and streams; prefers flowing water.

ID: brown-yellow back; silver sides; slender body; flattened head, with very little rise from head to back; pointed snout; subterminal mouth with barbel on each side; sickle-shaped fins; large, pointed pectoral fins; origin of dorsal fin directly over or just in front of origin of pectoral fins; forked caudal fin. *Juvenile:* dark stripe along body to end of caudal peduncle.

SIMILAR SPECIES: other chubs in the Rocky Mountains are smaller and do not have sickle-shaped fins.

pointed snout

flat head

origin of dorsal fin parallel with or just in front of pelvic fin origin

large pectoral fins

adult

LENGTH: *Average:* 9–12 in (23–30 cm). *Maximum:* 14 in (36 cm).

COLORADO PIKEMINNOW

Ptychocheilus lucius

If you want to invent a "fish that got away" story, you may consider the Colorado Pikeminnow as your subject—it historically grew up to 6 ft (1.8 m) long, making it the largest minnow native to North American waters. In the government publication "Historical Accounts of Upper Colorado River Basin Endangered Fish," Tim Merchant, from Green River, Wyoming, recalled that his grandfather used to catch Colorado Pikeminnows "as big as a junior high school kid" out of the river. • Today, few Colorado Pikeminnows of that size survive, and the species is listed as endangered by the United States government and by all of the states in which it occurs. Numerous factors contributed to its decline, including large dams (that fragmented its range, blocked movement to spawning grounds, isolated populations, inundated habitat, drastically altered flow regimes and caused channel drying), habitat degradation and establishment of a number of non-native predators and competitors throughout its native range in the Colorado River drainage basin. • Conservation efforts include building fish ladders around obstructions, restoring natural flow regimes, augmenting depleted populations with hatchery-reared individuals, suppressing problem non-native fishes and creating restrictions against sport fishing. Releasing water to coincide with spring snowmelt and then stabilizing summer flows for young fish mimics natural water flows. These efforts appear to be working. Scientists now believe that the Colorado Pikeminnow population

found in the Green River may be stabilizing or possibly increasing.

FEEDING: consume other fish almost as soon as they start feeding and become completely piscivorous once they reach 0.6 in (1.5 cm) in length, about 12–15 months after hatching; have taken angler's bait of small rodents, birds and chunks of meat.

SPAWNING: late June to July; make spawning migrations of up to 200 mi (320 km); gather and rest in eddies or deep pools; mate in riffles or shallow runs; no nest; eggs released over cobble; eggs hatch in 6–10 days; young drift downstream to nursery grounds, typically low-velocity areas and backwaters; mature at 5–6 years; historically lived over 50 years.

OTHER NAMES: White Salmon, Colorado Salmon; previously Colorado Squawfish.

DID YOU KNOW? In the late 1800s and early 1900s, Colorado Pikeminnows were so common, and individuals so large, they were commercially harvested from large rivers of the lower Colorado River drainage basin to feed miners and dam builders. Archaeological evidence suggests they were an important food source for aborigines of the lower Colorado River basin. Other names given to the fish, such as white salmon and Colorado salmon, attest to its edible

STATUS: rare; federally endangered; protected in all states within range.

HABITAT: main channels of large rivers; adapted to extremes in flow and turbidity; variety of water velocities, depths and substrates; backwaters and flood plains after spring runoff.

Trouts

Roundtail Chub

Northern Pikeminnow

large, toothless mouth

torpedo-shaped body

spawning

deeply forked caudal fin

qualities. • The Colorado Pikeminnow is thought to have evolved three million years ago, at the same time that woolly mammoths and American mastodons inhabited the earth.

ID: bluish gray or olive back; straw yellow or light olive sides; silver to white belly; compressed, torpedo-shaped body; broad, flat head; large, toothless, terminal mouth; dorsal and pelvic fins set well back; strong, deeply forked caudal fin. *Spawning male:* bronze color overall; nuptial tubercles abundant on head. *Juvenile:* black spot on caudal peduncle.

SIMILAR SPECIES: *Trouts* (pp. 112–45, 186–87): adipose fin; teeth. *Roundtail Chub* (p. 60): smaller mouth extends only to front of eye. *Northern Pikeminnow* (p. 72): larger scales; smaller maximum size; ranges do not overlap.

LENGTH: *Average:* 24 in (60 cm). *Maximum (historical):* 6 ft (1.8 m).
WEIGHT: *Average:* 15 lb (7 kg). *Maximum (historical):* 80 lb (36 kg).

NORTHERN PIKEMINNOW

Ptychocheilus oregonensis

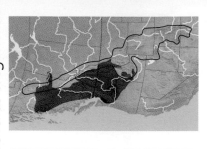

When the last ice age covered much of the Rocky Mountains and British Columbia, Northern Pikeminnows found refuge in the Columbia River and its tributaries. The climate in these ice-free regions of Washington, Oregon and Idaho was similar to today's climate. Since those times, the Northern Pikeminnow has triumphantly become one of the most common fishes within its range. • This large, predacious minnow has become so abundant, in fact, that several states have placed a bounty on it. Anglers are paid $3 to $6 per fish, in hopes that fewer Pikeminnows in the ecosystem will mean better survival rates for juvenile salmon. About one million Northern Pikeminnows were removed from the Columbia and Snake rivers in the 1990s, decreasing predation on salmon fry by an estimated 36 percent. The purpose of the bounty is to create a better balance for the two fish species; fisheries managers monitor the program so that Pikeminnow populations do not drop below self-sustaining levels. • Look for these powerful fish along the shorelines of lakes and rivers, hanging around protective cover such as rocks or piers. Calm, sunny days and clear lakes are best for viewing p[...] of pikeminnows cruising the shallows. Anglers will often get excited at seeing schools of these big gray predators, mistaking them for trout, but adept fishers will note the flat mouth and lack of adipose fin.

FEEDING: predacious; eats other fishes, especially shiners and sticklebacks; also eats terrestrial insects, crustaceans, freshwater clams, crayfish and occasionally plankton.

SPAWNING: late May to July; spawning takes place near lake shores or a short distance up tributary streams, in shallows over gravel; several males attend 1 female; no nest; greenish or orange, adhesive eggs settle in gravel beds; average of 40,000 eggs per female; eggs hatch in 7–9 days; males mature at 3–4 years, females at 4–6 years; live up to 19 years.

OTHER NAMES: Columbia River Dace; previously Northern Squawfish.

DID YOU KNOW? Although there are four species of pikeminnows in North America, two of which are found in the Rockies, fishwatchers can identify these fishes by their non-overlapping ranges.

STATUS: common; secure.

HABITAT: usually lakes; some slower rivers and streams; on the bottom; near shore in summer, moves to deeper water in fall; prefers still water; seeks cover, such as rocks.

Northern Pike

Peamouth

Flathead Chub

large, toothless, terminal mouth

adult

silvery or cream body

lighter sides

ID: dark green to olive back; lighter sides; silvery or cream belly; large, elongated body; rounded belly in older fish; large, toothless, terminal mouth; fine nuptial tubercles on head, back and lower fins. *Spawning male*: dorsal fins become yellow or orange. *Juvenile*: distinct black spot on caudal peduncle.

SIMILAR SPECIES: *Northern Pike* (p. 110): has teeth; dorsal fin near tail. *Peamouth* (p. 64): smaller mouth. *Flathead Chub* (p. 68): barbels near mouth; longer and pointed pectoral fins.

LENGTH: *Average*: 12 in (30 cm). *Maximum*: 27 in (69 cm).
WEIGHT: *Average*: 2–5 lb (0.9–2.3 kg). *Maximum*: 29 lb (13 kg).

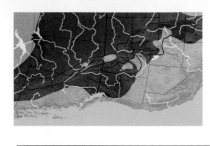

LONGNOSE DACE
Rhinichthys cataractae

Attempting to locate an adult Longnose Dace during the day is a challenge, because these minnows spend the daylight hours under rocks, hiding from predators such as Brook Trout. At night, Longnose Dace emerge to feed on aquatic insects and insect larvae. During the day, you are more likely to see schools of juveniles as they swarm in shallows. • Swimming close to the bottom of a fast-moving creek is relatively easy for the Longnose Dace; like most fishes that spend their time in fast water, it has a smaller swim bladder than lake fishes. As well, the Longnose Dace's wedge-shaped head helps to push the fish downward. • At one time, Longnose Dace on either side of the Continental Divide were considered two different species; modern methods of genetic analysis demonstrated that, rather than two species, there was one wide-ranging Longnose Dace species. The mouth area and base of the lower fins turn red on spawning males that live east of the divide, but the color is almost absent on Longnose Dace that live west of the divide. • *Rhinichthys* is Latin for "snout fish," and *cataractae* refers to a waterfall, specifically Niagara Falls, where the Longnose Dace was discovered. The name "dace" comes from "darce," an old version of "dart," which refers to the quick motions of this fish. • If local fishing rules allow it (always check first), use a small seine or dip net to catch a few of the usually abundant juvenile Longnoses. They prefer slow, gravelly sections along the edges of large Rocky Mountain rivers. If you manage to catch these tiny, gray fish, use a magnifying glass (or turn your binoculars backward) to see the great-looking little face with big eyes and a black, pencil-thin mustache.

FEEDING: nocturnal bottom feeder; eats aquatic insects, larvae, flies, midges and fish eggs.

SPAWNING: June to August; spawns mostly in streams, but in some lakes; male defends small territory and invites female by quivering his body at a sharp angle; up to 1200 transparent, adhesive eggs per female are broadcast over gravel or rocks; eggs are guarded by one parent until they hatch in 7–10 days; no parental care after hatching; mature at 2–3 years; live 5–6 years.

OTHER NAMES: Stream Shooter, Long-nosed Dace, Brook Minnow, Black-striped Minnow, Rock Minnow.

DID YOU KNOW? Hybridizations between Longnose Dace and other minnows are a common occurrence. Because Longnose Dace are broadcast spawners, their milt and eggs can mix with the eggs and milt of other minnows spawning in the same area.

STATUS: common; secure.

HABITAT: near the bottom of riffles in fast-flowing, cold streams; cold lakes; occasionally warm, slow, turbid waters.

Lake Chub

Speckled Dace

ID: silver; black mottling is thickest dorsally, lessening down sides; may have dark stripe along side; yellow or silver belly; conical head with pointed snout; small barbels (which may not be visible on smaller fish) at corners of distinctly subterminal mouth; rectangular dorsal fin; tip of upper jaw without groove separating it from tip of snout (frenum).

SIMILAR SPECIES: *Lake Chub* (p. 44): upper jaw separated from head by groove; larger, terminal mouth; breeding male has orange patch at base of pectoral fins. *Speckled Dace* (p. 76): upper jaw separated from head by groove; terminal mouth with frenum; nose more blunt.

conical head

subterminal mouth

black mottling

yellow or silver belly

adult

LENGTH: *Average:* 2–3½ in (5–9 cm). *Maximum:* 6½ in (17 cm).

SPECKLED DACE　　*Rhinichthys osculus*

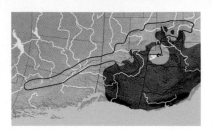

With a long snout and a small mouth that is angled downward in a frown, the Speckled Dace may appear to regard you with a disapproving expression. Perhaps this small minnow has a right to grimace; habitat degradation has caused the Canadian government to list it as a species of special concern. • Morphological characteristics of these minnows are so diverse that Speckled Dace were once separated into 12 different species. Forms began to evolve in various directions tens of thousands of years ago, when geological activity, such as volcanic eruptions, isolated populations. Varieties living in swift, high-gradient headwater streams of the Rockies developed streamlined bodies, slender caudal peduncles and enlarged, sickle-shaped fins to combat strong currents. Varieties found in less turbulent, lower-gradient rivers, such as the mainstem San Juan River, tend to be somewhat chubbier. • Speckled Dace are an important food for trout, where they co-occur. • The scientific name of the Speckled Dace describes its large snout (*Rhinichthys*) and small mouth (*osculus*).

FEEDING: omnivorous bottom feeder; active mainly at night; hides among rocks during the day; eats benthic insects and plant material; occasionally eats eggs or other fish larvae.

SPAWNING: most spawning in association with spring snowmelt, typically from May in southern portions of range to June or early July in more northern portions; male cleans detritus from small gravel area; female enters the nest and releases adhesive eggs; young fish mature at 1 year (second summer); live up to 3 years.

OTHER NAMES: none.

DID YOU KNOW? The Kendall Warm Springs Dace (*R. o. thermalis*) is a subspecies of the Speckled Dace that occurs only in a 1000-ft (300-m) section of a warm spring that flows into the Green River in the Bridger-Teton Forest of Wyoming. Because its habitat is so restricted, the Kendall Warm Springs Dace is listed as endangered. Several other subspecies of Speckled Dace with very limited ranges occur in the western United States. • The native range of the Speckled Dace is entirely west of the Continental Divide, whereas the range of its close relative, the Longnose Dace, is both sides of the divide.

STATUS: species of special concern in Canada; several isolated subspecies receive state protection; Kendall Warm Springs Dace receives federal protection in the United States.

HABITAT: varied; from riffles of high-gradient streams to quiet runs and sometimes backwaters; small creeks to large rivers; rarely in lakes; form large schools.

Longnose Dace

fleshy, subterminal mouth

dark flecks on body

spawning ♂

ID: extremely variable; grayish or dusky brown back and sides; dark flecks on body; creamy belly; lateral stripe may be prominent or weak; streamlined or chubby body; fleshy, subterminal mouth; groove between upper lip and snout; small, rounded barbels at corners of mouth (may be absent in Canadian populations). *Spawning male:* orange to red near mouth, anal fin base and lower caudal fin lobe.

SIMILAR SPECIES: *Longnose Dace* (p. 74): long, fleshy snout; no groove between upper lip and snout.

LENGTH: *Average:* 2–3 in (5–7.6 cm). *Maximum:* 4½ in (11 cm).

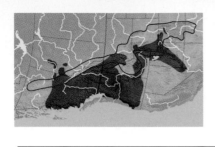

REDSIDE SHINER   *Richardsonius balteatus*

The native range of the Redside Shiner is largely west of the Continental Divide, but native populations occur east of the divide in British Columbia and Alberta. • The Redside Shiner is a schooling minnow, remaining in weedy areas during the day to avoid predation. If you happen to see schools of these little fish swimming through their shoreline habitats, you may notice that they are stratified by size. Young ones stay closest to the shore, often in waters only a few inches deep. As they get older and bigger, juvenile fish gradually venture into deeper waters, but only the largest adults feed at depths of more than a few feet. • Redsides are a very neat minnow for anglers to appreciate and to hone their subtle angling skills. Use the tiniest fly that your eyes will allow. Sink the fly into the clear lake water near a school of these small, gray fish. If you manage to land one, you'll be amazed at the chunky, deep shape and marvelous colors—especially those of a spawning male, with golden highlights offset by stunning crimson splashes.

FEEDING: eats crustaceans, aquatic and terrestrial insects and their young, as well as the young of other fish species.

SPAWNING: spring and summer; spawns in lakes and streams; in streams, males migrate first up tributaries, and females arrive a few days later; female is flanked by 1–2 males in riffles; female can produce up to 3600 eggs but will release 10–20 per spawning session; eggs adhere to vegetation and gravel and are covered by milt from the male; eggs hatch after 3–15 days, depending on water temperature; mature at 2–3 years; live 5–7 years; females live longer and grow larger than males.

OTHER NAMES: Red-sided Shiner.

DID YOU KNOW? Trouts and Redside Shiners are in some ways interdependent—Redside Shiners will eat juvenile trouts, but in turn, larger trouts will eat Redside Shiners.

STATUS: locally common; secure.

HABITAT: usually near shoreline in lakes; also large rivers and tributaries; requires vegetation for cover during the day.

ID: dark brown back, fading to yellow belly; deep body; small scales; keeled along belly between pectoral and anal fins; dark, downcurved lateral line; dark stripe through eye; large anal fin with 10 or more rays. *Spawning male:* bright yellow and red bands along sides and belly; nuptial tubercles on paired fins and head.

SIMILAR SPECIES: *Lake Chub* (p. 44): barbels at corners of mouth; anal fin has fewer rays; origin of dorsal fin just behind or even with origin of pelvic fins; less forked caudal fin; shallower body shape. *Red Shiner* (p. 46): lacks lateral band; smaller anal fin.

Lake Chub

Red Shiner

dark stripe through eye

deep body

bright yellow and red bands along sides

spawning ♂

large anal fin

LENGTH: *Average:* 4 in (10 cm). *Maximum:* 7 in (18 cm).

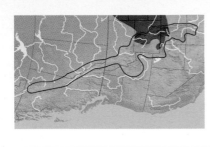

CREEK CHUB

Semotilus atromaculatus

If your main interests are watching fish behavior and wrestling, the Creek Chub may be the perfect fish for you. During spawning season, the pumped-up male waits patiently on the bottom for an attractive female to swim close by. Then, with a motion too rapid for the human eye, he locks her in a piscivorous embrace and flips her into an upright position. Using the nuptial tubercles on his expanded pectoral fin and body to provide grip, he clutches her until she releases several dozen eggs into his nest. The spent female recovers by floating belly up for several seconds before swimming away. • When you look into the waters of a clear, mid-elevation stream in spring, you may come across a long ridge of gravel that looks as if someone emptied a few buckets of small stones into the water. This engineering wonder is actually the nest of a Creek Chub. The male excavates the nest by forcefully swimming against the stream bottom to create a trench, then laboriously picking up small stones in his mouth and piling them a short distance upstream. When pairs spawn, the fertilized eggs sink to the bottom of the trench and are quickly covered with stones. • The Creek Chub reaches the western limits of its distribution in headwater streams of the Platte River in Wyoming and Colorado. • Creek Chubs typically inhabit small streams. The best times to see them are when males are constructing nests and during spawning.

SPAWNING: May to early July; spawns in streams in smooth water with small gravel and sand bottoms; male makes a trench 10–12 in (25–30 cm) wide and 3 ft (1 m) long or more by moving pebbles individually upstream; male embraces female, and she releases 25–50 eggs that sink into nest; both sexes spawn several times with different partners; male covers eggs with gravel; males mature at 3 years, females at 2–3 years; live up to 7 years.

FEEDING: omnivorous; feeds by sight; mainly eats insects and crustaceans with some plants; large adults eat small fishes.

OTHER NAMES: Horned Dace, Common Chub, Northern Creek Chub, Brook Chub, Silvery Chub, Mud Chub, Blackspot Chub.

DID YOU KNOW? The conspicuous nuptial tubercles on the spawning male's head inspired the Creek Chub's nickname "Horned Dace."

STATUS: common; secure.

HABITAT: prefers small, mid-elevation, clear streams; rarely shores of small lakes; uses gravel, sand or silt substrate.

ID: olive green back; silver sides with purple iridescence and dusky stripe; silver or white belly; thick, robust body; upper jaw extends past eye; small, flaplike barbel in fold above mouth; strong, hooked pharyngeal teeth; black spot at anterior base of dorsal fin. *Spawning male:* well-developed line of nuptial tubercles on each side of head and pectoral fins; head and sides may become tinted with orange, red, yellow, blue or purple.

SIMILAR SPECIES: *Pearl Dace* (p. 180): thinner, more elongate body; lacks spot on dorsal fin.

Pearl Dace

black spot on dorsal fin

thick body

dusky stripe

spawning ○

LENGTH: *Average:* 4 in (10 cm). *Maximum:* 12 in (30 cm).

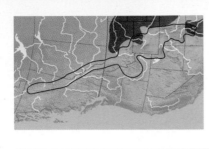

RIVER CARPSUCKER　*Carpoides carpio*

Though not a species that is characteristic of the Rocky Mountains, the River Carpsucker's range does extend into the foothills of the Rockies in Wyoming and New Mexico. • The entrance to the River Carpsucker's digestive system is extremely narrow because of a thick pad located near the mouth and throat that nearly fills the mouth and throat. As a result, the River Carpsucker's diet is restricted to tiny, decaying organisms and small invertebrates sucked from bottom silt. • Like many other fish species, River Carpsuckers are sensitive to sedimentation and changes in water temperature. They prefer quiet waters where submerged piles of brush and riparian vegetation offer protective cover and shade. When trees are removed from riparian areas, streamside habitat is altered. With fewer trees to provide shade, sunlight floods in and water temperatures rise. Without leaves and branches hanging over the stream, less organic material drops into the river. And without tree roots, banks become less stable and erode, altering the sediment load and flow patterns of the stream. All of these factors combine to change the composition of the aquatic environment, including the invertebrate and fish species that live there, sometimes resulting in a loss of diversity.

FEEDING: omnivorous bottom feeder; eats large amounts of detritus, diatoms, silt and algae; also eats insect larvae, mollusks and crustaceans.

SPAWNING: May to July; spawns over vegetation or debris in silt or sand; broadcast spawner; females usually produce 20,000–40,000 adhesive eggs; eggs hatch in 8–15 days; no parental care; mature at 3 years; usually live to 6 years, sometimes to 10 years.

OTHER NAMES: White Carp, Silver Carp, Cold Water Buffalo (southern United States).

DID YOU KNOW? Of the 48,170 recognized vertebrates found throughout the world, just over half are fishes. Forty percent of these fishes live in freshwater.

STATUS: locally abundant to rare.

HABITAT: quiet rivers, streams and lakes; reservoirs below 7000 ft (2100 m); associated with deep pools, backwaters and submerged brush piles.

Common Carp

nipple-shaped
lower lip

large scales

sickle-shaped
dorsal fin

adult

ID: olive to bronze back; silver sides; pale belly; short, blunt snout; large scales (less than 40 scales in lateral line); lower lip is nipple-shaped at center; long, sickle-shaped dorsal fin with more than 20 principal rays; first dorsal ray does not usually reach beyond middle of fin when pressed down.

SIMILAR SPECIES: *Common Carp* (p. 48): dorsal and anal fins have sawtooth spine; 2 barbels on each side of jaw. Ictiobus *spp.* (p. 184–85): brownish; no nipple on lower lip.

LENGTH: *Average:* 17 in (43 cm). *Maximum:* 25 in (64 cm).
WEIGHT: *Average:* 1–3 lb (0.5–1.4 kg). *Maximum:* 10 lb (4.5 kg).

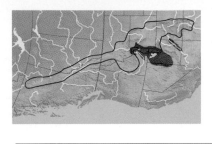

UTAH SUCKER
Catostomus ardens

For fishwatchers in the Rocky Mountains, spawning Utah Suckers may be among the most impressive and colorful fish species to behold. Can you imagine a continuous school of Utah Suckers 3 mi (4.8 km) long, 6 ft (1.8 m) wide and 24 in (60 cm) deep? Such a school was seen on the east side of Bear Lake, Utah, at 2:30 AM in mid-June, 1976! In the early 1800s, trappers and Native Americans gathered at Bear Lake during these extraordinary spawning runs to catch thousands of Utah Suckers. • Pioneers relied on the suckers of Utah and Bear lakes for food. During the breeding season, the fish have little fear, and fishwatchers have a good chance of getting a close-up view. Spawning takes place at night, with the best viewing opportunities after midnight. • Some good locations to find this fish are in the Heart Lake tributaries in Yellowstone National Park, Wyoming, in Bear Lake and Utah Lake in Utah and at St. Charles Creek, a tributary of Bear Lake, in Idaho. In fact, in St. Charles Creek, there are two separate runs of Utah Suckers. One run is composed of small, immature fish that are darker in color, and the other run is composed of larger, older spawners, recognizable by their faded colors and battered appearance.

FEEDING: omnivorous bottom feeder; eats algae attached to rocks; also eats plants and bottom-dwelling invertebrates.

SPAWNING: March to June in different parts of its range; spawns in tributaries; female is attended by 2 males; fish vibrate and release eggs and sperm; vibration stirs up gravel and buries eggs; young hatch in 1–2 weeks; fry move to a lake soon after hatching; live 10–12 years.

OTHER NAMES: Utah Mullet, Rosyside Sucker.

DID YOU KNOW? The species name *ardens* means "burning" and refers to the bright red lateral stripe that appears on spawning fish. This stripe often remains for months after the spawn.

STATUS: comparatively common in native range; sometimes abundant in lake habitats.

HABITAT: adaptable; wide range of habitats; lakes and streams; tolerates variety of currents; substrate ranges from mud or clay to gravel with little to a lot of aquatic plant life; cold, cool and warm water.

Largescale Sucker

White Sucker

ID: dark gray back; bronze-hued sides; white belly; densely speckled dorsal fin; silvery, diamond-shaped scales give checkered appearance; almost cylindrical in cross-section; large, short head; round snout; ventral mouth with fleshy, knobby lips; very deep groove in lower lip; coarse scales (60–73 in lateral line); usually 12–13 dorsal fin rays. *Spawning:* bright orange stripe along lateral line.

SIMILAR SPECIES: *Largescale Sucker* (p. 96): lightly speckled dorsal fin; pelvic fin connected to body with membrane. *White Sucker* (p. 90): lower lip much wider than upper lip.

round snout

fleshy, knobby lips

diamond-shaped scales

spawning adult

LENGTH: *Average:* 10½ in (27 cm). *Maximum:* 25 in (64 cm).
WEIGHT: *Average:* 2–4 lb (0.9–1.8 kg). *Maximum:* 12 lb (5.4 kg).

LONGNOSE SUCKER *Catostomus catostomus*

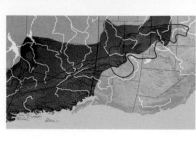

Suckers are believed to have originated in Asia and then expanded their range to North America when the Bering land bridge linked the two continents. Over the millennia, with a lot of swimming, the Longnose Sucker has extended its range as far south as the Colorado Rockies. Bait bucket releases have also helped it thrive. The Longnose Sucker has the most northern and broadest distribution of any other member of its family. • At one unenlightened time, sucker removal programs were all the rage (fewer suckers means more trout, or so thought many anglers), even in Rockies parks. After surviving those sad years, some unique populations of Longnose Suckers in isolated Rockies lakes may be just hanging on by their fin tips. • From late April to early June, Longnose Suckers advance in large numbers up tributaries to spawn. Migration to natal streams occurs mostly at night, although the actual spawning takes place during the day. These fish develop a bright red lateral stripe at this time. Both males and females spawn with more than one mate, and some fish will spawn an average of 40 times an hour! • The Longnose Sucker's scientific name refers to position rather than function; *catostomus* means "inferior mouth" in Latin, but the sucker mouth does not have any drawbacks. On the contrary, it is one of the best adaptations to feeding from a lake or river bottom. • When spring comes to the Rockies and small streams swell with snowmelt, Longnose Suckers will come out of the larger rivers and lakes for their annual spawning. Watch where a stream riffles over a shallow rocky area or where a beaver dam has created a little brushy waterfall. Longnoses will splash through these areas and rest in the slightly deeper holes nearby. The bright red stripe along their sides often causes streamside joggers to report sightings of landlocked Sockeye Salmon.

FEEDING: benthic feeder; eats mollusks, worms, crustaceans, detritus and aquatic insect larvae.

SPAWNING: April to July, depending on elevation; spawns in shallow tributaries and in gravelly shallows of lakes; female is flanked by 4–5 males, which take turns mating with her; male clasps female's pelvic fins or anal fin; no nest; white eggs stick to gravel; eggs hatch in 10–20 days; mature at 4–10 years; may live more than 20 years.

OTHER NAMES: Sturgeon Sucker, Northern Sucker, Western Longnose Sucker, Platte River Sucker, Gray Sucker, Red Sucker, Black Sucker, Red-sided Sucker, Finescale Sucker.

DID YOU KNOW? Longnose Suckers grow extremely slowly in northern waters. A 20-in (50-cm), 3-lb (1.4-kg) fish may be 25 years old!

STATUS: generally common and widespread; secure.

HABITAT: prefers cold lakes or rivers but may be found in warmer, turbid waters.

ID: slate gray or olive dorsally; white ventrally; small scales (more than 90 scales in lateral line); long, overhanging snout; deep cleft in lower lip; no lateral notch between upper and lower lips; large, rounded anal fin. *Spawning male:* thick, bright red lateral stripe above black stripe; darkened back. *Spawning female:* reddish wash along sides.

SIMILAR SPECIES: *White Sucker* (p. 90): mouth closer to end of nose; larger scales, especially toward caudal fin; scales both in front and rear of dorsal fin are equally large and obvious; no red lateral band on spawning male. *Mountain Sucker* (p. 98): mouth closer to end of nose; notch on sides of lips; shallow cleft in lower lip; cartilaginous scraper on lower jaw.

White Sucker

Mountain Sucker

long snout

reddish wash

spawning ♀

large, rounded anal fin

LENGTH: *Average:* 12–20 in (30–50 cm). *Maximum:* 25 in (64 cm).
WEIGHT: *Average:* 4 lb (1.8 kg). *Maximum:* 7 lb (3.2 kg).

BRIDGELIP SUCKER · *Catostomus columbianus*

Very little is known about this sucker, which inhabits the cold mountain streams and rivers of the Fraser River drainage of British Columbia, the Columbia River drainages of Idaho, Washington, Oregon and Nevada, and the Harney River system of eastern Oregon. The fact that the Bridgelip Sucker occurs mainly in the Fraser River and the Columbia drainage basin is reflected in the species name *columbianus*. • Within its limited range, the Bridgelip Sucker is found in a variety of environments. Some populations prefer small, fast-flowing streams with gravelly bottoms while others inhabit streams with slower-moving currents and sand or silt bottoms. Although Bridgelip Suckers are rarely found in lakes in the mountains, elsewhere, a few populations have adapted well to lake margins and reservoirs. • A good field mark for distinguishing the Bridgelip Sucker from other suckers found in the Rockies is the incomplete cleft in the lower lip. The Mountain Sucker also has this field mark, but it differs in having distinct notches where the upper and lower lips meet.

FEEDING: omnivorous; probably scrapes algae from rocks; also eats insect larvae and crustaceans.

SPAWNING: little known; late May to June; spawning behavior is probably similar to that of other suckers; mature when they reach 5 in (13 cm) long.

OTHER NAMES: Columbia Small Scaled Sucker.

DID YOU KNOW? The *Ligulus* tapeworm, probably the longest tapeworm in North America at 3.5 ft (107 cm), has infected some Bridgelip Sucker populations in the lower Crooked River in Oregon.

STATUS: common within its range; secure.

HABITAT: rivers and streams, usually cold and fast with gravelly bottoms; sometimes moderate currents with sand or silt bottoms; rocky riffles; backwaters; lake margins.

Mountain Sucker

Largescale Sucker

large, high eyes

round lower lip lobes

plump, rounded body

spawning

ID: olive brown back; pale yellow or white belly; plump, rounded body; large eyes, high on head; round snout; incomplete cleft in lower lip; membranous strip between base of pelvic fin and body; round lower lip lobes; small notches at corners of lips; small scales (97–111 in lateral line). *Spawning male:* orange stripe on sides. *Juvenile:* 3 dark blotches on sides.

SIMILAR SPECIES: *Mountain Sucker* (p. 98): visible indentations separate upper and lower lips. *Largescale Sucker* (p. 96): fewer than 80 scales in lateral line.

LENGTH: *Average:* 8–12 in (20–30 cm). *Maximum:* 15 in (38 cm).
WEIGHT: *Average:* ½ lb (0.25 kg). *Maximum:* 1½ lb (0.7 kg).

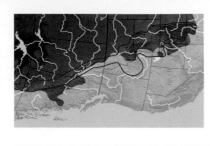

WHITE SUCKER   *Catostomus commersoni*

The White Sucker is a generalist species that is able to live in habitats ranging from cold streams to warm, and even polluted, waters. The White Sucker's native range is east of the Continental Divide; those found west of the Continental Divide in the mountain streams of Utah, Colorado, New Mexico and Montana have been introduced. Versatility benefits the White Sucker but poses a threat to other suckers native to the western Rockies. In the Colorado River basin, introduced White Suckers hybridize with both Flannelmouth Suckers and Bluehead Suckers, contaminating the gene pools of these native fishes. • During the spring spawning season, campers sleeping next to streams or shallow lakeshores may be roused by the splashing and jostling of hundreds of mating White Suckers. The suckers migrate upstream shortly after the ice breaks up. Animals such as other fish, eagles and bears depend on these spawning runs for food. Once hatched, the fry are a critical forage item in the diet of other young fish. • The best time to see these fish is during spawning season. White Sucker aficionados plan sucker-viewing trips for early spring, just after most ice has melted from the lakes. Look for a gravelly beach or a clear stream near a lake and watch carefully for the tan-colored, bullet-headed forms of these common suckers slowly drifting along. Following a single fish will usually lead the cautious fishwatcher to the favored sucker spawning grounds. There,

groups of White Suckers will be seen chasing and splashing, with an occasional fountain of water sprayed skyward by a cluster of wildly vibrating, egg-laying fish.

FEEDING: omnivorous bottom feeder; mostly active at dawn and dusk; eats mollusks, crustaceans, insect larvae, algae and aquatic plants.

SPAWNING: May to July, depending on elevation and temperature; migrates to shallow lake shores or smaller tributaries; prefers to spawn over gravel; 2–4 males flank 1 female while eggs and milt are released; spawn all day, frequently, over a period of 2 weeks; eggs hatch after 8–11 days; young remain at hatching site for 14 days; males mature in 5 years, females mature in 6 years; may live 14–17 years, but normally 10–12 years.

OTHER NAMES: Common Sucker, Mud Sucker, Brook Sucker, Black Sucker, Gray Sucker, Mullet, Black Mullet, Coarsescale Sucker.

DID YOU KNOW? White Sucker is processed and sold as "mullet" for human consumption. • *Commersoni* is derived from the name of an 18th-century French naturalist, Philibert Commerson, who explored much of the Southern Hemisphere for King Louis XV.

STATUS: common; secure.

HABITAT: variable; prefers cool, clean waters with sandy or gravel substrate; avoids rapid currents; uses shallow areas to feed.

ID: bronze, slate or olive back; white belly; rounded body; large scales; cone-shaped head; subterminal "sucker" mouth with bumpy (papillose) lips; lower lip much wider than high; 11–12 rays in dorsal fin; complete series (55–85) of lateral line scales. *Spawning male:* nuptial tubercles on head and belly but mostly concentrated on caudal peduncle and anal fin; flanks turn golden or even display red band; darker dorsally. *Juvenile:* 3–4 dark splotches on flanks.

SIMILAR SPECIES: *Longnose Sucker* (p. 86): longer snout; smaller or smoother scales (more than 80 in lateral line); small scales in front of dorsal fin (skin looks leather-like), with large scales only behind dorsal fin; red and black bands on sides while spawning. *Mountain Sucker* (p. 98): notches at sides of mouth between upper and lower lips.

Longnose Sucker

Mountain Sucker

cone-shaped head

subterminal "sucker" mouth

adult

LENGTH: *Average:* 10–16 in (25–41 cm). *Maximum:* 24 in (61 cm).
WEIGHT: *Average:* 2½ lb (1.1 kg). *Maximum:* 7 lb (3.2 kg).

BLUEHEAD SUCKER

Catostomus discobolus

The Bluehead Sucker takes the expression "scrape out a living" very seriously. It gets by almost entirely on algae and associated invertebrates, which it scrapes off rocks using the well-developed cartilaginous edge it has on each jaw. The Bluehead Sucker will feed between boulders, lying on its side or even upside down. In addition to the scraping edge, Bluehead Suckers have large, fleshy lips. • Normally, algae is eaten by tiny invertebrates, which are in turn eaten by larger creatures and so on, until the meal becomes substantial enough for an adult trout. As larger fish that eat primarily algae, suckers eliminate the in-between steps in the food chain but still provide a hungry trout with a sizeable snack. • The Bluehead Sucker is native to the Colorado River drainage, the Snake River system and the Lake Bonneville basin. It is declining in Arizona, Wyoming and Utah; introduced White Suckers hybridize with native Blueheads and threaten genetic integrity. • In a roundabout way, the Bluehead Sucker's Latin name is probably a reference to this fish's pendant-shaped upper lip. *Disco* comes from an ancient Greek word meaning "thrower of the discus," while *bolos* means "lump." • Look for foraging suckers in deep, rocky pools or in riffles where the current is strong. Bluehead Suckers normally disappear at the slightest disturbance; however, during spawning season, these fish lose their wariness, and fishers may be able to spot them splashing in riffle shallows.

FEEDING: omnivorous; feeds in deep, rocky pools or most commonly in riffles where current is strong; scrapes algae off rocks with cartilaginous edge on each jaw; also eats aquatic insects and invertebrates living on rocks.

SPAWNING: late spring to early summer, depending on elevation and water temperature; spawns in cobbled riffles during daylight; single female is typically joined by 2 males; use anal fins to "sweep" spawning substrate free of fine sediment; each female produces 5000–8000 eggs; fertilized eggs settle among interstitial spaces of riffle; mature at 2–3 years (usually 3 years); live 10–12 years.

OTHER NAMES: Chiselmouth Sucker, Western Chiselmouth Sucker.

DID YOU KNOW? A subspecies of the Bluehead Sucker, the Zuni Bluehead Sucker, is a natural hybrid of Bluehead and Rio Grande suckers. This mixing of two forms occurred during the Pleistocene when the headwaters of a Rio Grande tributary were captured by the headwaters of the Rio Nutria, a tributary to the Zuni River that flows into the Little Colorado River.

STATUS: rare; species of special concern in Wyoming and Utah; secure in Colorado and New Mexico.

HABITAT: medium to large, moderate-gradient, cool-water streams and rivers; occasionally in warmer-water, lower-gradient streams; rocky riffles and runs.

Mountain Sucker

ID: blue-gray head; olive brown back; brassy sides; may have brown mottling on sides; light yellow belly; medium-sized scales (75–120 along lateral line); pronounced snout overhangs mouth; large lips, especially pendant-like upper lip; deep notches on either side of mouth where upper lip meets lower lip; cartilaginous scraping edge on both jaws; moderately slender caudal peduncle. *Spawning male:* yellow-orange lower fins; red lateral stripe.

SIMILAR SPECIES: *Mountain Sucker* (p. 98): larger scales; adult is smaller; interradial membranes of caudal fin not pigmented.

pronounced snout

spawning ♂

yellow belly

slender caudal peduncle

LENGTH: *Average:* 6–12 in (15–30 cm). *Maximum:* 18 in (46 cm).
WEIGHT: *Average:* ½–1 lb (0.25–0.5 kg). *Maximum:* 2 lb (0.9 kg).

FLANNELMOUTH SUCKER *Catostomus latipinnis*

While establishment of non-native fishes, environmental degradation and habitat changes to the Colorado River basin have affected all native fishes, the Flannelmouth Sucker appears to be coping somewhat better than most other endemic species. Although it has not experienced the declines many other native fishes have, it still faces challenges to its persistence. Spawning and rearing areas have been negatively affected by dams, which diminish natural flow variation and temperature. As well, both introduced and native fishes prey heavily upon larvae and juveniles. • The introduced and highly adaptable White Sucker poses yet another threat. In addition to competing with native fishes for food and habitat, White Suckers hybridize with Flannelmouths, contaminating the genetic heritage. • Early settlers used suckers as food, harvesting great numbers during spawning season. The excess fish were preserved in salt, giving rise to the saying, "I'm thirsty as a sucker in a salt bale."

• The Flannelmouth Sucker may be seen feeding in shallows of large rivers over cobbled substrate near twilight.

FEEDING: bottom feeder; eats algae, aquatic plants and sometimes benthic invertebrates.

SPAWNING: spring, probably June; spawns over cobble and gravel bars when water temperatures are 54–60° F (12–15° C); 9000–23,000 eggs per female; adhesive eggs sink between crevices; no parental care; males mature earlier and are fertile longer; mature at 4–5 years; live 12–15 years.

OTHER NAMES: Buglemouth.

DID YOU KNOW? The species name *latipinnis* means "broad fin."

STATUS: common; secure.

HABITAT: large, swift rivers; deep riffles and runs; murky pools with few plants; mud, sand or gravel bottoms; young remain close to shore in shallows.

ID: reddish brown dorsally; yellow-orange ventrally; upper tail and sides are blue-gray or greenish; small head; small eyes, high on head; large, fleshy lips; elongated lower lip lobes; slightly sickle-shaped dorsal fin; medium-sized scales (90–116 in lateral line); scales smaller near caudal fin.

SIMILAR SPECIES: *Utah Sucker* (p. 84): shorter and thicker caudal peduncle; fewer (60–73) scales in lateral line; smaller caudal fin.

Utah Sucker

large, fleshy lips

small, high eyes

adult

slightly sickle-shaped dorsal fin

LENGTH: *Average:* 21 in (53 cm). *Maximum:* 30 in (76 cm).
WEIGHT: *Average:* 1–3 lb (0.5–1.4 kg). *Maximum:* 5 lb (2.3 kg).

LARGESCALE SUCKER *Catostomus macrocheilus*

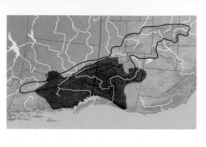

The Largescale Sucker is native to the Pacific Northwest and is found throughout the Columbia, Fraser and Peace river systems. Usually found only west of the Continental Divide, Largescale Suckers occasionally cross into the eastern Rockies via the Peace River. Like several other sucker species, the Largescale Sucker migrates to spawn. • Largescale Suckers are born with terminal mouths and feed upon zooplankton at the edges of rivers while they are young. Juveniles probably serve as one of the many forage species for predaceous fish and birds as well as mammals such as bears. When the suckers have grown to about 1 in (2.5 cm) long, the mouth moves to a sub-terminal position, and they become bottom feeders. Grown suckers use their ventral, fleshy lips to find food items such as benthic aquatic invertebrates and detritus.

FEEDING: benthic feeder; grazes for aquatic invertebrates, insects and detritus.

SPAWNING: June to July, usually just after Longnose Sucker and White Sucker; spawns in shallow water over sand or gravel in streams; female is flanked by multiple males; female releases up to 20,000 adhesive eggs per spawning season; no nest or parental care; eggs hatch in 2 weeks; males mature at 4 years, females at 5 years; live up to 15 years.

OTHER NAMES: Coarsescale Sucker, Columbia River Sucker.

DID YOU KNOW? Sensitive papillae cover the mouths of most suckers, including the Largescale Sucker. These little bumps serve as feelers for food in the same way that barbels do on other fish.

STATUS: common; secure.

HABITAT: large rivers and streams with moderate current; deep pools with sand and gravel bottoms.

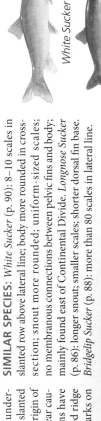

White Sucker

Longnose Sucker

Bridgelip Sucker

white belly

scales larger nearing tail

adult

ID: contrast between dark dorsal area and white under-parts; oval-shaped in cross-section; 11–14 scales in slanted row above lateral line; origin of dorsal fin ahead of origin of pelvic fins; dorsal fin has 13–16 rays; scales larger near cau-dal fin; less than 80 scales in lateral line; pelvic fins have membranous connections with body; slightly raised ridge along back behind head. *Juvenile:* 3 dark lateral marks on flanks.

SIMILAR SPECIES: *White Sucker* (p. 90): 8–10 scales in slanted row above lateral line; body more rounded in cross-section; snout more rounded; uniform-sized scales; no membranous connections between pelvic fins and body; mainly found east of Continental Divide. *Longnose Sucker* (p. 86): longer snout; smaller scales; shorter dorsal fin base. *Bridgelip Sucker* (p. 88): more than 80 scales in lateral line.

LENGTH: *Average:* 13–17 in (33–43 cm). *Maximum:* 24 in (60 cm).
WEIGHT: *Average:* 2–4 lb (1–2 kg). *Maximum:* 7 lb (3.2 kg).

MOUNTAIN SUCKER

Catostomus platyrhynchus

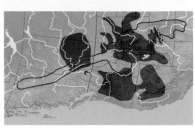

What little we know about the Mountain Sucker could make this species a poster fish for the protection of streamside habitat. The Mountain Sucker depends on intact streamside vegetation to keep riverbanks from eroding so that silt does not suffocate developing eggs. Juvenile fish also rely on vegetation for cover. The Mountain Sucker rarely grows more than 8–9 in (20–23 cm) long, making it one of the smallest suckers. • The Mountain Sucker was once known as two separate species—the Flatnose Sucker and Jordan's Sucker. Flatnose Suckers lived on the west side of the Continental Divide, in the Snake River drainage basin in Idaho, and Jordan's Suckers were native to the east side, in the upper Missouri drainage basin. • A deep notch on each side of the mouth where the upper lip meets the bottom lip distinguishes the Mountain Sucker from most other suckers found in the Rocky Mountains. Look carefully and you can see that the bottom lip looks similar to the tail, or fluke, of a whale. • Fishers may see dull flashes of the Mountain Sucker's sides as it turns upside down or sideways to scrape algae off the sides of boulders with the cartilaginous sheaths on its jaws. This fish is nowhere abundant, so fishers should pay careful attention to any chocolate–bar–sized suckers they spot in clear mountain streams.

FEEDING: eats mostly algae from the surrounding boulders; occasionally eats invertebrates.

SPAWNING: June and July; spawns in riffles, sometimes beneath deep pools; a large female may produce up to 3000 eggs per spawning season; no parental care; adhesive eggs stick to the bottom; after spawning, small schools of parents spend time in deep pools before migrating back to the larger river; eggs hatch after 8–14 days; young remain in pools or under streamside vegetation for cover from predators; males mature at 2–3 years, females at 4–5 years; males live up to 7 years, females up to 9 years.

OTHER NAMES: Plains Mountain Sucker, Northern Mountain Sucker, Redside Sucker, Jordan's Sucker, Flatnose Sucker.

DID YOU KNOW? The Mountain Sucker was one of the species collected by Lewis and Clark in Montana in 1805, but no one paid enough attention to this tiny fish to identify it until nearly 100 years after it was captured.

STATUS: locally common; secure in most of its range; species of special concern in Colorado.

HABITAT: clear, cold mountain streams; rocky riffles and runs; occasionally alpine lakes or big rivers; prefers sandy or cobble bottoms.

ID: brown or gray with dark splotches on back; yellowish sides; white belly; long, rounded snout; mouth covered with bumps (papillae); lateral notches where upper lip meets bottom lip; small cleft in bottom lip; cartilaginous ridges on jaw; dorsal fin is higher than length of its base; 80 or more scales on lateral line; unique bony projection at base of pelvic fin. *Spawning:* nuptial tubercles on ventral fins and bottom of caudal peduncle (more pronounced on male); male has bright red stripe above dark lateral stripe.

SIMILAR SPECIES: *Longnose Sucker* (p. 86): continuous lips; deep cleft in lower lip. *White Sucker* (p. 90): larger scales; shorter snout; continuous lips; deep cleft in lower lip.

Longnose Sucker

White Sucker

cartilaginous ridges on jaw

bony projection at base of pelvic fin

bright red stripe above dark lateral stripe

spawning ♂

LENGTH: *Average:* 5–7 in (13–18 cm). *Maximum:* 12 in (30 cm); 8 in (20 cm) in Montana and Wyoming.
WEIGHT: *Average:* 2–4 oz (50–100 g). *Maximum:* 9 oz (250 g).

RIO GRANDE SUCKER

Catostomus plebeius

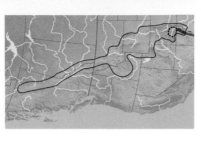

Formerly common in the Upper Rio Grande drainage basin in Colorado and New Mexico, the Rio Grande Sucker is now much reduced in range and abundance in the Rocky Mountains, largely the consequence of the non-native White Sucker. Hybridization with the introduced White Sucker has greatly diminished the range of the Rio Grande Sucker in Colorado; it now occurs only in the endorheic San Luis Valley and two small habitats in the Rio Grande drainage basin. Although the Rio Grande Sucker has also declined in New Mexico, it is more common there than in Colorado. Recovery efforts at Hot Creek State Wildlife Refuge in Colorado include removal of White Suckers and stocking of native Rio Grande Suckers. • Human alteration of habitat in the form of road building, forestry, recreation and livestock grazing has affected this species. When livestock enter the streams to drink or cool off, they trample the banks and stream-bed causing erosion, changing water quality and ruining spawning sites. In some study areas, livestock exclusion fences protected streams by allowing cattle access to limited areas only. • Rio Grande Suckers are most common in riffles, but may be seen, particularly when young, in slower-velocity runs. Where water is clear, they can be observed darting among cobble of riffles, scraping rocks for diatoms.

FEEDING: feeds in fast water over rock or gravel; scrapes algae from rocks; also eats diatoms, benthic invertebrates and small crustaceans.

SPAWNING: spawns in spring, over gravel in clear streams; spawning habits similar to other suckers; mature at 3 years; live up to 7 years; if conditions appropriate, may also spawn in fall.

OTHER NAMES: none.

DID YOU KNOW? When fisheries managers use controversial chemicals such as Rotenone to control exotic fish—a practice more common in the 1960s than today—native fishes, such as the Rio Grande Sucker, will also be adversely affected. Managers will usually rescue non-target native fishes beforehand and keep them in a hatchery for later return. For restoration of native trouts, the application of these chemicals often is the only appropriate tool.

STATUS: endangered in Colorado; declining in New Mexico.

HABITAT: small to medium-sized, clear, gravel- and cobble-bottomed, usually mid-elevation streams; downstream of rocky riffles during the day, into riffles at night; occasionally in backwaters; avoids areas high in silt or organic detritus.

Mountain Sucker

White Sucker

ID: olive to dusky brown back; white or pale yellow belly; bicolored or mottled; small, bumpy lips; lower lip has 3 rows of bumps (papillae); small cartilaginous ridges inside lips; cartilaginous ridge on both jaws; thick caudal peduncle; clear caudal fin. *Spawning:* red lateral stripe and jet black above on male; both sexes get nuptial tubercles.

SIMILAR SPECIES: *Mountain Sucker* (p. 98): lower lip shaped like whale tail; front of upper lip usually lacks bumps. *White Sucker* (p. 90): larger scales; lacks cartilaginous ridge on jaws; lacks later notches on mouth.

small, bumpy lips

mottled or bicolored

red lateral stripe

thick caudal peduncle

spawning

LENGTH: *Average:* 4–6 in (10–15 cm). *Maximum:* 8 in (20 cm).
WEIGHT: *Average:* 2 oz (50 g). *Maximum:* 4 oz (125 g).

RAZORBACK SUCKER   *Xyrauchen texanus*

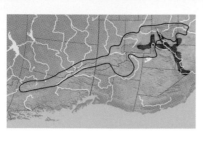

With a unique keel-like hump, there is no mistaking the Razorback Sucker. Count yourself lucky if you get to see one though, because this fish is endangered throughout its range. Historically, the Razorback Sucker occupied the mainstem Colorado River and its larger tributaries (Gila, Salt and Green rivers) from the Gulf of California to Wyoming. Few remain in the mainstem Upper Colorado and Green rivers, and much of the population is composed of aging adult fish. Most surviving Razorback Suckers are in Lake Mohave, Nevada, in an artificial impoundment. • Historically, this fish used its powerful caudal fin to propel it on long migrations to spawning areas, where it produced millions of young. Today, few of the traditional spawning sites remain in the Rockies: only Split Mountain on the Green River and a site near Grand Junction on the Colorado River. Dams and agriculture diversions have degraded habitat, blocked migration routes and changed spring runoff patterns to the detriment of the Razorback Sucker. • The Upper Colorado Recovery Implementation and San Juan Recovery Implementation programs (joint federal, state, tribal and NGO efforts) represent major efforts to conserve the Razorback Sucker. Augmentation of extant populations with young captured from Lake Mohave or reared at Dexter

National Fish Hatchery and removal of non-native predators are two of the primary efforts being made to recover the Razorback Sucker.

FEEDING: eats plant debris, zooplankton and aquatic invertebrates.

SPAWNING: late winter to early spring, during early spring snowmelt; once undertook long spawning migrations, though few areas are usable today; spawns over gravel shorelines in bays and windswept shallows; no nest, but a depression may form during spawning; female deposits few eggs at a time, but spawns repeatedly; transparent, adhesive eggs sink among gravel; young use flood plains as nursery habitat; mature at 3–6 years; males mature earlier than females; live to over 40 years.

OTHER NAMES: Humpback Sucker, Buffalofish.

DID YOU KNOW? Like Colorado Pikeminnows, Razorback Suckers were so common in the early 20th century that they were commercially harvested from the Gila and Salt rivers, both of which are lower Colorado River tributaries.

STATUS: endangered under federal Endangered Species Act; protected in every state throughout its range.

HABITAT: large, turbid rivers with strong currents; constructed impoundments; use boulders for cover.

Humpback Chub

ID: dark brown to olive back; pinkish brown sides; yellow to orange belly; colorful pink to orange fins; mouth covered with bumps (papillae); large, keel-like hump behind head; large dorsal fin; powerful, forked caudal fin. *Spawning:* black or brown above; tubercles on anal fin and caudal fin; males have bright yellow belly.

SIMILAR SPECIES: no other sucker has keel-shaped hump behind head. *Humpback Chub* (p. 54): fewer than 10 dorsal rays.

bumpy mouth

large, keel-like hump behind head

yellow to orange belly

large dorsal fin

spawning adult

LENGTH: *Average:* 20–23 in (51–58 cm). *Maximum (historical):* 3 ft (91 cm).
WEIGHT: *Average:* 10 lb (4.5 kg). *Maximum:* 16 lb (7.3 kg).

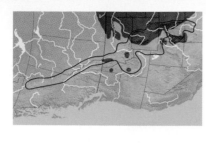

BLACK BULLHEAD *Ameiurus melas*

If you find yourself staring into a stagnant pool or small lake and watching a fish swim in confused circles, you are probably looking at a Black Bullhead. Instead of heading forward in one direction like most other fishes, these catfish swim randomly along, seemingly without a care in the world. Young Black Bullheads appear in early summer and school for two to three weeks or sometimes more. Like a compact, jet-black ball, the school swims effortlessly through the water then veers without warning, as if united by a collective consciousness. • These opportunistic scavengers usually feed at night, gobbling almost anything edible, including plants, insects, frogs and other fishes. The Black Bullhead's best-known feeding habit is swallowing hooks; in *Fishes of the Central United States*, Tomelleri and Eberle report that this fish seems "more at home on the hook than in its free and natural state." • Black Bullheads are sometimes the most abundant species in small ponds or shallow lakes. They do not do quite so well in larger water bodies because other species are able to outcompete them for food.

FEEDING: omnivorous bottom feeder; opportunistic scavenger; feeds at night on a variety of foods including plants, insects, crustaceans, fishes, frogs and snails.

SPAWNING: May to July; spawns in hollowed out depression in sand or gravel substrates of backwaters; makes depression in substrate for nest, often in vegetation; female lays gelatinous mass of 2500–4000 yellowish, adhesive eggs; eggs hatch in 7 days; one or both adults guard eggs and care for young; young remain in tight school, guarded by male, for 2–3 weeks or most of summer; mature at 2–3 years; live up to 9 years.

OTHER NAMES: Bullhead, Polliwog, Stinger, Chuckle-head, Riversnapper, Mudcat, Slick, Common Bullhead, Horned Pout, Yellowbelly Bullhead.

DID YOU KNOW? This fish's large head earned it the name "Bullhead." The name comes from England, where it refers to freshwater sculpins, which also have oversized noggins. • The poison glands associated with the pectoral fin spines (hardened rays) can produce a sting to the unwary handler.

STATUS: common; secure.

HABITAT: pools and backwaters; mud-bottomed ponds and shallow lakes; slow streams; stagnant, turbid waters; tolerates low oxygen levels and high water temperatures (up to 90° F or 35° C).

ID: black or dark olive overall; yellow or greenish ventrally; 4 pairs of black, gray or black-spotted barbels hang from "chin"; often pale bar on caudal peduncle; fin membranes darker than rays; one spine (hardened ray) in dorsal and pectoral fins; caudal fin not forked (square edges, truncate); flap-like adipose fin.

SIMILAR SPECIES: *Stonecat* (p. 108): narrow, keel-like adipose fin. *Channel Catfish* (p. 106): black spots on sides; deeply forked caudal fin.

Stonecat

Channel Catfish

gray or black-spotted barbels hang from "chin"

fin membranes darker than rays

caudal fin not forked

adult

LENGTH: *Average:* 3–10 in (7.5–25 cm). *Maximum:* 14 in (36 cm).
WEIGHT: *Average:* less than 1 lb (0.5 kg). *Maximum:* 8½ lb (3.9 kg).

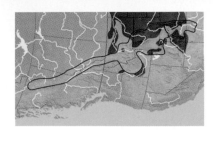

CHANNEL CATFISH

Ictalurus punctatus

The Channel Catfish was named for the spots that cover most of its body (*punctatus* means "spotted" in Latin). However, the name is somewhat confusing because fish over 12 in (30 cm) long often do not have spots. Perhaps the name "Varied Catfish" would be more suited to this species, which changes considerably with size, sex, season and geographic location. • As the most cultivated warm-water fish in North America, this fish has been well studied, especially in the United States. The Channel Catfish has been broadly distributed beyond its native range, often to the detriment of native fishes. In the Upper Colorado River and San Juan River drainage basins, considerable effort is expended to remove these unwelcome fish from habitats occupied by imperilled native fishes. • Aquatic insects, crustaceans, plant material and other fish are some examples of the many organisms that fall prey to this fish.

FEEDING: omnivorous bottom feeder; sometimes feeds at the surface; feeds both at night and during the day, grazing on or pursuing the most available food; uses barbels and sight to search for macrophytes, crustaceans, mollusks, insects, plants and other fishes.

SPAWNING: late May through early July when water temperature reaches 70–85° F (21–30° C); often occupies dark, secluded areas such as undercut banks, hollow logs, barrels or abandoned muskrat dens; may migrate to find a suitable den; male prepares nest and guards eggs; female releases 3000–8000 yellow eggs, depending on her size; eggs gradually turn brown and hatch in 5–10 days; hatchlings remain on bottom for 2–5 days until yolk sac is absorbed; mature at 3 years; may live 15 or more years.

OTHER NAMES: Channel Cat, Spotted Catfish, Northern Catfish, Lake Catfish.

DID YOU KNOW? Three thousand years ago, Native peoples used the spines of Channel Catfish as sewing tools. The spines were fashioned into needles by smoothing away the barbs and rounding the base. When the base broke off, the spine could still be used as a tool for piercing leather.

STATUS: common; secure.

HABITAT: warm to cool pools of medium to large rivers; lakes; sometimes brackish water; sand or gravel bottoms; may seek shelter in deep holes during the day and hide in logs or between rocks.

8 long "whiskers"

adult

deeply forked caudal fin

long base of anal fin

ID: yellowish green or light slate gray body; light gray belly; dark spots usually on sides; slender; scaleless; 8 long "whiskers"; small, compressed head; long snout; long, deep caudal peduncle; first ray of dorsal and pectoral fins modified to form spine; prominent adipose fin, free from back posteriorly; deeply forked caudal fin; long base of anal fin.

SIMILAR SPECIES: other Rockies catfishes lack deeply forked caudal fin.

LENGTH: *Average:* 14–21 in (36–53 cm). *Maximum:* 4.5 ft (1.3 m).
WEIGHT: *Average:* 2–4 lb (0.9–1.8 kg). *Maximum:* 37 lb (17 kg).

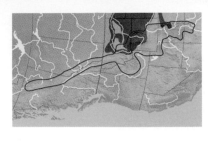

STATUS: widespread; may be locally common; species of special concern in Colorado.

HABITAT: slow-moving water that contains large rocks and boulders; usually gravel or silty bottoms.

STONECAT *Noturus flavus*

Aside from getting your fingers stuck in the mouth of a Northern Pike, being stung by a member of the catfish family is the only pain that a Rocky Mountain fish might inflict, and that of the Stonecat is the most painful. This fish is the largest member of the "madtom" group of catfishes, notorious for their stinging pectoral fins. A poison gland at the base of the first few spines on that fin delivers a wasp-like sting if the fish is not handled properly. • This fish is mostly a "feeler feeder," using its eight barbels to sense benthic creatures such as aquatic insect larvae. Stonecats feed mainly at night, and their sense of sight is rarely used in feeding. In fact, three other members of the madtom family are completely blind, relying entirely on their barbels to find food. • The Stonecat is most often found in moderate-sized cool to warm streams in cobbled riffles. Perhaps the Stonecat's affinity for hiding around boulders during the day is the reason for its name. • Stonecats, like other catfishes, do not have scales—they have a smooth skin. • Sighting the only madtom catfish in the Rockies makes a special day in the life of a fish lover. Carefully wade along the warmer shallows in the Marias or Missouri rivers, watching for big brown "tadpoles" among fist-sized rocks. Don't disturb the fish, because they are quite likely adults guarding their eggs, which are stuck to the underside of a rock. Take care in your identification, because sculpins and baby Burbot can be easily mistaken for these little madtoms.

FEEDING: largely at night; uses barbels to locate aquatic insect larvae, especially stonefly, caddisfly and midge larvae; occasionally eats small fishes, fish eggs, detritus and plant material.

SPAWNING: June to August; female spawns with a single male; she deposits about 500 eggs in a gelatinous clump under a large rock or log in a moderate current; one parent, usually the male, guards the eggs until hatching, which takes place in 1–2 weeks; mature at 3–4 years; live up to 9 years.

OTHER NAMES: Stone Catfish, Doogler, Whitecat, Deepwater Bullhead, Mongrel Bullhead, Stonecat Madtom, Beetle-eye.

DID YOU KNOW? Although there are 25 species of stinging madtom catfishes in North America, they are mainly found in warmer waters of the eastern United States. The Stonecat is the only madtom found in the Rockies. The population in St. Vrain Creek, Colorado, likely represents the southernmost population of this species in the Rockies.

ID: scaleless; typically gray or brownish yellow back; yellowish white belly; eyes almost on top of head; 4 pairs of barbels: 2 pairs on bottom of mouth, 1 pair on sides of mouth and 1 pair near nares; long, keel-like adipose fin is connected to body throughout its length (adnate); anal fin is about same length as adipose fin; squared caudal fin has light-colored margin.

SIMILAR SPECIES: *Burbot* (p. 146): 1 barbel on lower jaw; smaller, rounded caudal fin; skin has dark mottling; pelvic fins far forward on body, below or in front of pectorals; 2 dorsal fins, the first short and the second very long; anal fin is as long as second dorsal fin. *Channel Catfish* (p. 106): deeply forked caudal fin; adipose fin not connected to caudal fin. *Black Bullhead* (p. 104): adipose fin not connected to caudal fin; thicker body.

Burbot

Channel Catfish

Black Bullhead

4 pairs of barbels

adult

long adipose fin equal in length to anal fin

squared caudal fin

LENGTH: *Average:* 6–8 in (15–20 cm). *Maximum:* 12 in (30 cm).
WEIGHT: *Average:* 4 oz (100 g). *Maximum:* 1 lb (0.5 kg).

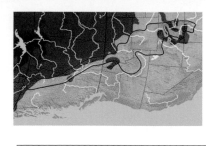

NORTHERN PIKE *Esox lucius*

The Northern Pike's hunting style is to lie in wait in shallow water, camouflaged among aquatic vegetation until an unsuspecting fish swims by. With a quick stab of its long snout, the Northern Pike grabs the prey in its heavily toothed jaws. Not only fishes fall prey to this carnivore's voracious appetite—ducklings, shorebirds and rodents are also victims. • The Northern Pike has unfairly earned a bad reputation because of its talent as a predator. Tales of vicious attacks on everything from swans to humans have followed it around its vast circumpolar range (its distribution is one of the largest in the world among freshwater fishes). • There is a myth among anglers that Northern Pike are not as easily caught in August because they lose their teeth. In fact, these fish do lose their teeth, but never all at the same time. Anglers find a decrease in the amount of biting Northern Pike in August because of an increase in available prey and a warming of the water. By late summer, the fish have usually moved to deeper, cooler waters. • Northern Pike have been introduced to waters on both sides of the Continental Divide as a fine food and sport fish. They are stocked for sport-fishing in warmer lakes and reservoirs throughout the southern Rockies. In Canada, they are uncommon in the mountains and foothills. • If you canoe slowly in the shallow, weedy bays of certain lakes or reservoirs in the southern Rockies, you'll see adults hanging motionless amongst the reeds or along the edge of a dense aquatic plant bed. Young are seen closer to shore, right next to overhanging

vegetation or undercut banks. • During spawning season, they will rise out of the murky water and slowly swirl through the vegetation or quickly burst up and over a beaver dam's spillway. You may get the thrill of seeing a three-foot-long (metre-long) behemoth cruising up the shallow water, pushing along a bow wave.

FEEDING: carnivorous; ambushes prey by hiding within aquatic vegetation; hunts during the day, mainly by sight; prefers Yellow Perch and other small fish; will also eat whatever is available, including birds, rodents and amphibians.

SPAWNING: April to May; prefers heavily vegetated, shallow bays or even flooded areas; 1 female is flanked by 2 or more males; female releases 50–60 eggs during each spawning act, which is repeated many times over several days; female produces about 30,000 eggs; no nest; eggs stick to vegetation; hatch after 2 weeks; young adhere to protective vegetation for 1 week; males mature in 3–5 years, females in 4–6 years; live up to 25 years.

OTHER NAMES: Jackfish, Shovelnose, Water Wolf.

DID YOU KNOW? Because the Northern Pike does not discriminate between endangered and common species as prey, an active program to remove Northern Pike from Upper Colorado River drainage streams is underway.

STATUS: sporadic in the Rockies; sensitive to over-fishing.

HABITAT: vegetated edges of typically clear lakes and rivers; backwaters or warm stretches of rivers with low to moderate current.

ID: body color varies from silver to yellowish green to dark brown, usually with light spots on a darker background; elongated body; rounded in cross-section; flattened head; long, flat snout contains sharp, backward-slanted teeth, even on roof of mouth; "cheek" and upper half of operculum are scaly; rounded dorsal fin is far back on body, equal with rounded anal fin; forked caudal fin; female is larger than male. *Juvenile:* vertical stripes instead of spots.

SIMILAR SPECIES: none in the Rockies.

long snout with sharp teeth

adult

rounded dorsal fin parallel with anal fin

LENGTH: *Average:* 18–30 in (46–76 cm). *Maximum:* 4.5 ft (1.3 m).
WEIGHT: *Average:* 4–23 lb (1.8–10 kg). *Maximum:* 38 lb (17 kg).

COHO SALMON
Oncorhynchus kisutch

In 1948, the Montana Fish and Game Department became the first institution in North America to successfully raise Coho Salmon, normally an ocean-going fish, entirely in freshwater. Today, Coho survive in many reservoirs and lakes in the Rockies and around the world, though most populations are maintained by annual releases of hatchery stocks. • Male Coho Salmon have two distinct life history patterns. Most males, called hooknoses, return to freshwater streams at age three or older to breed. Hooknoses are characterized by their exaggerated snout and enlarged teeth, which they use to aggressively fight off other males for access to spawning females. Other males, called jacks, reach maturity at age two. These salmon use their small size to their advantage, hiding behind rocks or debris and then sneaking in during the spawning act to fertilize the eggs without conflict. • Wild Coho Salmon have earned the nickname "Creekfish" because some populations migrate only short distances and spawn in small tributaries. Although these Coho may avoid the problems associated with dams and irrigation diversions that other salmon encounter, loss and alteration of riparian habitats remain a serious problem. • Watch for schools of light orange, parr-marked young as they dart near the shores of lakes in spring and summer. Coho fry (little speckled fish with red tails) are the schoolyard bullies of western foothills streams. Catch a tiny fly or mosquito, toss the hapless insect into a Coho pool and watch the fight as frenzied coho fry collide with each other as they race for the tidbit. A good spot to view Cohos is at Cascade Reservoir in Idaho.

FEEDING: predaceous; diet mainly consists of fishes and a few invertebrates; young feed on insects and plankton.

SPAWNING: October to December; adults become very aggressive during spawning; female digs redd in gravelly area of creek; both adults swim into nest and release milt and 440–5700 large, orange-red eggs; female may spawn with up to 4 different males; no parental care; adults die after spawning; eggs hatch in early spring after 35–50 days; fry emerge from March to July and remain in freshwater for 1–2 years; mature at 3–5 years; live up to 5 years.

OTHER NAMES: Silver Salmon, Coho, Hooknose, Silver, Creekfish, Blueback (young only), Medium Red Salmon.

DID YOU KNOW? The name "salmon" originated from the Latin word *salire*, meaning "to jump." Caesar's soldiers were apparently the first to use the name as they watched migrating schools of Atlantic salmon.

STATUS: uncommon and vulnerable in Canada; endangered in Idaho; stocked annually in Idaho and New Mexico.

HABITAT: landlocked Coho are stocked in large, cold freshwater lakes and reservoirs.

ID: steel blue to green overall; white on belly; black spots above lateral line and, if present, on upper caudal fin lobe; elongated snout; terminal mouth; sharp, well-developed, black teeth; white lower gums; long, thin dorsal adipose fin; broad caudal peduncle; usually 13 or more anal fin rays; tips of caudal fin are pointed. *Spawning male*: back and head darken; dirty red stripe along side; elongated head; thick, hooked snout; lower jaw enlarged and deformed.

SIMILAR SPECIES: *Chinook Salmon* (p. 116): usually larger; black lower gums; black spots on entire tail. *Kokanee* (p. 114): lacks distinct black spots; may have black speckles.

Chinook Salmon

Kokanee

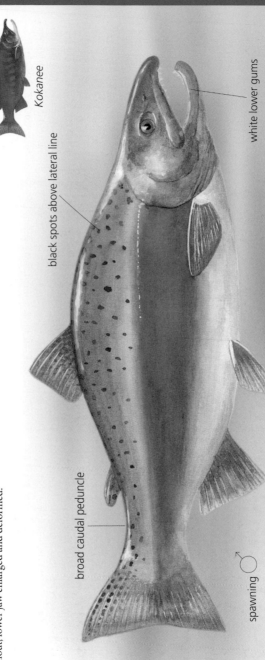

black spots above lateral line

white lower gums

broad caudal peduncle

spawning ♂

LENGTH: *Average:* 18–24 in (46–61 cm). *Maximum:* 38 in (97 cm).
WEIGHT: *Average:* 8–12 lb (3.6–5.4 kg). *Maximum:* Sea-run form: 31 lb (14 kg); Landlocked form: rarely exceeds 5 lb (2.2 kg).

KOKANEE • SOCKEYE SALMON *Oncorhynchus nerka*

Unlike anadromous Sockeyes, Kokanees have not developed their "sea legs" and remain in freshwater for their entire lives. Most *O. nerka* in the Rockies are Kokanee. They occur naturally where Sockeye no longer have access. In addition to areas of natural occurrence, Kokanee Salmon have been stocked in a number of cold, high-elevation lakes. Only a few Sockeye populations migrate all the way to the mountains, swimming up the Fraser River in British Columbia or up to Redfish Lake in the Sawtooth Mountains of Idaho. • The Kokanee is generally smaller and showier than the Sockeye. It was originally recognized as a separate species, *Salmo kennerlyi*, until scientists decided that separating the two forms was pointless. Intermediate or "residual" forms of the species also exist. Under certain circumstances, residual Kokanee fry will follow Sockeye on their ocean migrations, and a few infertile Sockeye will stay behind in the lakes. • Intolerant of warm water, Kokanee are normally found 16–100 ft (5–30 m) beneath the surface of large, cold lakes. At dawn and dusk, when the water surface has cooled, Kokanee migrate vertically to feed on zooplankton and insects. As water passes through the gills, zooplankton is strained out with fine combs called gill rakers.

FEEDING: pelagic feeder; usually eats zooplankton; sometimes grazes for crustaceans, tiny plants and insects.

SPAWNING: *Stream spawning:* August to December for Kokanee; September to October for Sockeye; female excavates redd in pea-sized gravel; both adults swim into nest and release milt and 370–1800 orange-red eggs; female may dig several redds and spawn with other males; no parental care; both parents die after spawning; eggs hatch from March to May; mature at 4 years; live to 8 years. *Shore spawning:* no redd; eggs fall between spaces in gravel.

OTHER NAMES: *Kokanee:* Kickininee, Kennerly's Salmon, Little Redfish, Land-locked Sockeye, Silver Trout, Yank. *Sockeye:* Blueback, Blueback Salmon, Red Salmon.

DID YOU KNOW? What do Kokanee and carrots have in common? The flesh of both is colored orange by a pigment called carotene. The skeletal structure of the zooplankton that Kokanee eat is packed full of carotene, which gives the Kokanee's flesh a brilliant orange-red hue.

STATUS: *Kokanee:* not at risk but susceptible to increases in sediment and water temperature; stocked. *Sockeye:* E.S.A. threatened species.

HABITAT: *Kokanee:* prefers open water; inhabits upper layers of open lakes in summer; uses all depths during spring and fall. *Sockeye:* open ocean; spawns in freshwater.

Chinook Salmon

Coho Salmon

ID: steel blue to dark gray head and back; bright silver sides; may have black marks on dorsal fin; dark fin membranes; robust, streamlined body; bluntly pointed head; small, well-developed teeth; anal fin has long base and angled trailing edge; 13 or more anal fin rays. *Spawning male:* head and body compressed; turned up, hooked snout; small hump before dorsal fin; back and sides are dirty red or sometimes yellow to green in Kokanee.

SIMILAR SPECIES: *Chinook Salmon* (p. 116) and *Coho Salmon* (p. 112): black spots on back and at least on upper lobe of caudal fin.

hooked snout

spawning ♂

small hump before dorsal fin

dirty red back and sides

long base of anal fin

LENGTH: Kokanee: *Average:* 8–14 in (20–35 cm). *Maximum:* 26 in (66 cm). Sockeye: *Average:* 22–25 in (55–65 cm). *Maximum:* 33 in (84 cm).
WEIGHT: Kokanee: *Average:* 4 oz–1½ lb (100–600 g). *Maximum:* 6½ lb (3 kg). Sockeye: *Average:* 4–7 lb (2–3 kg). *Maximum:* 15½ lb (7 kg).

CHINOOK SALMON

Oncorhynchus tshawytscha

As the largest Pacific salmon, the Chinook has rightfully earned the nickname "King Salmon" by tipping the scales at a whopping 125 lb (57 kg). Only ocean-going Chinook reach these large sizes, however. Because of a lack of suitable prey, landlocked specimens remain much smaller, usually weighing less than 20 lb (9 kg). • A single river can have several Chinook runs during different seasons because of the species' variable spawning patterns. Generally, fish that migrate farther upstream turn up at the river mouth earlier. While some fish swim only short distances to spawn, others, such as the Fraser River Chinook, may migrate 600 mi (960 km) or more. Depending on the food and habitat of the fish, the color of its flesh may also vary from white to red. • German naturalist Wilhelm Stellar first described a Pacific salmon (*Oncorhynchus* spp.) during an exploration of the Kamchatkan Peninsula in the 1740s. The Kamchatkan names in his field notes were used as species names instead of trying to pronounce the species name *tshawytscha* (pronounced "cha-vee-cha"), some jokingly call the Chinook the "Tongue-twister Salmon." • All through August, you can see these giant fish spawning in their home stream. A good place to view them is Swift Creek in Valemont, British Columbia. These majestic fish dig redds, chase intruders and eventually die along the shallow streambanks. All those stinky, decomposing salmon carcasses are needed to create a food web to support millions of tiny salmon fry in a few months. A mountain stream would be a terrible place for baby Chinooks to grow up if it were not for the rich nutrients that the parents carried upstream from the far-distant ocean. What a great display of the wonderful ecological linkages of nature. Powerfully smelly, but amazing.

FEEDING: in freshwater, young feed at all levels from bottom to water surface; main portion of diet is invertebrates such as terrestrial insects and chironomids; in ocean, feed on squid, shrimp and fish.

SPAWNING: March through May; spawns near riffles in large rivers or tributaries; both sexes behave aggressively; female digs a redd up to 12 ft (3.7 m) long and 12 in (30 cm) deep; parents swim into nest, vibrate and release milt and 4500–10,000 large, orange-red eggs; female guards nest but usually dies within days; eggs hatch in spring; alevins spend 2–3 weeks in nest; commonly spawn at 4 years old; may spawn at 5–7 years.

OTHER NAMES: Chinook, King Salmon, King, Tyee, Spring Salmon, Tongue-twister Salmon, Quinnat.

DID YOU KNOW? In 1872, the Chinook Salmon became the first Pacific salmon to be stocked around the world. For many years, the only self-sustaining, anadromous population to survive was on New Zealand's South Island.

STATUS: stocked; E.S.A. threatened species.

HABITAT: anadromous; most spend 1–2 years in freshwater and then 2–3 years at sea; widely stocked in freshwater lakes, but do not usually produce self-sustaining populations.

ID: blue-green or gray overall; silver belly; black spots on back and entire tail; large, laterally compressed, stream-lined body; small, circular scales; blunt snout; terminal mouth; black lower gums; well-developed teeth; upper jaw extends beyond eye; widely spaced gill rakers; long, thin adipose fin; square anal fin; 13 or more anal fin rays. *Male:* small males may be dull yellow. *Spawning male:* dark olive brown; enlarged, hooked jaw; gaping mouth; extended snout; changes are less obvious in freshwater stocks. *Juvenile:* 6–12 parr marks.

SIMILAR SPECIES: *Coho Salmon* (p. 112): shorter anal fin; white gums; no black spots on lower lobe of caudal fin. *Kokanee* and *Sockeye Salmon* (p. 114): lack distinct black spots.

Coho Salmon

*Kokanee &
Sockeye Salmon*

extended snout

spawning ♂

black spots on back and tail

square anal fin

LENGTH: *Average:* 33–36 in (84–91 cm). *Maximum:* 5 ft (1.5 m).
WEIGHT: *Sea-run form: Average:* 30–40 lb (14–18 kg). *Maximum:* 126 lb (57 kg). Landlocked form: *Average:* 15–18 lb (6.8–8.1 kg). *Maximum:* 44 lb (20 kg).

CUTTHROAT TROUT

Oncorhynchus clarki

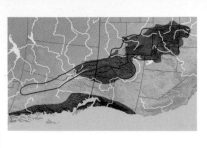

The two orange or red lines in the folds on each side of the Cutthroat Trout's lower jaw are often used to distinguish this species from other black-spotted trouts. However, these slashes may not be present on young Cutthroats and they may disappear in a matter of hours when the fish dies. The only reliable way to tell if you have a Cutthroat is to feel for the minute teeth just behind the base of the tongue. • No fewer than 14 subspecies of Cutthroats, naturally isolated through time, have been described, but many of these are now threatened with extinction. Habitat loss, stream degradation, whirling disease (see Rainbow Trout) and competition, hybridization and predation by introduced fishes have taken a toll on native Cutthroats. Declining East Slope trout populations were restocked with a mixture of the Yellowstone Cutthroat subspecies, Rainbow Trout and hybrids of the two. The successful introductions contaminataed the native Cutthroat Trout gene pool and put many native and pure Cutthroats in danger of extinction. Pure populations of Westslope, Greenback, Rio Grande and Colorado River subspecies survive mainly in the headwaters of a few mountain streams within their historical ranges. • In recent years, government agencies have made efforts to protect and expand a number of populations of this fish. • To see a Cutthroat Trout, hide beside a shady pool in a cool foothills stream in August and toss a grasshopper toward the upstream end. Watch carefully just below the grasshopper in the dark water. If you've been calm and quiet, the resident Cutthroat will slowly rise up to sniff out your offering. If it meets with his approval, the insect will disappear in a gentle slurp. Often, however, the trout will merely look carefully and slip back into the depths.

FEEDING: eats aquatic and terrestrial insects, crustaceans, frogs and small fishes (mostly trouts, salmon, speckled and longnose daces, chubs, suckers, sculpins and sticklebacks) and their eggs.

SPAWNING: April to May; spawns in gravel-bottomed streams; female digs a redd 12 in (30 cm) across and 6 in (15 cm) deep by turning to her side and beating her tail; lies in nest and releases 500–1500 eggs for fertilization by male; female dislodges gravel upstream of nest to cover eggs; eggs hatch after 6–7 weeks; young remain under gravel for the first few weeks; mature at 3–4 years; live up to 8 years.

OTHER NAMES: Native Trout, Red-throated Trout, Short-tailed Trout, Harvest Trout, Black-spotted Trout. *Well-known subspecies:* Westslope, Yellowstone, Lahontan, Snake River, Colorado, Rio Grande, Greenback trouts.

DID YOU KNOW? The novel *A River Runs Through It* by Norman MacLean involves native Cutthroat Trout in Montana. When the movie was made, filmmakers used hatchery-raised Rainbow Trout because of the low numbers and small size of the remaining Cutthroat Trout.

STATUS: all declining; several subspecies listed as threatened by the E.S.A.; others protected by individual states; several others extinct.

HABITAT: mountain streams and tributaries; alpine lakes; clean, clear, oxygen-rich water; some individuals stay within gravelly "home territory," only 60 ft (18 m) wide, for their entire lives.

Rainbow Trout

SIMILAR SPECIES: *Rainbow Trout* (p. 120): no minute teeth at base of tongue; absence of gular slash an unreliable field mark.

ID: marked differences in color and spotting patterns within and among subspecies; light yellow body; irregularly shaped black spots, sometimes few or absent, but usually concentrated above lateral line and near head; pinkish "cheek"; pink extends down lateral line; bright red streaks in gular folds of lower jaw; minute teeth at base of tongue; tiny scales, typically more than 100 in lateral line. *Spawning male:* large male may have "hook jaw"; often bright red abdomen. *Juvenile:* 10 parr marks along lateral line; some individuals retain parr marks as adults.

small head and mouth

adult

LENGTH: *Average:* 10–15 in (25–38 cm). *Maximum:* 3 ft (1 m).
WEIGHT: *Average:* 5 lb (2.3 kg) or less. *Maximum:* 41 lb (19 kg).

RAINBOW TROUT   *Oncorhynchus mykiss*

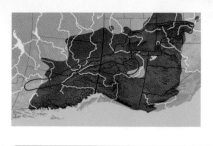

The Rainbow Trout is one of the most commercially raised sport fish in North America. It is highly respected by fly fishers because of its spectacular jumps and fighting strength. • Its colorful appearance varies in hue with lifestyles and habitats, as do the Rainbow Trout's various names. Silvery-colored Steelhead Trout live in saltwater for most of their adult lives but spawn in freshwater. Redband Trout live in streams in the Canadian Rockies and develop brick-red side bands at spawning. Kamloops Trout can weigh up to 52 lb (23.6 kg) in the productive montane lakes of the British Columbia interior. • Humans have spread this trout from western North America so that it now lives on six continents, making it the most widely introduced species in the world. But human interference has had ecological consequences. Throughout the Rockies, many rivers were stocked with non-native Rainbow Trout. The stocked individuals hybridized with and out-competed local fishes, including Cutthroats, and today only small pockets of native, pure fish species remain. • Wild Rainbow Trout in several mountain states have been particularly hard hit by whirling disease, another consequence of stocking and fish culture. Characterized by tail chasing or "whirling" and a darkened tail (blacktail), the disease is caused by a parasite that digests the infected fish's cartilage and often leads to devastating population declines. • Find a foothills stream overgrown with stream-side shrubs. Position yourself with the sun at your back and a clear view of a riffle as it drops into a little pool. As your eyes become accustomed to the shadows in the water, you'll realize that some of the shadows are actually tiny Rainbow Trout. If your binoculars can focus close enough, you might see the bright white tips on the trouts' fins as well as fine black speckling across the sides.

FEEDING: eats mainly aquatic and terrestrial insects, crustaceans, snails, leeches, other fishes and eggs if available.

SPAWNING: usually March to late June; spawns in flowing water; usually in fine gravel of a riffle; female digs a large redd with her caudal fin; flanked by 1–2 males, she releases 800–1200 eggs; female covers eggs with gravel; eggs hatch in late July to mid-August; mature at 2–3 years; live up to 13 years. *Steelhead:* some return to sea after spawning; young spend 2–3 years in freshwater and 1–4 years in ocean; mature in 2–4 years; few live beyond 5 years.

OTHER NAMES: Steelhead Trout, Kamloops Trout, Pacific Trout, Silver Trout, Redband Trout, Redside, Gerrard Trout.

DID YOU KNOW? Because of the cold, unproductive, tiny streams that they love, Alberta's native Rainbow Trout, found in the Athabasca River from its headwaters in the Rocky Mountains to the southern slopes of the Swan Hills, includes some of the slowest growing and smallest Rainbows.

STATUS: introduced populations: common; secure. *Native populations:* of concern.

HABITAT: cool, oxygen-rich waters; moderately flowing streams; prefers stretches of swift-flowing water, edge of strong currents, head of rapids or strong riffles; also moderately deep lakes and ponds.

ID: bluish to olive back; silver and yellowish green sides with dark spotting throughout body and fins; may have pink line on side that turns red while spawning; pink blush on "cheek"; 12 or fewer anal fin rays; more than 100 scales in lateral line. *Steelhead:* silvery and bright when emerges from sea; torpedo-like body shape. *Juvenile:* 8–12 parr marks, which may remain in adulthood at higher elevations.

SIMILAR SPECIES: *Cutthroat Trout* (p. 118): basibranchial teeth near back of tongue; red slash along gular fold. *Golden Trout* (p. 122): smaller; more golden color; dark spots below lateral line are concentrated near caudal fin; exist in only a few mountain lakes.

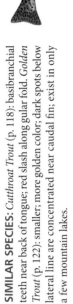

Cutthroat Trout

Golden Trout

pinkish "cheek" and body

bluish to olive back (highly variable)

squarish to slightly forked (variable)

adult

LENGTH: Rainbow: *Average:* 12–18 in (30–46 cm). *Maximum:* 36 in (91 cm). Steelhead: *Average:* 20–33 in (51–84 cm). *Maximum:* 4 ft (1.2 m). **WEIGHT:** Rainbow: *Average:* 1–3 lb (0.5–1.4 kg). *Maximum:* 52 lb (24 kg). Steelhead: *Average:* 4–20 lb (1.8–9 kg); varies depending on race. *Maximum:* 46 lb (21 kg).

GOLDEN TROUT

Oncorhynchus mykiss aquabonita

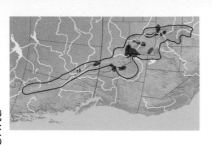

With a yellowish green back, gold sides and a brilliant pink stripe, the Golden Trout radiates with color. This fish was recently classified as a unique subspecies of the Rainbow Trout. • Although the Golden Trout has been introduced to Rocky Mountain lakes in Colorado, Idaho, Wyoming, Montana and Alberta, this beautiful fish is native only to the South Fork Kern River of California's Sierra Nevada range. The native population has been declining, and protective measures are in place to coax its numbers back up. • Because the Golden Trout prefers water temperatures of 55–63° F (14–17° C), it is found only in cold mountain lakes and streams. Usually it lives at elevations over 1 mi (1.5 km), where it grows quite slowly. When the Golden Trout is the only trout species in a lake it may flourish, but it does not compete well with other trout species. • For anglers, the Golden Trout is a rare and highly prized fish, surrounded by many rules and regulations. • Most mountain lakes with Golden Trout are quite a distance from the nearest parking lot, but the hike is well worth the effort. A stunning color pattern and crystal-clear mountain water makes for excellent viewing. During spawning in late June or July, watch carefully along the shore of alpine lakes, or slip quietly alongside the outflow streams, looking first for the shadow of a fish in the bright summer sunshine, then spotting the slowly undulating form of a Golden Trout as it hovers in the current or cruises for summer bugs.

FEEDING: eats aquatic insects and larvae; zooplankton.

SPAWNING: June to late July or when water temperature reaches 50° F (10° C); female digs more than one redd in gravelly area of small mountain stream; lays 500–2000 eggs; more than one male will fertilize eggs; eggs hatch in September; mature at 3–4 years; live up to 7 years.

OTHER NAMES: California Golden Trout.

DID YOU KNOW? *Aquabonita* means "beautiful water" in Spanish, a fitting name for this colorful fish.

STATUS: rare; native Little Kern subspecies is listed as threatened by the E.S.A.

HABITAT: cold, well-oxygenated, high-elevation lakes and streams; gravelly and rocky shores; prefers water temperatures of 55–63° F (14–17° C).

ID: colorful, golden body; red along lateral line and belly; yellow-green back; black spots along back and dorsal fin, concentrated near caudal fin; orange and white tips on lower fins; possible large, oval marks along lateral line, up to 10 per side; small scales; 12 or fewer anal fin rays.

SIMILAR SPECIES: *Rainbow Trout* (p. 120): black spots over entire body; pinkish "cheek"; larger scales. *Cutthroat Trout* (p. 118): red slash along gular fold; spots over most of body, especially above lateral line; basibranchial teeth.

Rainbow Trout

Cutthroat Trout

parr marks

spots concentrated near tail

adult

LENGTH: *Average:* 6–10 in (15–25 cm). *Maximum:* 19½ in (50 cm).
WEIGHT: *Average:* 10–14 oz (280–400 g). *Maximum:* 4½ lb (2 kg).

BROWN TROUT *Salmo trutta*

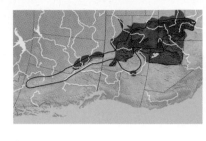

Early European settlers introduced the Brown Trout to North America and elsewhere. Many of the fish were forms either from Germany or from Scotland. Today, the populations are mixed and indistinguishable and have spread through much of the United States and Canada, but some trout that resemble the original forms remain in Yellowstone National Park, Wyoming. • Brownies are drift feeders that have a preference for streams with cover and an intermediate waterflow. They are voracious predators that have become a problem for the native species that they out-compete. In fact, Brown Trout are responsible for the elimination of several native North American salmonids. • This species seems to need warmer habitats than other Rocky Mountain trout. The most northerly Brown Trout in North America are in foothill streams in the Rocky Mountain House area of Alberta (a bit south of 53° N). Brownies stocked north of this point seldom spawn successfully. Because they can handle warmer water temperatures and higher turbidity than other trouts, they may be present in streams disturbed by logging or industrial activity. • The Brown Trout's closest native relative is the Atlantic Salmon. In some parts of the world, the Brown Trout can be anadromous, living in the ocean as adults and only returning to freshwater streams to spawn. • A great time to view Brown Trout is during spawning in fall. Visit spawning flats on rivers known to have Brownies, such as Madison and Firehole drainages in Yellowstone National Park in Wyoming and Bill Griffiths Creek on the Bow River near Canmore, Alberta. By simply standing along the shore, you can watch females digging redds and great chase scenes as the males battle for the right to spawn.

FEEDING: opportunistic drift feeder; hides under cover and darts out to catch prey; highly territorial; largest fish occupy best feeding territories; eats insects, shrimp, mollusks, fishes, amphibians and rarely small mammals, birds and snakes.

SPAWNING: September to January, usually when water temperatures fall below 45–50° F (8–10° C); spawns over shallow, gravelly beds in side channels of streams or at the outlets of lakes; female digs 1 redd, lays 1200–6000 eggs and covers them with gravel; most young hatch from March to late April; mature usually at 3 years; live up to 15 years, but usually 6–13 years.

OTHER NAMES: German Brown Trout, English Brown Trout, German Trout, English Trout, von Behr Trout, Loch Leven Trout, European Brown Trout, Spotted Trout, Brownie.

DID YOU KNOW? In 1880, Fred Mather, a representative of the US Fish Commission (now the US Fish and Wildlife Service), went fishing in Germany with Baron Friedrich Felix von Behr, president of the German Fish Culturalist

STATUS: common; secure.

HABITAT: often streams with gentle flow; deep pools; under abundant cover such as overhanging vegetation, undercut banks and snags; also large rivers, beaver ponds and lakes; tolerates turbidity and water temperatures up to 75° F (24° C).

Bull Trout

Rainbow Trout

Cutthroat Trout

adult

red spots with blue halos

square caudal fin has no spots

Association. Mather liked the Brown Trout they were catching so much that he arranged to have eggs shipped to the United States. That variety of trout is known as "von Behr Trout" after Fred's fishing buddy.

ID: golden brown, blue-green or olive back and sides; may have silver sides; white to yellowish underside; body, gill cover and most fins often covered with orange-red spots with bluish halos and dark, X-shaped or crescent-shaped spots or occasionally pale spots; 12 or fewer anal fin rays; square caudal fin has no spots.

SIMILAR SPECIES: *Bull Trout* (p. 126): spots on body are lighter than olive background color; bottom fins have white leading edges; forked caudal fin. *Rainbow Trout* (p. 120) and *Cutthroat Trout* (p. 118): pinkish hue, especially near "cheek"; dark spots smaller and more plentiful; no orange-red, blue-haloed spots; few or no spots on gill cover; caudal fin forked and covered with black spots.

LENGTH: *Average:* 10–16 in (25–41 cm). *Maximum:* 34 in (86 cm).
WEIGHT: *Average:* 1–2 lb (0.5–0.9 kg). *Maximum:* 18 lb (8.1 kg).

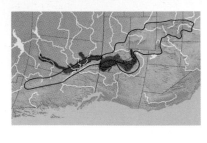

BULL TROUT

Salvelinus confluentus

Bull Trout were once common in all streams with headwaters in the Rocky Mountains of Alberta, Idaho and western Montana. At the turn of the 20th century, these beautiful fish were also widely distributed well into the central plains. Since then, Bull Trout have declined in numbers and distribution. These large fish are unusually easy to catch, making them vulnerable to overfishing. Today, all remaining populations are protected from harvest by anglers. The saying "no black, put it back" refers to the lack of black markings on the Bull Trout's dorsal fin. • Other factors contributing to the Bull Trout's decline include habitat loss, blocked migration routes (caused by dams and culverts) and reduced water quality and quantity through industrial activity or agricultural soil erosion. Competition and interbreeding with the introduced Brook Trout is also a serious problem. • While spawning, the female digs her redd then covers the fertilized eggs with gravel. The smaller females can only move little pebbles found at shallow creek edges, and their eggs may become stranded when winter flows are low. Fortunately, stronger females are able to move larger gravel and can bury their eggs in safer, deeper midstream waters. • During September, you can get a great view of these species while they are spawning. You'll see big Bull Trout defending their gravel nests ("redds") and small Bull Trout hiding out and trying to avoid their cannibalistic relatives. One good location to observe these fish is Kananaskis Provincial Park in Alberta.

FEEDING: piscivorous; Bull Trout and Mountain Whitefish are a classic predator-prey match; also feeds on other fishes, aquatic insects, crustaceans and mollusks; may take surface insects.

SPAWNING: September to October; migrates to small, shallow creeks in August; female digs large redd in gravel, lays 1300–9000 eggs and covers them after spawning; eggs hatch from March to April; young stay in nursery creeks for 2–3 years; mature at 4–5 years; adults often spawn every other year; live up to 20 years.

OTHER NAMES: Mountain Char, Western Brook Trout, Inland Char.

DID YOU KNOW? Bull Trout were considered the same species as the coastal Dolly Varden (*Salvelinus malma*) until 1978, when it became clear that no interbreeding takes place between the freshwater-loving Bull Trout and its sea-loving cousin.

STATUS: uncommon; E.S.A. threatened species; sensitive in Alberta.

HABITAT: clear, cold, oxygen-rich waters; small headwater streams; large, gravelly rivers with low sediment loads; cool lakes; often the only species in the fastest, steepest sections of mountain streams.

Brown Trout

Brook Trout

blunt snout

long, downturned upper jaw

no markings on dorsal fin

adult

white leading edge on lower fins

shallowly forked caudal fin

ID: olive green to tan body with silvery overtones; pale yellow to red spots on back and sides; lower fins with white leading edge; no black marks on dorsal or caudal fins; blunt snout; long, downturned upper jaw; 12 or fewer anal fin rays; shallowly forked caudal fin with pointed to rounded tips. *Spawning male:* orange to red sides.

SIMILAR SPECIES: *Brown Trout* (p. 124): black markings on dorsal fin; light body with large, irregular dark spots and orange-red, blue-haloed spots; square caudal fin. *Brook Trout* (p. 128): dark spots on dorsal fin; lighter color overall; worm-like markings on back; red, blue-haloed spots.

LENGTH: *Average:* 8–31 in (20–79 cm). *Maximum:* 3 ft (1 m).
WEIGHT: *Average:* up to 18 lb (8.1 kg). *Maximum:* 40 lb (18 kg).

BROOK TROUT

Salvelinus fontinalis

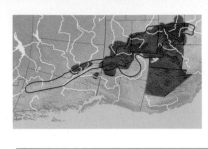

The unique vermiculations, or "worm tracks," on the backs of Brook Trout set these handsome fish apart in mountain waters. Brookies prefer small, cold, clear, slow-moving waters. However, they tolerate a wide range of conditions including beaver ponds and small lakes that are low in oxygen. • Native to eastern North America, Brook Trout were the first fish to be introduced elsewhere in North America and have spread widely. They are a non-native fish that competes with native fish. Most jurisdictions have tried Brook Trout eradication programs, including using anglers to selectively harvest Brookies, building barrier dams and electrofishing all Brookies above the dams. These programs met with limited success. • Introduced Brook Trout spawn at younger ages than the closely related native Bull Trout, which causes many mixed populations and overcrowding. When overcrowding occurs, competition and hybridization can be a serious problem for native Bull Trout. The separation in spawning times (Bull Trout mostly in September, Brook Trout mostly in November) is probably what keeps Brookies and Bulls from hybridizing even more. • The Brook Trout is actually a char—it is the only char in the Rockies to have "jelly donuts" (red or yellow dots with blue halos) on its sides. • Head high up into the Rockies in late fall. Find a tiny side-channel or tributary stream and walk slowly along, looking for fish not much longer than your hand. When you spot one, crawl up to the stream edge and watch carefully. The spawning colors of these small fish are astounding. Males will sport brick-red bellies and glowing blue doughnut spots, with sharply contrasting white and black lines on the edges of their bright red fins. They'll even have hooked jaws like a great Pacific salmon, but all reduced down to a fish the size of a candy bar.

FEEDING: omnivorous; feeds primarily on aquatic and terrestrial invertebrates; also eats fishes, frogs, snails, snakes, and eggs and young of its own species.

SPAWNING: October to November; usually spawns over gravel beds of shallow streams or lakeshores; male arrives first and defines a territory; female builds a redd up to 8 in (20 cm) deep over 2 days; average female lays 300–500 eggs; eggs hatch from April to May; mature at 1.5–3 years; live up to 7 years.

OTHER NAMES: Eastern Brook Trout, Speckled Trout, Specks, Mud Trout, Spotted Trout, Speckled Char, Brook Char, Squaretail, Brookie, Aurora Trout, Mountain Trout, Native Trout.

DID YOU KNOW? The following quandary is an excellent example of conservation problems. The Brook Trout is imperilled in much of its native range, partially as a consequence of the introduction of Rainbow and Cutthroat trout. And yet, the introduction of Brook Trout into areas outside its native range presents a problem for fish native to the area in which is introduced, such as Cutthroat and Bull trout.

STATUS: common; secure.

HABITAT: creeks, rivers, mountain lakes and beaver ponds; clear, shallow areas with water temperatures below 70° F (21° C); takes cover under banks or overhanging bushes and behind rocks.

Lake Trout

Bull Trout

adult

vermiculations on back

red spots with blue halos

white leading edge on lower fins

ID: olive green to dark brown back; silvery white underparts; "worm tracks" (vermiculations) on back; sides have red to yellow tinge; light spots throughout body, including head; blue halos around red and yellow dots on sides; ventral fins with white leading edge followed by black line; 12 or fewer anal fin rays; squared caudal fin. *Spawning male:* crimson or orange wash to belly; hooked jaw.

SIMILAR SPECIES: *Lake Trout* (p. 130): no "worm tracks" on body; whitish spots cover entire body; deeply forked caudal fin. *Bull Trout* (p. 126): no "worm tracks" on body; no spots on dorsal fin; white leading edge on paired fins not followed by black line; white to pinkish spots.

LENGTH: *Average:* 6–10 in (15–25 cm). *Maximum:* 33 in (84 cm).
WEIGHT: *Average:* 2½–11 oz (70–310 g). *Maximum:* 14½ lb (6.6 kg).

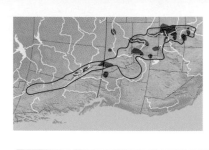

LAKE TROUT

Salvelinus namaycush

In summer, these large, solitary fish follow the retreat of colder water to the bottom of a lake, rarely making excursions into the warm surface layer. The best opportunity to see them in the wild is in spring and fall, because Lake Trout will use shallow waters when the water is cold throughout a lake. • Large Lake Trout are often over 20 years old, but one granddaddy of a specimen was found to be 62 years old! All Lake Trout mature late in life and may spawn only once every two to three years, making recovery from overfishing difficult. Lake Trout from a cold alpine lake in Jasper National Park, Alberta, have been recorded at 28 years old and only 13 in (33 cm) long. These little Lakers have only about two months of ice-free summer to fatten up on a few mosquito larvae before everything slows down to the winter world under the ice again. • In fall, the spawning urge brings Lake Trout into shallows where diligent fish lovers can observe their graceful forms. Spawning is nocturnal, so the best time for viewing Lake Trout is in early morning when the water is calm and the fish have not yet left the shallows after their night's activities. As you canoe quietly along the shallows, watch for long, grayish fish with pale white leading edges on their pectoral and pelvic fins. To overhead fishwatchers, those lines on the fins show up very well, sometimes better than the fish themselves.

FEEDING: piscivorous; also eats crustaceans and aquatic insects; young feed first on zooplankton, then on shrimp and aquatic insects.

SPAWNING: October and November; spawns at night, usually in shallow water less than 40 ft (12 m) deep, over boulders or cobble; does not require running water; male cleans silt from an area with his body, tail or snout but constructs no nest; female lays up to 6000 eggs; eggs sink to bottom between rubble and hatch after 4–5 months; mature at 6–7 years; can live to 25 years or more.

OTHER NAMES: Laker, Mackinaw, Great Lakes Trout, Great Lakes Char, Salmon Trout, Landlocked Salmon, Gray Trout, Great Gray Trout, Mountain Trout, Togue, Namaycush, Masamacush, Forktail.

DID YOU KNOW? Every day, a large Lake Trout eats the equivalent of at least two adult-sized Kokanee. • Lake Trout in Yellowstone Lake, Wyoming (stocked illegally by a misguided fish-lover), are now such a threat to the native Cutthroat Trout that Wyoming has a "Must-Kill" angling regulation for any Lakers caught.

STATUS: somewhat common in a reduced area; very sensitive to overfishing.

HABITAT: mostly restricted to deep, cool lakes; occasionally shallow rivers and lakes in northern North America; feeds at the surface in spring and fall, but otherwise stays below 50 ft (15 m) deep.

Brook Trout

Bull Trout

large, terminal mouth

adult

covered in whitish, irregular spots

deeply forked caudal fin

ID: generally dark gray or olive brown back; paler underparts; head and body are covered in whitish, irregular spots; slightly orange lower fins with dull white leading edge; large, terminal mouth; large, protruding eyes; 12 or fewer anal fin rays; deeply forked caudal fin. *Juvenile:* 5–12 dark, irregular parr marks along lateral line.

SIMILAR SPECIES: *Brook Trout* (p. 128): "worm tracks" on back; pale spots and reddish, blue-haloed spots on sides; distinct black markings on dorsal fin; spawning male has red belly; caudal fin only slightly forked. *Bull Trout* (p. 126): red or orange spots on sides; caudal fin not as deeply forked.

LENGTH: *Average:* 18–25 in (46–64 cm). *Maximum:* 49 in (1.3 m).
WEIGHT: *Average:* 2–6 lb (0.9–2.7 kg). *Maximum:* 102 lb (46 kg).

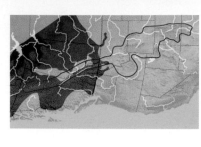

LAKE WHITEFISH   *Coregonus clupeaformis*

Although the Lake Whitefish is a dweller of the deep, you are more likely to encounter this species than other whitefishes. On a calm evening, you may see the dorsal fin cutting through the surface momentarily, when the fish rises gently to swallow a floating insect. Its well-known shape is formed by a small head that flows through a hump on the back into a broad body. The size of the hump depends on the age of the fish. • The best identifier for different forms is the number and length of gill rakers. Fish that live in open water will evolve to have extended gill rakers that are better for filtering plankton. Lake Whitefish caught near the surface tend to have higher gill-raker counts than forms that nibble food from the lake bottom. • This was the first native fish in the Canadian Rockies to be the focus of a re-introduction program. In the "trout-only" days of early fisheries management, some lakes were poisoned to remove unwanted species that might compete with stocked trout. During fall 2000 and fall 2001, biologists re-introduced adult Lake Whitefish to Lac Beauvert in Jasper National Park, Alberta, from a nearby lake that had been overlooked in the poisoning days. This move signaled a brighter future for Lake Whitefish and acknowledged the importance of fish in Rocky Mountain ecosystems. • Get to a lakeshore in the Rockies on an October night when the moon is full and the crisp air is dead calm. Carefully watch along a gravel beach for schools of Lake Whitefish to slip out of their deep-water homes and move into the shallows. You'll see brief chases, frenzied egg-laying

and effortless gliding. If you can get up close, you may see rows of beautiful, whitish "pearls" along the fishes' sides. These are breeding tubercles and form only on mature fish during spawning time.

FEEDING: benthic feeder; takes larval insects (particularly *Chironomidae* midges), snails, clams, fish eggs and some-times smaller fishes; some individuals are pelagic feeders, sifting for lake shrimp and other plankton and occasionally taking insects from the surface; young feed on plankton.

SPAWNING: late September to early winter; spawns when water temperatures fall to about 46° F (8° C) or below in water 6½–13 ft (2–4 m) deep on rocky reefs and sandy shoals of large lakes; occasionally migrates into tributaries; no nest; eggs incubate over winter and hatch April to May; mature at 4–5 years in northern lakes; live up to 30 years, but seldom more than 15 years.

OTHER NAMES: Humpback Whitefish, Common White-fish, Eastern Whitefish, Great Lakes Whitefish, Inland Whitefish, Labrador Whitefish.

DID YOU KNOW? In the fur-trade era journals of early Rocky Mountain travelers, the Lake Whitefish was usually called by its Cree name, *Tittameg*. This abundant fish was the main fuel of both dog teams and hungry voyageurs in the western mountains.

STATUS: common; secure.

HABITAT: cool, deep water at the bottom of large lakes; mostly at depths of about 33 ft (10 m), some as low as 320 ft (100 m); occasionally in rivers.

ID: bluish back, changing to white and silver flanks and underside; laterally compressed body; subterminal mouth; anterior ray of dorsal fin extends past base of posterior ray when pressed down; small head; 2 flaps of skin between nares; large fish develop hump behind head; forked caudal fin. *Juvenile:* lacks parr marks along lateral line.

SIMILAR SPECIES: *Mountain Whitefish* (p. 136): upturned snout; more pointed snout when spawning; 1 flap of skin between nares; anterior ray of dorsal fin does not extend past base of posterior ray when pressed down. *Pygmy Whitefish* (p. 134): smaller; rounded snout; 1 flap of skin between nares; anterior ray of dorsal fin does not extend past base of posterior ray when pressed down.

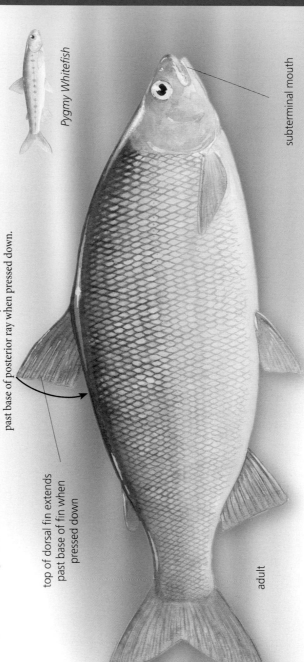

Mountain Whitefish

Pygmy Whitefish

subterminal mouth

top of dorsal fin extends past base of fin when pressed down

adult

LENGTH: *Average:* 15 in (38 cm). *Maximum:* 24 in (60 cm).
WEIGHT: *Average:* 2½–4½ lb (1.1–2 kg). *Maximum:* 10 lb (4.5 kg).

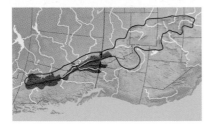

PYGMY WHITEFISH

Prosopium coulteri

We know very little about the Pygmy Whitefish, a small and inconspicuous fish that lives deep in lakes and mountain streams. In 1892, Carl H. Eigenmann found the species in the Kicking Horse River at Field, British Columbia, during a sampling trip along the Canadian Pacific Railway. It was later found at other locations along the Rockies and in Alaska, but it was not until 1952 that the Pygmy Whitefish was discovered in eastern Canada, living fairly deep in Lake Superior. • The Pygmy Whitefish seems to have two disconnected distributions, one following a line from the Great Lakes to Canada's Great Bear Lake, and the other following a diagonal line along the Rockies. Those people familiar with glacial history will recognize the pattern of the last ice age, which separated the two regions and forced the fish into southern streams. When the two separate ice shields melted and retreated, large, cold lakes formed and offered ideal conditions for the Pygmy Whitefish. As the climate warmed further, this species remained only in the mountains and at the bottom of cool, large lakes. • For most of the year Pygmies are invisible, hiding deep down in cold Rocky Mountain lakes. It is only during fall spawning runs that the lucky fisher might spot these tiny whitefish in the shallows of a clear stream or along the gravelly shore of a mountain lake. Your best bet is during the evening,

or possibly on a bright, moonlit night. Sit, wait, and watch with a good flashlight ready, but don't turn the flashlight on unless you see tiny forms flitting about in the murk. Their small size, big eyes and chubby, round face should help you distinguish Pygmies from the more common Mountain Whitefish. If you see some, celebrate and be sure to call your local fisheries biologist.

FEEDING: mainly bottom feeder; takes zooplankton, aquatic insect larvae, crustaceans, small mollusks and eggs of trout and whitefish.

SPAWNING: October to January, depending on latitude; presumably spawns in shallow water in either lakes or streams; female produces 100–600 eggs per spawning season; eggs are shed over gravel; hatch in spring; mature at 1–3 years, usually at 2 years; live up to 8 years.

OTHER NAMES: Coulter's Whitefish, Brownback Whitefish.

DID YOU KNOW? The Pygmy Whitefish is difficult to tell from a young Mountain Whitefish and probably has been overlooked in many places in the Rockies.

STATUS: rare.

HABITAT: mountainous lakes; moderate to swift, silty or clear streams; prefers deep, cold lakes; usually stays deeper than 20 ft (6 m); sometimes in shallows.

Mountain Whitefish

Lake Whitefish

rounded snout; slightly subterminal mouth

top of dorsal fin doesn't extend past base of fin when pressed down

small adipose fin

spawning adult

ID: dark brown back; silvery sides; whitish belly; elongate body is rounded in cross section; small head; rounded snout; slightly subterminal mouth; 70 or fewer scales in lateral line; anterior ray of dorsal fin does not extend past base of posterior ray when pressed down; 11–12 dorsal fin rays; small adipose fin. *Spawning male:* nuptial tubercles on head and paired fins. *Juvenile:* several parr marks along lateral line.

SIMILAR SPECIES: *Mountain Whitefish* (p. 136): larger adipose fin; bulbous snout; smaller scales (70 or more in lateral line). *Lake Whitefish* (p. 132): much larger; more laterally compressed; double nasal flap; anterior ray of dorsal fin extends past base of posterior ray when pressed down.

LENGTH: *Average:* 4–5 in (10–13 cm). *Maximum:* 10 in (25 cm).
WEIGHT: *Average:* 1 oz (20–30 g). *Maximum:* 4 oz (100 g).

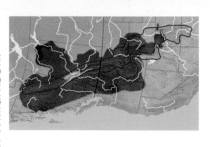

MOUNTAIN WHITEFISH
Prosopium williamsoni

Mountain Whitefish, known affectionately as Rockies, are common in every major river system in the northern Rocky foothills. In Colorado and Utah, it is native only in westslope streams (Green River in Colorado; Provo and Logan drainage basins in Utah). This coldwater fish has endured habitat changes and increased fishing pressures remarkably well. However, whitefish are sensitive to environmental or chemical pollution and are sometimes likened to a canary in a coalmine. • Some Mountain Whitefish can be sedentary, but many populations are known for their migratory behavior. In fact, Mountain Whitefish seem in perpetual migration between seasonal feeding habitats and spawning grounds, and they move in large groups from pool to pool. Spawning runs are legendary among residents living near the rivers on the eastern slopes of the northern Rockies. Pods of whitefish school upstream rivers in fall, en route to their spawning grounds either in the main stem of a river or slightly into its tributaries. One Rocky tagged in Alberta swam several hundred miles to its spawning stream. • Occasionally, you may come across a thinner Mountain Whitefish with a slightly upturned snout. Known as a "Bugle-nose" or "Pinocchio," this distinct fish pokes its specialized snout between rocks on the river bottom and—depending on which expert you talk to—"flips" or "vacuums" up invertebrates. • Anytime from mid-September to freeze-up, watch along the shallow downstream margins of deep pools. You'll probably see a fish or two drift out of the deeper, turbulent water and hover over the shallow gravel beds. They are masters of fast water, seeming to drift without effort in the rushing flow.

FEEDING: largely benthic feeder; eats invertebrates including aquatic insect larvae and mollusks; sometimes eats fish eggs and smaller fishes; will take terrestrial insects from the surface in streams or plankton in mid-water.

SPAWNING: late September to February; migrates to spawning grounds in the mainstem of fast rivers or in tributaries; sometimes gravelly lake shores; courtship begins in evening, with spawning at night; no nest; eggs sink into spaces between gravel; about 5000 eggs per female; eggs hatch from March to late April when the ice breaks; young form schools; mature in 3–4 years; live up to 18 years (oldest known age of 29 years).

OTHER NAMES: Rocky Mountain Whitefish, Williamson's Whitefish, Mountain Herring; Yellowstone River populations historically called Sterlet or Steret.

DID YOU KNOW? The belief that whitefish and trout are in direct competition for food is largely unfounded. For thousands of years, whitefish and trout have lived quite well together in streams, probably because each species prefers a different microhabitat.

STATUS: common, locally abundant; secure.

HABITAT: resident or migratory; rivers and fast, clear or silty areas of large streams; requires deep pools at least 16 ft (4.9 m) long; also cold, deep lakes; usually stay above 65 ft (20 m) deep.

ID: dark brown or blue back; silvery sides; slender; cylindrical body; 70–90 scales in lateral line; small head; bulbous snout; subterminal mouth; single flap of skin between nares; anterior ray of dorsal fin does not extend past base of posterior ray when pressed down; forked caudal fin. *Juvenile:* 7–11 large, oval parr marks (sometimes with a few spots above).

SIMILAR SPECIES: *Lake Whitefish* (p. 132): 2 nare flaps; subterminal mouth; anterior ray of dorsal fin extends past base of posterior ray when pressed down. *Pygmy Whitefish* (p. 134): smaller; larger scales (fewer than 70 in lateral line); rounded snout; slightly subterminal mouth.

Lake Whitefish

Pygmy Whitefish

small head

bulbous snout

top of dorsal fin doesn't extend past base of fin when pressed down

adult

LENGTH: *Average:* 6–18 in (15–45 cm). *Maximum:* 23 in (58 cm).
WEIGHT: *Average:* 1–3 lb (0.5–1.4 kg). *Maximum:* 5½ lb (2.5 kg).

BEAR LAKE WHITEFISH   *Prosopium abyssicola*

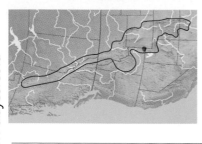

The Bear Lake Whitefish is a small whitefish, endemic to Bear Lake on the Utah-Idaho border. When fully grown, most adults are only about the length of your hand. The young grow extremely fast in the first two years, but growth slows significantly after that. • As the Latin name implies, Bear Lake Whitefish remain at "abyssal" depths of 60–100 ft (18–30 m), even to spawn. Your only chance of catching a glimpse of these fish may be on the occasional summer night when they migrate vertically to feed in the surface waters. Otherwise, Bear Lake Whitefish depend almost completely on the small invertebrates that live on the soft bottom. • Bear Lake Whitefish are sometimes eaten by Lake Trout and Cutthroat Trout, but they face few threats from humans. They live too deep to be taken by anglers, and so far only small amounts of toxic pesticides and fertilizers enter the lake from nearby residences or farms.

FEEDING: varied diet includes bottom-dwelling aquatic invertebrates, insect larvae and aquatic worms; occasionally eats fishes.

SPAWNING: late January to early March; spawns deep below surface over gravel substrate; no nest; broadcast spawner; female produces an average of 2000 eggs; young mature at 3–4 years; live up to 13 years.

OTHER NAMES: none.

DID YOU KNOW? There are many organic alternatives to the pesticides and fertilizers used on lawns and gardens. Wherever you live, the chemicals you add to the earth will seep into the groundwater and eventually drain into a stream or lake, causing the water quality to deteriorate.

STATUS: sensitive in Idaho and species of concern in Utah because of restricted range.

HABITAT: cold, deep water; usually stays 60–100 ft (18–30 m) deep.

Bonneville Whitefish

Bonneville Cisco

ID: back may be tinged with green; silvery sides; white belly; slender body; cycloid scales; small mouth; lower jaw covered by upper jaw when mouth closed; 68–79 scales in lateral line; deeply forked caudal fin. *Spawning:* green color of back deepens.

SIMILAR SPECIES: *Bonneville Whitefish* (p. 140): pointed snout; smaller scales (76–90 in lateral line); grayish dorsally; more often in shallow water; young have dark spots. *Bonneville Cisco* (p. 142): sharply pointed snout; lower jaw projects beyond or equals length of upper jaw.

lower jaw covered by upper jaw when mouth closed

green-tinged back

deeply forked caudal fin

spawning adult

LENGTH: *Average:* less than 8 in (20 cm). *Maximum:* 12 in (30 cm).
WEIGHT: *Average:* 2–4 oz. (50–100 g). *Maximum:* 8 oz (200 g).

BONNEVILLE WHITEFISH

Prosopium spilonotus

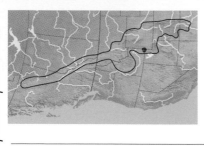

Bonneville Whitefish are found only in Bear Lake, a large lake on the Utah-Idaho border. Like most coldwater bodies, the lake is stratified into three layers. Bonneville Whitefish spend most of their lives in the middle layer, where water temperatures change rapidly with the seasons. With large swim bladders, these fish can regulate buoyancy and remain deep below the surface. Bonneville Whitefish occasionally rise when they visit the mouths of tributary streams, and schools congregate in the shallows during the winter spawning season. • Several researchers believe that this whitefish, evolved from the Mountain Whitefish, but exactly where and when they diverged is unclear. • Ancient Bonneville Whitefish bones have been found in Lake Bonneville fossil beds, leading researchers to believe that this fish evolved in the Bonneville basin and then spread into Bear Lake through the Snake River during the last glacial epoch when Lake Bonneville was much larger. Since the retreat of the glacier, Bear Lake provides the only suitable habitat for the Bonneville Whitefish.

FEEDING: varied diet includes midge larvae, bottom-dwelling aquatic invertebrates and aquatic worms; occasionally eats terrestrial insects (excluding midges), fishes and eggs of other fish species.

SPAWNING: late November to early December; schools move to shallows to spawn; break into groups of 5–6 males with 1 female; eggs are broadcast over gravel or sand bars; average of 600–900 eggs per female; mature at 3–4 years; live up to 10 years.

OTHER NAMES: none.

DID YOU KNOW? Bear Lake is the only lake in the Rocky Mountains with four endemic fish species: the Bear Lake Whitefish, the Bonneville Whitefish, the Bonneville Cisco and the Bear Lake Sculpin.

STATUS: common in Bear Lake; vunerable species because of restricted range.

HABITAT: cold, deep water; usually stay at 60–100 ft (18–30 m) deep.

ID: grayish back; silvery sides; white belly; dark spots on back and sides, which may fade or disappear when fish is 10 in (25 cm) long; elongated body; cycloid scales; short head; large, blunt snout extends slightly past lower jaw; small mouth; large eyes; 9–11 anal fin rays; deeply forked caudal fin.

SIMILAR SPECIES: *Bear Lake Whitefish* (p. 138): more pointed snout; larger scales (68–79 on lateral line); may be greenish dorsally. *Bonneville Cisco* (p. 142): lower jaw projects beyond upper jaw. *Mountain Whitefish* (p. 136): 12–13 anal fin rays.

Bear Lake Whitefish

Bonneville Cisco

Mountain Whitefish

large, blunt snout extends past lower jaw

white belly

deeply forked caudal fin

adult

LENGTH: *Average:* 8–12 in (20–30 cm). *Maximum:* 23 in (58 cm).
WEIGHT: *Average:* less than 2 lb (0.9 kg). *Maximum:* 4 lb (1.8 kg).

BONNEVILLE CISCO
Prosopium gemmifer

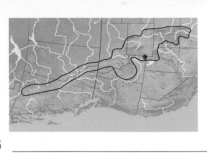

The unique Bonneville Cisco is endemic to Bear Lake (Idaho-Utah border) and is the most abundant species in the lake. Attempts to stock this fish in other mountain waters such as Flaming Gorge Reservoir (Utah-Wyoming) and Lake Tahoe (California-Nevada) have met with little success. • Like the Bear Lake Whitefish and the Bonneville Whitefish, the Bonneville Cisco normally remains well below the surface in deep, cool waters. However, once Bear Lake has iced over, hundreds of thousands of these ciscos move to shallower waters for a short, two-week spawning period. The males arrive first, followed by schools of females that swim parallel to the shore, varying their distance in response to turbulence, ice cover and the presence of fishermen. Males remain longer on the spawning grounds and always outnumber the females. Although one might suspect the vulnerable males would be reduced with overfishing, sex ratios within the lake somehow remain equal.

FEEDING: feeds mainly on zooplankton; occasionally eats midge larvae and other invertebrates.

SPAWNING: late January to early February; spawns in shallows but sometimes in water up to 65 ft (20 m) deep; broadcasts eggs over gravel substrate; 2000–3000 eggs per female; mature at 3 years; usually live up to 7 years, occasionally to 11 years.

OTHER NAMES: Peak-nose.

DID YOU KNOW? The species name *gemmifer* means "set with gems" and refers to the shiny yellow and gold appearance of the spawning fish.

STATUS: common and secure in Bear Lake.

HABITAT: deep, cold waters; usually stay at 60–100 ft (18–30 m) deep.

Bear Lake Whitefish

Mountain Whitefish

Bonneville Whitefish

large eyes

lower jaw extends
beyond upper jaw

gold-streaked sides

elongated body

spawning adult

ID: green-blue back; silver sides; white belly; elongated body; large, cycloid scales (69–74 in lateral line); distinctly pointed snout; lower jaw extends beyond upper jaw; large eyes; deeply forked caudal fin. *Spawning:* sides streaked with gold and yellow; nuptial tubercles.

SIMILAR SPECIES: *Bear Lake Whitefish* (p. 138), *Mountain Whitefish* (p. 136) and *Bonneville Whitefish* (p. 140): lower jaw does not project beyond upper jaw; mouth opens on level below eye.

LENGTH: *Average:* 5–7 in (13–18 cm). *Maximum:* 9 in (23 cm).
WEIGHT: *Average:* 2 oz (55 g). *Maximum:* 3 oz (85 g).

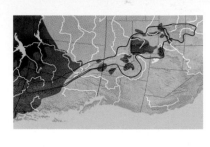

ARCTIC GRAYLING   *Thymallus arcticus*

The Arctic Grayling's large dorsal fin, the aquatic equivalent of deer or moose antlers, and its vivid coloration identify this species immediately. During spawning, this fish ventures from lakes and large rivers to smaller tributaries. In spawning streams, each male aggressively defends its selected spawning ground. Any male intruder will be challenged, first with a threat display that shows off the raised dorsal fin and gaping mouth. If this move proves ineffective, the intruder will be shoved, nipped and chased off the territory. A female can enter the nest by adopting a submissive pose, with her dorsal fin depressed and her tail and body resting on the streambed, allowing the male to curve his dorsal fin over her. • A fish of cold, clear streams, the Arctic Grayling is vulnerable to changes in the environment. This fish needs to see its food to catch it, so clean, clear water is important. The Arctic Grayling is on the southern edge of its range in Canada, so climate change may result in water that is too warm. The range of the native Arctic Grayling in Montana has been reduced to less than eight percent of its original area. Competition from introduced salmonids is also a problem for this species. • A brisk set of rapids in an otherwise slow Rocky Mountain foothill stream is perfect for finding Graylings. Toss a small grasshopper into the head of the rapids and watch as Graylings frantically rush for the insect, often overshooting and launching themselves out of the water.

Occasionally, two overly enthusiastic fish will collide in midair as they go for the same morsel. If you have a fly rod (and it's open season), catch one of these northern fish to marvel at the color pattern.

FEEDING: opportunistic feeder; picks up terrestrial insects such as beetles, ants, wasps and grasshoppers from the water's surface (often more than half of diet); also eats aquatic insects, small fishes and eggs, crustaceans and mollusks; may eat shrews and voles.

SPAWNING: varies over range, but usually May to June, sometimes earlier; migrates to smaller, gravelly streams just after ice break-up when water temperatures reach 44–50° F (7–10° C); spawns during the day, mostly afternoon; no nest; lays up to 12,000 adhesive eggs; eggs hatch after 11–22 days; young stay in same stream until freeze-up; mature at 2–5 years; most live to 8 years, some to 10 years.

OTHER NAMES: Grayling, American Grayling, Montana Grayling, Bluefish, Back's Grayling, Sailfin, Arctic Trout.

DID YOU KNOW? The Latin name *Thymallus* refers to the supposed odor of thyme in the fresh fish, but few, if any, biologists working with Arctic Grayling have ever smelled that odor. Graylings may look beautiful, but they smell awful.

STATUS: common; of special concern in some areas (fluvial form in Montana, for example); vulnerable to overfishing

HABITAT: clear, cold waters of large rivers, rocky creeks and lakes; occasionally enters milky glacial waters; in lakes, usually found near the surface.

Mountain Whitefish

SIMILAR SPECIES: *Mountain Whitefish* (p. 136): 12 or fewer dorsal fin rays.

ID: dark purple to dark blue back; silver to dark blue sides with pink wash; black stripe on belly; black "X," "Y" or diamond markings on anterior part of body; long, large, bluish purple dorsal fin, edged with red or orange, has rows of orange spots and a few emerald green spots; elongated, laterally compressed body; large eyes; 15–25 dorsal fin rays; dorsal fin base longer than head; forked caudal fin. *Spawning male:* will get quite dark, sometimes jet black, with dull red caudal fin.

LENGTH: *Average:* 6–12 in (15–30 cm). *Maximum:* 30 in (76 cm).
WEIGHT: *Average:* 1–3 lb (0.5–1.4 kg). *Maximum:* 6 lb (2.7 kg).

long, large dorsal fin

black spots near front of body

adult ♂

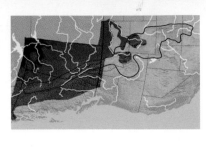

BURBOT
Lota lota

Lota lota could describe the amount of dorsal or anal fin on the Burbot, but *lota* is actually a form of the 16th-century French word for this fish, *lotte*. The common name also comes from Old French—*burbotte* means "to wallow in mud." Some fishwatchers favor the nickname "Lawyer" because of the fish's heavy mucus covering, which makes it extra slimy. • Burbots satisfy their ravenous appetites by eating progressively larger fishes as they grow—in the stomach of one 15-in (38-cm) Burbot, a 12-in (30-cm) Walleye was found! • Spawning occurs under the privacy of ice cover, but Burbots do not seem shy about the whole process. Up to 12 adults will gather to participate in a "communal love-fest," simultaneously releasing eggs and milt in one large, wriggling session. A single female can carry one million eggs or more! • In comparison to other Rockies fishes, Burbots are unusual because they grow faster in winter until they hit maturity. Growth then becomes slow and not very noticeable. • Young Burbots can often be found along rocky shorelines and in tiny streams near large lakes and rivers, especially in late summer and early fall. Flip over large rocks and logs to see these cute little cods that look like big tadpoles at first glance and are easily scooped up by hand or with a small dip net. Replace the fish along with its rock or log when you're finished ooh-ing and aww-ing over its beauty. Adult Burbots are often observed by ice fishers in late winter. If you peer down a darkened ice-fishing hole over a shallow, sandy lake-bottom, you may see individuals slowly swimming by or a cluster of swarming, mating fish swirling past.

FEEDING: mostly piscivorous, nocturnal feeder; eats mostly fishes, but also molluscs and crustaceans.

SPAWNING: January to March; spawns under ice over sand or gravel; groups gather together at night to simultaneously release eggs and milt; 50,000–2,000,000 eggs are released; eggs settle on bottom; no parental care; eggs hatch in April or May; mature at 3–4 years; live up to 15 years.

OTHER NAMES: Ling, Eelpout, Lawyer, Methy, Maria, Loche, Freshwater Cod, Sandling, Dogfish, Spineless Cat, Mother-of-eels, Gudgeon, Mudblower, Cuskfish.

DID YOU KNOW? The Burbot was and still is eaten by people in the North, especially in Siberia, where the Burbot's skin has even been put to use as a window replacement.

STATUS: common; some populations have declined drastically owing to dam construction and overfishing.

HABITAT: usually large, cold lakes and rivers; deep water in summer; shallow water in winter; prefers to hide around boulders.

ID: dark olive or green with irregular, lighter mottling along entire body; yellowish belly; long, round, eel-shaped body; terminal mouth; 1 median "chin" barbel; 1 barbel from each nare; all fins are soft rayed; pelvic fins are positioned in front of pectorals; first dorsal fin is short; second dorsal fin is elongated almost to caudal fin; anal fin is similar to second dorsal fin; rounded caudal fin.

SIMILAR SPECIES: *Stonecat* (p. 108): 4 "chin" barbels; adnate adipose fin; range overlaps only in the Missouri River tributaries in Montana and Wyoming.

Stonecat

second dorsal fin equal to anal fin

1 barbel on "chin" and 1 barbel from each nare

rounded dorsal fin

adult

LENGTH: *Average:* 12–32 in (30–81 cm). *Maximum:* 40 in (1 m) in the Rockies; nearly 4 ft (1.2 m) in Alaska.
WEIGHT: *Average:* 3–5 lb (1.5–2 kg). *Maximum:* 17 lb (7.7 kg) in the Rockies; 60 lb (27 kg) in Alaska.

WESTERN MOSQUITOFISH *Gambusia affinis*

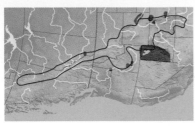

In addition to having an appetite for mosquito larvae, the Western Mosquitofish is an aggressive and adaptable fish. These last two attributes were unknown (or unimportant, compared to the thought of less mosquitoes) to government officials when they began introducing this popular aquarium fish to the Rockies over a century ago. The fish does eat mosquito larvae, but not enough to warrant its destructive presence in certain delicate mountain ecosystems. Introduction has occurred around the globe, resulting in damage to ecosystems and even the extinction of some species. • The Western Mosquitofish is a member of the livebearer family. Eggs hatch in the female's body cavity, and she gives birth to a litter of free-swimming young. A courting male will partially wrap his dorsal and anal fins around his mate, curve his body into an "S" shape, then dart behind her and attempt to insert his gonopodium—a slender, tubular structure used for fertilization. The female can store sperm in a specialized internal pouch and use it to fertilize several broods. Once she has spawned, the female becomes unreceptive, but she will sometimes breed again less than an hour after giving birth! • In Banff National Park, Alberta, Parks Canada has built a viewing platform in the Cave and Basin Marsh so visitors can get a good look at Western Mosquitofish, African Jewelfish and Sailfin Molly, the three introduced fishes in

the marsh. The Mosquitofish were introduced in 1924 to spare the bathing tourists from biting bugs. Oddly enough, the best time to view this tropical fish in Banff is during the frigid Canadian winter. Much of the lake freezes over, and these little Floridian imports cluster around the hot springs like skiers in a hot tub.

FEEDING: carnivorous; feeds just under water surface; renowned for eating mosquito larvae; also eats diatoms, crustaceans, zooplankton, insects and larval fishes, including its own.

SPAWNING: spring and summer (year-round in thermal water); male fertilizes female using specialized gonopodium (several anterior rays of anal fin are modified for internal fertilization); eggs are brooded within female's body for 21–28 days; young are born alive; up to 315 per litter; mature in 4–6 weeks; young born early in the season reproduce that summer; live to 15 months.

OTHER NAMES: Mosquitofish.

DID YOU KNOW? When the Panama Canal was built, mosquitofishes were stocked in the area to reduce malaria, a recurrent fever transmitted by mosquitoes.

STATUS: scattered; some populations are maintained by annual stocking; self-sustaining populations in some thermal waters.

HABITAT: warm, shallow, sluggish or stagnant waters; vegetated backwaters, pools, streams and edges of lakes; brackish sloughs; tolerates polluted waters where other fishes are absent; can develop resistance to pesticides.

ID: gray to yellow-brown back; silver sides with blue and yellow sheen; teardrop mark under large eyes; dorsally opening, supraterminal mouth; seemingly swollen belly, especially on female; rounded caudal fin with rows of dark spots; spots on dorsal fin. *Male:* smaller than female; gonopodium; origin of dorsal fin is far behind origin of anal fin. *Female:* anal fin rays are relatively equal length; origin of dorsal fin is only slightly behind origin of anal fin.

SIMILAR SPECIES: *Green Swordtail* (p. 190): male has long, slender projection on caudal fin. *Shortfin Molly* (p. 189), *Sailfin Molly* (p. 189) and *Variable Platyfish* (p. 190): no black teardrop under eye.

supraterminal mouth

seemingly wollen belly

rounded caudal fin

adult ♀

LENGTH: *Average:* 1–2 in (2.5–5 cm). *Maximum:* Male: 1½ in (3.8 cm). Female: 2½ in (6.4 cm).

BROOK STICKLEBACK *Culaea inconstans*

The Brook Stickleback is very common in central and eastern Alberta. It gets progressively scarcer as you move toward the foothills and mountains, but it has trickled into British Columbia and isolated areas of Montana. It's found on both sides of the Continental Divide where it has been introduced. Relic populations also exist in the South Platte drainage basin of Colorado. • The Brook Stickleback is able to live in a wide range of environmental conditions, from cold alpine lakes to warm, saline prairie potholes. It will often take the first opportunity to disperse, even into a farmer's flooded field that may eventually leave it high and dry. Its low-oxygen tolerance allows it to survive in small pools over winter by using the oxygen-rich water that surrounds trapped gas bubbles. The Brook Stickleback has been found in artesian wells, which indicates that individuals are present even in underground streams! • Muskrats, shrews, salamanders, grebes, predaceous insects, fishes and snakes all eat Brook Sticklebacks. These fish burrow into the mud to escape from predators, as well as in search of invertebrates for themselves to eat if times are really tough. • Look for this fish near the edge of a water body with plenty of vegetation. If you happen upon a pond with a high density of Brook Sticklebacks, you may be lucky enough to see a "food fight"—if food is scarce, an individual will try to tear food from another's mouth. Sticklebacks demonstrate a range of interesting behaviors from territorial displays and nest building to parental care. They are one of the few species of fish that "hover." They will hang suspended in the water column, fanning their pectoral fins and tracking some distant target—usually, a tiny member of the plankton community. Observant fishers may see a darting attack on the almost invisible water bug. Sticklebacks are often territorial, so if the fish darts away when you first appear, be patient and it will often hover back into view.

FEEDING: eats aquatic invertebrates and their larvae, crustaceans and very small fish eggs and juvenile fish, including its own species.

SPAWNING: May to July; spawns in areas with aquatic vegetation; male defends a territory and builds a small, oval-shaped nest with vegetation and his own kidney secretions; female is wooed or pushed into male's territory; he pokes his nose into her abdomen area to induce her to release eggs into the nest; she exits out the back of the nest, which he then repairs; female mates every 3 days for 1 month, releasing about 2000 eggs in total; male defends eggs and aerates them until they hatch; eggs hatch in about 21 days, or 8–9 days at 65° F (18° C); mature after first year; live up to 4 years.

OTHER NAMES: Black Stickleback, Common Stickleback, Pinfish, Five-spined Stickleback.

STATUS: common; secure.

HABITAT: varied; small, clear, cold streams or springs with vegetation; ponds, saline sloughs, rivers, creeks and lake edges.

DID YOU KNOW? In 1950, it was discovered that the Brook Stickleback's original generic name *Eucalia* had already been given to a butterfly, so the new name *Culaea* was coined. • Up to one-third of the body weight of some Brook Sticklebacks can be attributed to *Schistocephalus*, a larval tapeworm.

ID: dark brown to olive with mottling on back and sides; beige belly; transparent fins; terminal or supraterminal mouth; 5 free (no connecting membranes) dorsal spines, 1 pelvic spine and 1 short anal spine; origin of dorsal fin is even with origin of anal fin; rear margin of caudal fin is truncate; very narrow caudal peduncle. *Spawning male:* black bands through eyes; very dark overall. *Spawning female:* varied and splotchy colors.

SIMILAR SPECIES: *Nine-spine Stickleback:* 9 free dorsal spines; much darker; in northern British Columbia, along the eastern foothills.

Nine-spine Stickleback

terminal or supraterminal mouth

4–6 dorsal spines

adult

dorsal fin equal to anal fin

very narrow caudal peduncle

LENGTH: *Average:* 2 in (5 cm). *Maximum:* 3½ in (9 cm).

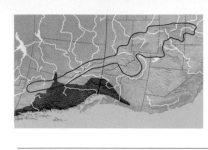

PRICKLY SCULPIN *Cottus asper*

With bulging eyes, swollen lips and oversized pectoral fins, no Prickly Sculpin is going to win any beauty contests. In fact, these little monsters are remarkably well adapted to their benthic environment. With eyes on top of their heads, sculpins can see predators approaching from above. Instead of using the movements of their bodies to advance, as other fish do, sculpins use their large pectoral fins to propel forward quickly. Prickly Sculpins appear almost docile until the slightest disturbance instantly sends them darting toward cover. • Benthic-feeding sculpins have been given a bad rap for eating salmon and trout eggs, and Prickly Sculpins are one of the few family members that support this claim. Anglers who bait their hooks with salmon roe may sometimes find a Prickly Sculpin staring up from the end of their line, but only the largest adults eat fish eggs. Prickly Sculpins usually prefer invertebrates. Conversely, cannibalistic trout actually consume more of their own eggs, and sculpins are an important forage food for these larger fish. • These little bottom-dwellers are almost perfectly camouflaged among the silty rocks and can really only be seen when they move, and unfortunately for us, they move mainly at night. Gently wading along quiet streams and carefully turning over rocks is your best bet for viewing these fish. Watch for a tiny puff of silt and a blur of motion. Sculpins won't swim far, and the keen-eyed naturalist will see the little fish settle into a new hiding spot. If the water is particularly clear, you may be able to see the rough skin that gives Prickly Sculpins their name.

FEEDING: benthic feeder; most active at night; eats aquatic insect larvae and other bottom invertebrates.

SPAWNING: usually mid-March to late July; uses areas with boulders, cobble or flat rocks; male selects nest site under a rock; female deposits 700–4000 orange eggs in a jelly-enclosed cluster on ceiling of nest; 1 male may mate with up to 10 females; male may guard up to 30,000 eggs in 1 nest; eggs hatch in 15–16 days; mature at 3 years; live to 7 years.

OTHER NAMES: Prickly Bullhead, Bullhead.

DID YOU KNOW? The Latin name *asper* means "rough" and refers to the small prickles that cover most of this sculpin's body.

STATUS: common; secure.

HABITAT: cool, oxygen-rich streams; prefers quiet waters and avoids currents; also lakes.

Mottled Sculpin

Slimy Sculpin

entire body may be
covered with prickles

"cheek" spine

bars on all fins except pelvic fin

adult

ID: highly variable; olive gray back; pale yellow or white belly; 3 dark bands under second dorsal fin; bars on all fins except pelvic fin; vague mottling; entire body may be covered with prickles; palatine teeth; preopercular ("cheek") spine; lateral line is usually complete; pelvic fins have spine; lateral line on first dorsal fin; male is darker overall.

SIMILAR SPECIES: *Mottled Sculpin* (p. 154): incomplete lateral line. *Slimy Sculpin* (p. 158): no palatine teeth.

LENGTH: *Average:* 7 in (18 cm). *Maximum:* 12 in (30 cm).

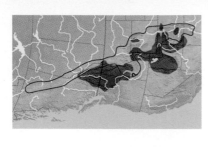

MOTTLED SCULPIN   *Cottus bairdi*

The female Mottled Sculpin literally falls "head over tails" for her mate. After entering his burrow, she turns upside down to deposit her sticky eggs on the underside of the rock or ledge that covers the den. The female must be tactical because cannibalistic males will swallow small females. Once the female has released her eggs, the swollen-headed male drives her off, intent on attracting other mates to his burrow. • No stranger to variation and closely related to the Shorthead Sculpin, this species keeps scientists on their toes. The Mottled Sculpin may in fact be a combination of many species. In the Rockies, a true population of Mottled Sculpins can be found in the Flathead River, which flows from southeastern British Columbia into Montana. These sculpins were long believed to be Shorthead Sculpins, and they commonly hybridize with the Slimy Sculpins found farther upstream. A very closely related sculpin (known as the St. Mary's Shorthead Sculpin) is found in the Rocky Mountain foothills in Alberta in the St. Mary's and Milk rivers. • The Mottled Sculpin is named for Spencer Fullerton Baird, who was the first Fish Commissioner in the U.S.

FEEDING: benthic feeder; prefers aquatic insect larvae and mayfly nymphs but also eats other insects and invertebrates, plant material, macrophytes, annelids, crayfish and crustaceans.

SPAWNING: spawns in spring; tiny eggs are laid in a rock crevice or nest burrow covered with gravel or rock; adhesive eggs stick to underside of burrow; male may mate with and guard the eggs of several females; eggs hatch in 20 days; mature at 2–3 years; live up to 4 years.

OTHER NAMES: Bullhead, Blob, Miller's Thumb, Columbia Sculpin, Gudgeon, Freshwater Sculpin.

DID YOU KNOW? The nickname "Miller's Thumb" refers to the sculpin's profile, which resembles the thumb that has been crushed between the millstones used by a miller.

STATUS: common on both sides of the Continental Divide; vulnerable in BC.

HABITAT: bottom dweller; cool streams or montane lakes between or beneath rocks; most abundant in slow currents; requires high oxygen levels; prefers clean, rocky substrate such as boulders, pebbles or sand.

Slimy Sculpin

Shorthead Sculpin

large eyes and mouth

spiny first dorsal fin

soft second dorsal fin

slightly rounded tail

spawning ♂

ID: considerable variation; brown overall; paler sides and whitish belly; dark spots on back and sides; few scales; sturdy body tapers at tail; wide, flattened snout; large eyes; large mouth; upper lip protrudes slightly; incomplete lateral line; 2 dorsal fins, first spiny, second soft with long base; slightly rounded tail; teeth on roof of mouth. *Spawning male:* enlarged head; first dorsal fin edged with red or orange.

SIMILAR SPECIES: *Slimy Sculpin* (p. 158): caudal peduncle length always exceeds postorbital length (distance from bony edge of operculum to eye); no other field marks are consistently reliable because of extreme variation in the species. *Shorthead Sculpin* (p. 160): fewer mottles; usually prefers smaller tributaries.

LENGTH: *Average:* 3 in (7.6 cm). *Maximum:* 5 in (13 cm).

PAIUTE SCULPIN   *Cottus beldingi*

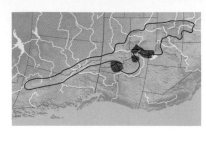

Imagine yourself an unsuspecting caddisfly, muddling quietly along through the picturesque waters of a Rocky Mountain stream. Suddenly, you are engulfed by a menacing black shadow. This scenario is the reality for many benthic invertebrates ambushed by bottom-dwelling Paiute Sculpins. Like many fishes, the Paiute Sculpin is an opportunistic feeder, and its diet largely depends on what food is most available. Depth can play an important part in the diet. In shallow areas, Pauite Sculpins usually concentrate on aquatic insect larvae. Snails are a favorite food for sculpins that dwell between 100–200 ft (30–61 m), and at depths below that, a large number of segmented worms called Oligochetes are consumed. • Sticking close to bottom cover, sculpins move along with a series of darting motions by paddling their large pectoral fins. Because trouts prey upon sculpins, anglers often try to imitate these sculpin movements with their lures as they reel in their line.

FEEDING: bottom feeder; ambushes prey; forages at night; feeds on aquatic insect larvae and other benthic forms such as snails, algae, water mites, aquatic beetles and worms.

SPAWNING: spring; spawns near riffles and often near the mouth of a stream; may spawn in deep water in lakes; male selects nest site; female deposits eggs on ceiling of nest; young mature at 2 years.

OTHER NAMES: Piute Sculpin.

DID YOU KNOW? When you dunk your dip net into the upper Colorado River in summer, one percent of the tiny aquatic life forms you scoop up are sculpin larvae.

STATUS: common; secure.

HABITAT: clear, cold water with rocky riffles; prefers gravelly lakes and streams; sometimes lives on other substrates; associated with trouts.

ID: brown or brownish gray back; paler belly; heavy, black and white mottling; 5–7 crossbars on back; black marks on all fins; may have bands on sides; large head with body tapering to tail; large mouth; small teeth on roof of mouth; large eyes; 1 preopercular ("cheek") spine; complete or mostly complete lateral line; rounded caudal fin is truncate on rear margin.

SIMILAR SPECIES: *Mottled Sculpin* (p. 154) and *Torrent Sculpin* (p. 166): well-developed palatine teeth; 2–3 saddle marks on back under second dorsal fin. *Slimy Sculpin* (p. 158): usually 3 preopercular spines. *Wood River Sculpin* (p. 164): no preopercular spines.

Mottled Sculpin

Wood River Sculpin

Slimy Sculpin

Torrent Sculpin

large head

"cheek" spine

rounded caudal fin

adult

LENGTH: *Average:* 4 in (10 cm). *Maximum:* 5 in (13 cm).

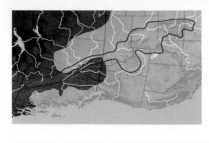

SLIMY SCULPIN   *Cottus cognatus*

From above, the Slimy Sculpin looks like an arrow: its large, pointed head tapers to a thin tail. A closer look reveals fanlike pectoral fins and a bullish face. Members of the sculpin family are masters of camouflage. The dark mottling on their gray bodies blends in perfectly with the gravelly bottoms that these fish frequent. Most of their movement occurs at night, when they feed on the bottom-dwelling invertebrates and chase after insect and fish larvae. During the day, "Slimies" remain still under rocky hide-outs, avoiding predators such as Lake Trout, Burbot and Northern Pike. • In the Rocky Mountains, spawning begins in late spring with males cleaning out a small territory. Challengers that arrive are met with short, quick charges in their direction until the loser retreats, his breeding colors fading with his withdrawal. Females are welcomed into the territory, where they deposit their eggs on the ceiling of the nest, under the well-guarded rocks. More than one female may visit a nest, and the male will guard his area for up to five weeks. • Wherever a road crosses a stream is always a good place for fishers to stop and check out the local species, especially Slimy Sculpins, which are particularly fond of living under bridges. It will take a few moments for your eyes to adjust to the gloom under the bridge, but then walk slowly along the shallows, looking for a tiny bit of red (the fish's gills just peeking out from under the gill cover)

or the distinctive eye peering up at you. Culverts are another favored habitat of Slimies, but only ones with nicely embedded rocks and tiny silty pools. Avoid the all-metal culvert tubes that are more fish-barrier than fish-friendly.

FEEDING: occasional benthic feeder; eats crustaceans, aquatic insects (especially 2-winged flies, caddisflies, mayflies, stoneflies and dragonflies), small fish and detritus.

SPAWNING: May to June; male cleans and defends a small, gravelly territory; female enters the territory and male presses her up to the ceiling of the nest to deposit up to 1400 eggs; male may mate with several females; male guards eggs; eggs hatch after 4 weeks; live up to 7 years.

OTHER NAMES: Cottus Big Fin, Stargazer, Northern Sculpin, Slimy Muddler, Miller's Thumb, Bear Lake Bull-head.

DID YOU KNOW? Found in Siberia and Alaska, as well as between the two continents on St. Lawrence Island in the Bering Strait, the Slimy Sculpin provides good evidence that the Bering land bridge once existed. Many scientists believe that this land bridge was the primary route Asian animals used to populate North America during the ice age.

STATUS: common; secure.

HABITAT: gravelly or rocky bottoms of cold, northern streams and lakes.

ID: dark brown to light gray body with dark mottling; whitish belly; transparent fins with dark lines; rounded body tapers to tail; slimy skin; almost no prickles; large, triangular head; terminal mouth; 3 preopercular ("cheek") spines; short, incomplete lateral line; large pectoral fins; 2 dorsal fins touch; long pelvic fins with 12–13 rays; anal fin has long spines; square caudal fin. *Spawning male:* darker color; first dorsal fin is outlined orange.

SIMILAR SPECIES: *Mottled Sculpin* (p. 154) and *Shorthead Sculpin* (p. 160); palatine teeth. *Spoonhead Sculpin* (p. 168): flat, wide head; 1 preopercular spine curves up strongly; complete lateral line; evident prickles along most of body.

Mottled Sculpin

Shorthead Sculpin

Spoonhead Sculpin

2 dorsal fins touch

adult

square caudal fin

LENGTH: *Average:* 3 in (7.6 cm). *Maximum:* 5 in (13 cm).

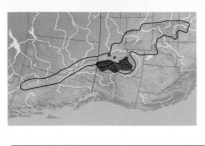

SHORTHEAD SCULPIN   *Cottus confusus*

While looking for food and watching out for its many predators, the Shorthead Sculpin is oblivious to the confusion it is causing ichthyologists. With an uncanny ability to blend into its benthic environment, the Shorthead Sculpin can vary considerably in color or structure and is easily confused with the Mottled Sculpin. The two species can occur together, though the Shorthead Sculpin is often found farther upstream or in smaller creeks, and the Mottled Sculpin usually remains in the main river. The Shorthead Sculpin typically occurs in fast, cold waters, such as those of the Columbia River drainage or Montana's cool streams, but may be dispersing into the slow, silty waters of northern Montana and southern Alberta via irrigation canals. • Creeks throughout the Rockies contain populations of this sculpin, but the critical habitat needs of the Shorthead Sculpin are not known. It is considered a threatened species in Canada, and water quality is a growing concern.

FEEDING: benthic feeder, eats small aquatic invertebrates.

SPAWNING: spring, perhaps May; male defines a territory with rocks; female deposits eggs underneath the surface of the rocks; female produces an average of 100–250 eggs per season; mature in 2–3 years; live 6–7 years.

OTHER NAMES: Short-head Sculpin.

DID YOU KNOW? All sculpins lack a swim bladder and for good reason—they spend almost all of their time camouflaged near the bottom of water bodies and do not need to move up and down the water column.

STATUS: uncommon; COSEWIC threatened species; species of special concern in Montana.

HABITAT: usually riffles of fast, cold streams; sometimes larger rivers or slower moving water at the shoreline; generally farther upstream than other sculpins; needs rocks for spawning.

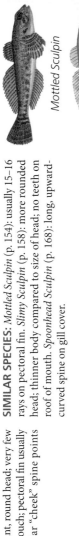

Mottled Sculpin

Slimy Sculpin

Spoonhead Sculpin

ID: irregular mottling on body; blunt, round head; very few or no prickles on body; dorsal fins touch; pectoral fin usually has 13–14 rays; small preopercular "cheek" spine points backward; teeth on roof of mouth.

SIMILAR SPECIES: Mottled Sculpin (p. 154): usually 15–16 rays on pectoral fin. Slimy Sculpin (p. 158): more rounded head; thinner body compared to size of head; no teeth on roof of mouth. Spoonhead Sculpin (p. 168): long, upward-curved spine on gill cover.

"cheek" spines point backward

dorsal fins touch

adult

LENGTH: Average: 2–4 in (5–10 cm). Maximum: 4½ in (11.5 cm).

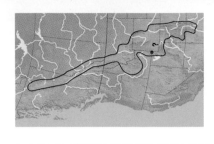

BEAR LAKE SCULPIN
Cottus extensus

In terms of sheer numbers, the Bear Lake Sculpin leaves a lot of other local fishes behind. Although this sculpin is one of the most abundant species in Bear Lake (on the Utah-Idaho border), second in numbers only to the Bonneville Cisco, the Bear Lake Sculpin is considered a sensitive species. The main reason for protecting this sculpin is its restricted natural range. Once found only in Bear Lake, a second population has been stocked in Flaming Gorge Reservoir (on the Utah-Wyoming border) and is established. • Some Bear Lake Sculpins live in the shallows, but most are found near the bottom of this deep mountain lake. To hide from voracious predators, such as Cutthroat Trout, Lake Trout and Bonneville Whitefish, they bury themselves under bottom silt during the day. But every night, from dusk to dawn, these little sculpins venture out and swim up to the middle of the water column. Surprisingly, they do not feed there; this daily vertical migration is believed to speed and aid digestion.

FEEDING: bottom feeder; eats zooplankton, aquatic invertebrates and midge larvae.

SPAWNING: late winter to early May; spawns near shore; deposits eggs on the underside of rocks; returns to deep water after spawning; live to 5 years.

OTHER NAMES: Bullhead.

DID YOU KNOW? During the last two million years, isolated Ancient Lake Bonneville Sculpin populations evolved into the Bear Lake Sculpin and the now extinct Utah Lake Sculpin. Some scientists think these fish may have changed morphologically in only 12,000 years, a comparatively short time.

STATUS: abundant in Bear Lake but considered sensitive in Utah and critically imperiled in Idaho because of its restricted range.

HABITAT: most live 50–175 ft (15–54 m) deep; some live in shallows; use soft bottom for cover during the day; migrate to mid-water from dusk to dawn.

Mottled Sculpin

ID: tan or light brown overall; lighter sides and underparts; sometimes dark spots or blotches on upper sides; slimmer body than other sculpins; short head; prickles cover sides but not belly; teeth on roof of mouth; 3 preopercular ("cheek") spines; first dorsal fin is spiny, second is soft; incomplete lateral line; rounded caudal fin is truncate on rear edge.

SIMILAR SPECIES: no other sculpins are found in Bear Lake. *Mottled Sculpin* (p. 154): more robust head and body; dorsal fins meet at base; mottling is more distinct; few prickles on body.

spiny first dorsal fin

soft second dorsal fin

prickles cover sides but not belly

rounded caudal fin

adult

LENGTH: *Average:* 3 in (7.6 cm). *Maximum:* 5 in (13 cm).

WOOD RIVER SCULPIN *Cottus leiopomus*

Few studies have been done on the Wood River Sculpin since the species was first recognized in 1893. What we do know is that this sculpin is only found swimming beneath the cottonwood-lined banks of the Little Wood River and the Big Wood River in Idaho's Rocky Mountains. With a small range and an uncertain future, the Wood River Sculpin is listed as a species of special concern. Habitat degradation in the form of encroaching development and water diversions are some of the main threats to the water quality of the Wood River. Land stewardship groups are making attempts to restore sections of the Big Wood River to a more natural condition. Efforts include removing steep, constructed banks that are creating deep channels in the river, adding rocks mid-river to improve habitat for fish and planting native bushes to help reduce bank erosion. Trees and shrubs that grow near streams are almost as essential to fish as the water itself. Vegetation stabilizes the banks, helps control runoff and provides shade to keep the water cool.

FEEDING: probably the same as other sculpins; bottom-dwelling invertebrates.

SPAWNING: no studies have been done; probably similar to other sculpins.

OTHER NAMES: none.

DID YOU KNOW? The Wood River Sculpin was probably used as trout bait by Native Americans who lived in the Wood River Basin.

STATUS: locally common; species of special concern in Idaho because of limited range.

HABITAT: cool, swift creeks and small rivers; over gravel and rubble; riffles.

ID: grayish olive overall with dark brown or black mottling; broad, short head; slender body tapers toward tail; incomplete lateral line; no teeth or very small teeth on roof of mouth; first dorsal fin has 7 spines.

SIMILAR SPECIES: no other sculpins are found in the Wood River; other sculpins have preopercular spines.

no teeth or very small teeth on roof of mouth

7 spines on first dorsal fin

adult

LENGTH: *Average:* 2½ in (6 cm). *Maximum:* 4½ in (12 cm).

TORRENT SCULPIN   *Cottus rhotheus*

Well-developed prickles cover the body and sometimes the tail of most Torrent Sculpins, but there are a few exceptions to the rule. Thousands of years ago, geological activity and retreating glaciers scraped waterfalls throughout the Rocky Mountains and isolated several Torrent Sculpin populations above falls. Amazingly, all of these widely scattered, segregated populations have lost their prickles. Sculpins are often hard to tell apart because their color and structure varies with their environment. One clue for separating sculpin species is the palatine teeth, paired bones that extend out and back on the roof of the mouth. To feel for palatine teeth, use the side of a needle and brush it against the roof of the fish's mouth. On the Torrent Sculpin, you will feel long patches of palatine teeth between the teeth of the jaws.

FEEDING: adults feed primarily on immature aquatic insects; larger adults eat minnows, especially Redside Shiners and Northern Pikeminnows; young eat planktonic crustaceans, algae and insects.

SPAWNING: probably June; male defends a territory in the rocks; female deposits eggs on the underside of the rocks; male guards eggs; mature at 2 years; live to 6 years.

OTHER NAMES: Bullhead.

DID YOU KNOW? The Latin species name *rhotheus* means "rushing of the torrent" and refers to the surging waters that these sculpins inhabit.

STATUS: common; secure.

HABITAT: riffles of cold, clear streams; sometimes near rocky beaches of large lakes.

ID: brown or gray body; light sides; dark mottling; 2 saddle-like patches on back, under second dorsal fin; bands of pigment run across fins; large head; body tapers toward tail; well-developed prickles on sides, back and usually tail; strong, well-developed teeth; teeth on roof of mouth; 1 preopercular ("cheek") spine curves up gently; complete lateral line. *Spawning male:* edge of first dorsal fin is thicker and tinged with orange.

SIMILAR SPECIES: *Slimy Sculpin* (p. 158): incomplete lateral line; no palatine teeth.

Slimy Sculpin

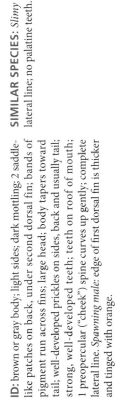

prickles on sides, back and usually tail

large head

"cheek" spine curves up gently

spawning ♂

LENGTH: *Average:* 4 in (10 cm). *Maximum:* 6 in (15 cm).

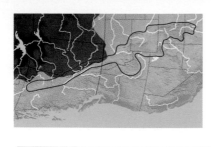

SPOONHEAD SCULPIN   *Cottus ricei*

On the sides of the Spoonhead Sculpin's large, flat head are pairs of preopercular ("cheek") spines, which likely make some predators think twice before gulping down this fish. One pair of medially curved spines is larger than the other, giving the appearance of buffalo horns. Another adaptation against heavy predation is the small prickles that cover the bodies of Spoonheads, which also help protect this scaleless fish in its rocky habitat. • The Spoonhead Sculpin is found almost exclusively within Canada, east of the Continental Divide. During an ice age 18,000 years ago, the northern Rocky Mountains were covered almost entirely by the Laurentide ice sheet. South of the glacier, the Spoonhead Sculpin and many other wildlife species were pushed to a large ice-free area in the Great Plains, which extended east from the foothills to the Mississippi River. When the glacier retreated, carving deep lakes and rivers in its wake, the Spoonhead Sculpin gradually repopulated the foothills and Rockies until the unconquerable barrier of the Continental Divide was reached. • Go looking for Spoonheads in fall, when the high country is getting its first snowfall. The large rivers that Spoonheads call home will be getting low and clear as the glacier-fed headwaters finally stop the summer-long melting that has been silting up the water. Very slowly wade upstream in the gravelly, silty shallows. Spoonheads will be lying next to (and even under) rocks, almost invisible in their mottled, drab colors. Patience will ultimately pay off, however, and it is a real thrill to spot one of these little fish before it puffs away into the deeper, darker water. The big cheek spine is quite noticeable if one will let you get close enough.

FEEDING: assumed to eat aquatic insects and benthic invertebrates such as mollusks.

SPAWNING: late summer to early fall; male defends a territory containing rocks; female places up to 1200 orange, adhesive eggs underneath the rocks; male guards and fans the eggs until they hatch in 2–3 weeks; mature in 2 years; live up to 6 years.

OTHER NAMES: Cow-faced Sculpin, Muddler.

DID YOU KNOW? As you go farther north, the color of the Spoonhead Sculpin becomes darker. • This fish's common and scientific names are easy to remember if you can remember that Spoonheads have a spoon handle on their head, and spoons are used for eating rice.

STATUS: uncommon; may be at risk; species of special concern in Montana.

HABITAT: among rocks in rivers, streams and lakeshores; some turbid streams; also deeper lake waters.

Mottled Sculpin

ID: dark brown to olive back; color fades along sides to white belly; dark splotches cover body; well-developed prickles over entire body; large, triangular head; pair of "bison horns" curve upward and inward; small, beady eyes; no palatine teeth; lateral line is complete to base of caudal fin; enlarged, fan-like pelvic fins; 2 touching dorsal fins; small, square caudal fin.

SIMILAR SPECIES: *Mottled Sculpin* (p. 154): lacks "bison horns" on gill covers; incomplete lateral line.

small, beady eyes

large preopercular spine curves upward

dorsal fins touch

small, square caudal fin

adult

LENGTH: *Average:* under 3 in (7.6 cm). *Maximum:* 5 in (13 cm).

GREEN SUNFISH

Lepomis cyanellus

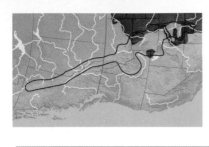

STATUS: common; secure.

HABITAT: low elevations; quiet, slow streams and ponds; lake shores; tolerates turbid water, low oxygen and high temperatures.

Ubiquitous in east-central North America, the Green Sunfish has been introduced to relatively warm, low-elevation water bodies in the Rocky Mountains. Although showy and colorful, Green Sunfish are often thought of as thieves in the aquatic world. Legendary as talented bait-stealers, these little gluttons are the most adaptable of all sunfishes. Because Green Sunfish compete aggressively with more sought-after game fishes, they are often regarded as nuisance fish. • This species excels in digestion and reproduction. Green Sunfish have no problem swallowing fish three-quarters their size. Reproduction is what these fish do best, occasionally multiplying until there is not enough food to share, causing individuals to become stunted at tiny lengths. • Even though spawning males vigorously defend their territories and attack other males, an area 50 square feet (4.6 square meters) may be dense with as many as 25 nests. Once the spawning has taken place, fighting subsides and the males concentrate on fanning the eggs or guarding the young. • In ponds with clear water, these fish may be seen around brush piles.

FEEDING: stays near protection of rocks, boat docks or weeds to feed; eats insects, mollusks, crustaceans and fishes.

SPAWNING: May into July; spawns repetitively, every 8–10 days; male constructs oval nest close to rocks, weeds or logs and defends territory; female enters nest to deposit yellow, adhesive eggs, which hatch in 3–5 days; male guards and aerates nest, protects young; mature at 2–3 years; live to 7 years.

OTHER NAMES: Bluespotted Sunfish, Blue Sunfish, Buffalo Sunfish, Goggle-eye, Redeye, Rubbertail, Ricefield Slick, Blue Bass, Green Perch, Branch Perch, Sun Perch, Shade Perch.

DID YOU KNOW? *Lepomis* means "scaled operculum." Scales are found on the "cheeks" and gill covers of all fishes in this genus. *Cyanellus* means "blue" and refers to the fish's blue-green sheen.

Bluegill

Pumpkinseed

large mouth reaches to under the eye

spines in front of dorsal fin

light edge of fins

spawning

ID: yellow-brown overall with green hue; yellowish white belly; dark blotches at rear of dorsal and anal fins; robust, laterally compressed body; large mouth reaches to under eye; operculum is stiff to rear margin; scaly head; fewer than 55 scales in lateral line; 10 or more spines at front of dorsal fin, rear of fin is soft; 3 anal spines; rounded pectoral fin. *Spawning male:* edges of dorsal, anal and caudal fins lighten.

SIMILAR SPECIES: *Bluegill* (p. 192) and *Pumpkinseed* (p. 191): longer, pointed pectoral fin; mouth does not reach to under eye. *Rock Bass* (p. 191): 5–6 anal spines.

LENGTH: *Average:* 5 in (13 cm). *Maximum:* 9 in (23 cm).
WEIGHT: *Average:* less than 1 lb (0.5 kg). *Maximum:* 2 lb (0.9 kg).

YELLOW PERCH *Perca flavescens*

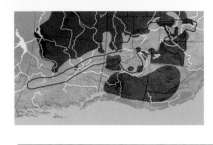

The Yellow Perch is native to the Rockies in Alberta, but it was introduced to other provinces and states in the Rockies from waters east of the mountains. Its recognizable black saddles have earned it nicknames such as "Raccoon Perch" and "Bandit Fish." • This common perch is a prey species for almost every larger piscivorous predator, particularly Walleye and Northern Pike, in the Rockies—even whitefishes have been found with Yellow Perch in their stomachs. Young Yellow Perch hide out in the vegetated shallows of lakes. If they escape the hungry mouths of basses or mergansers, the now larger perch graduate to deeper waters, only to face new predators such as Lake Trout. • Spotting a school of Yellow Perch in the mountains may be a challenge, but the eggs of Yellow Perch offer a unique viewing opportunity for fishwatchers. The female lays gelatinous ribbons of accordion-folded eggs, which can be as long as a human is tall, and drapes these zigzag ribbons over aquatic vegetation, an excellent strategy to keep the precious eggs away from suffocating bottom silt. Predators avoid these egg masses as unpalatable. Occasionally, winds or waves cast segments of these curious ribbons ashore, a unique find for lucky beachcombers. • The Yellow Perch is a much sought-after commercial and recreational food fish year-round. Its tastiness likely contributes to its popularity as a sport fish. There is a risk of overfishing in the northern part of its range because of its slow growth and late maturity. • Although not native to most waters of the Rocky

Mountains, the few lakes where Yellow Perch have been stocked (and are usually undesired) often provide great viewing. Canoe along weedy shallows on a warm, mid-summer afternoon. Watch the little striped bandits sneak into a clump of algae to nab unsuspecting water fleas, or furtively swim out across a few feet of open water, risking death-by-pike. Swimming Yellow Perch will often suddenly stop and briefly raise their spiny dorsal fin like an antenna array. Some scientists hypothesize that this fin may be used as a sensory organ to "sniff" the water for stray molecules from predators or prey.

FEEDING: adult eats smaller fishes, crayfish, leeches, mollusks and aquatic insect larvae; young feed on zooplankton.

SPAWNING: April and May after ice breakup; spawns in shallow, sheltered, vegetated areas in bays or tributaries; 1 female is flanked by group of males; 10,000–50,000 eggs are released in sticky strings and draped over vegetation, brush or rocks while being fertilized; no parental care; eggs hatch in 10–20 days; males mature in 2–3 years, females in 4–6 years; live to 11 years.

OTHER NAMES: Bandit Fish, Convict, Ringed Perch, Raccoon Perch, Jack Perch.

DID YOU KNOW? Students of biology may be more familiar with the Yellow Perch than they realize. Yellow Perch

STATUS: locally abundant; secure.

HABITAT: common in cool lakes, less common in slow-moving rivers; frequently in deep waters; young remain among weeds off shorelines.

are often pictured in biology textbooks and dissected in science laboratories.

ID: dark green back; yellow flanks; white belly; 6–7 vertical black saddles; no canine teeth; preopercle is serrate on rear margin; pelvic fins are thoracic; 2 separated dorsal fins, the first spiny, the second fleshy; 2 anal spines; 1 pelvic spine; slightly indented caudal fin.

SIMILAR SPECIES: *Walleye* (p. 174) and *Sauger* (p. 196): shallower bodied; larger; black and gold flecks cover body; no vertical bars; white tip to bottom of caudal fin; glassy eyes; large canine teeth on jaws.

Walleye

Sauger

6–7 large, black saddles

spiny first dorsal fin

fleshy second dorsal fin

slightly indented caudal fin

adult

LENGTH: *Average:* 8–10 in (20–25 cm). *Maximum:* 14 in (36 cm).
WEIGHT: *Average:* 7–10 oz (200–300 g). *Maximum:* 3 lb (1.4 kg).

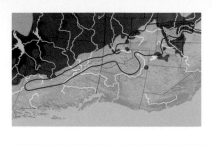

WALLEYE · *Sander vitreus*

Like other sport fishes of the Rockies, Walleye are stocked in specific habitats, mostly in lakes and reservoirs. In some areas, such as the west slopes of Colorado, Walleye are no longer stocked, but remnant populations have survived. • In the northern parts of the Rockies (Alberta and British Columbia), the slow growth of Walleye makes them unsuitable for put-and-take stocking. Anglers (and managers) seldom want to wait 5 to 10 years for these tasty fish to get to catchable sizes in those unproductive mountain waters. • Native Walleye in Alberta are more at home in the boreal forest streams and parkland lakes, but a few do get up into the foothills rivers and a few low-elevation mountain lakes. • The best Walleye viewing is during their spawning run, but Walleye spawn at night during early spring, when the water is cold and the weather in the Rockies is generally bad. Occasionally, however, you may be rewarded with a clear, warm night and frenzied Walleye splashing right against the shore. Their glassy eyes show up like glowing beacons in a flashlight's beam. Later in summer, Walleye will sometimes be seen in clear, shallow water, usually on the margin of a river pool. They typically give you only a moment's glimpse before ghosting back into deeper, darker water, but the white tip on their lower tail fin as they depart is a perfect good-bye wave and positive identification of this species.

FEEDING: mostly piscivorous; occasionally eats insects and other aquatic invertebrates.

SPAWNING: April to May; spawns in moderate to fast-running water in streams or over rocky shoals in lakes; males migrate to spawning area first; spawning occurs at night; female is flanked by 1 or more males; no nest; female rushes into shallow water and turns on her side to release her eggs; female can carry about 20,000–90,000 and even over 600,000 eggs per season; eggs settle into gravel until they hatch in 12–18 days; mature at 2–4 years, with males maturing 1 year earlier than females; live up to 30 years.

OTHER NAMES: Pike-perch, Wall-eyed Pike, Yellow Pickerel, Yellow Walleye.

DID YOU KNOW? This fish gets its name from the term "walleyed," which refers to bulging eyes. The Walleye's large, glassy eyes are a result of a membrane at the back of the eye that allows the Walleye to see in dark water. The specialized eye is extremely sensitive to bright daylight.

STATUS: uncommon to common, depending on the area; vulnerable to overfishing.

HABITAT: large rivers and relatively deep lakes; prefers low amounts of light.

Yellow Perch

Sauger

large, glassy eyes

adult

dark spot at base of first dorsal fin

white spots on tips of anal and caudal fins

ID: dark back; black and gold flecks throughout body; white underparts; tip of anal fin is white; cone-shaped head; large, glassy eyes; large, terminal mouth with canine teeth on jaws; separate pectoral fin bases; 2 dorsal fins, the first spiny, the second fleshy; back end of first dorsal fin has dark spot at base; forked caudal fin has white spot on end of lower lobe.

SIMILAR SPECIES: *Yellow Perch* (p. 172): deeper body; vertical bars on sides; no canine teeth on jaws. *Sauger* (p.196): smaller; blotches on sides.

LENGTH: *Average:* 16–24 in (41–60 cm). *Maximum:* 36 in (90 cm).
WEIGHT: *Average:* 2½–4½ lb (1–2 kg). *Maximum:* 15 lb (6.8 kg).

OTHER ROCKY MOUNTAIN FISHES

PACIFIC LAMPREY *Entosphenus tridentatus*

This ancient, parasitic fish once migrated up the Columbia and Snake Rivers (in BC, ID, MT) to spawn in the same tributaries that salmon and Steelhead historically spawned. As the numbers of dams along these waterways increased, lamprey numbers declined, and it is doubtful that many reach rivers in the mountains today. Pacific Lamprey are born in fresh water, then burrow into mud downstream of the nest for 5 or more years before transforming into adults. Most populations are anadromous, and spend part of their lives in the Pacific Ocean, anywhere from the Aleutian Islands to Baja California and across to Japan. In the foothills, a few landlocked populations existed in reservoirs until the 1970s, but today angler reports of lamprey scars on game fishes, such as Rainbow Trout and Kokanee, are virtually nonexistent.

ID: elongate, cylindrical body becomes more compressed near caudal fin; smooth, leathery skin; cartilaginous skeleton; funnel-like, subterminal mouth; tongue and mouth are lined with sharp teeth; lacks jaws; cleft separates two dorsal fins; inconspicuous anal fin; blue gray to brown overall; pale ventrally.

SIZE: *Average length:* 21 in (53 cm). *Maximum length:* 27 in (68 cm). Landlocked populations are usually less than 8 in (20 cm).

SHOVELNOSE STURGEON *Scaphirhynchus platorynchus*

With the construction of the Yellowtale Dam, natural populations of the Shovelnose Sturgeon were extirpated from the Bighorn River. However, the Wyoming Fish and Game Department reintroduced fingerlings above the dam in the late 1990s. These stocked sturgeons occur mainly in the tributaries to the Bighorn River and frequent areas where slow to moderate currents flow over mixed substrate. They are fairly common in the Tongue River, but occurrence varies from common to rare in other streams. Because sturgeons mature late in life, it is still too early to tell if these fish are reproducing.

ID: body round in cross section; covered with rows of bony plates; flat, shovel-shaped snout; 4 fringed barbels; long, thin caudal peduncle; asymmetrical caudal fin; light brown back, sides and fins; white below.

SIZE: *Maximum length:* 3½ ft (1.1 m). *Maximum weight:* 10½ lb (4.8 kg).

AMERICAN EEL *Anguilla rostrata*

Historically, American Eel found their way up the Pecos and Rio Grande rivers of New Mexico, but were extirpated from the state in the 1940s. Around the same time, a few privately stocked ponds in Colorado also contained eels that occasionally escaped into the upper Rio Grande and Chama rivers. The American Eel is endangered throughout the Rio Grande, as dams and impoundments have blocked migration routes required for spawning. From rivers, these eels swim downstream great distances to the Sargasso Sea in the Atlantic Ocean, where they spawn and then die. Young eels make their way from the spawning grounds back to the coastal streams of North America, a long journey that takes a year or more. While the males remain in the brackish coastal waters throughout their lives, females migrate upstream, sometimes for hundreds of miles.

ID: long, snakelike body; dorsal fin begins half way down back and curves around body to join anal fin; pelvic fins absent; yellow brown overall; pale ventrally.

SIZE: *Average length:* 12–36 in (30–91 cm). *Maximum length:* 5 ft (1.5 m). *Average weight:* 6 lb (2.7 kg).

GIZZARD SHAD *Dorosoma cepedianum*

Gizzard Shad are commonly stocked as forage for other introduced fishes such as Walleye. In different states, they may be stocked annually in varying locations, depending on management practices and winter mortality rates. In the past, Gizzard Shad have been introduced to various water bodies in the mountains, including lakes near Pueblo in Colorado, Willard Reservoir in Utah and Seminoe Reservoir in Wyoming. These extremely prolific fish can produce several hundred thousand eggs per year, but young often do not survive the cold winter temperatures of mountain lakes. Gizzard Shad are native to the Great Lakes region and the central United States.

ID: strongly compressed body; blunt snout; subterminal mouth; last dorsal ray is long and pointed, and extends parallel to back; silver blue on back; silver sides with blue iridescence; up to eight dark stripes on upper sides. *Juveniles:* large purple blue spot just above gill cover.

SIZE: *Average length:* 10 in (25 cm). *Maximum length:* 22½ in (57 cm). *Maximum weight:* 4½ lb (2 kg).

CENTRAL STONEROLLER *Campostoma anomalum*

The Central Stoneroller is mainly found in the eastern United States, but it can range into the mid-elevation mountain streams of the southwest, to elevations of 8000 feet (2400 meters). This species is native to the Wyoming's North Platte River and a few headwater streams in Colorado and New Mexico, including the Pecos, Canadian and Arkansas drainages but has also been introduced to other areas. Central Stonerollers are usually found in permanent streams, where they are associated with rocky riffles.

ID: long, bulbous snout; upper jaw extends past lower jaw; large scales; pectoral fin low on body; orange and black markings on fins; dark gray above fades to yellow below. *Spawning male:* black band on dorsal and anal fins; 1–3 large nuptial tubercles on snout.

SIZE: *Average length:* 3–6 in (7.6–15 cm). *Maximum length:* 8 in (20 cm).

GOLDFISH *Carassius auratus*

The Goldfish is one of the three most cultivated baitfish in the United States, but in some States, including New Mexico, using it as bait is illegal. Even where outlawed, the practice is still widespread. Bait bucket introductions along with released aquarium or ornamental fish can devastate native fish populations, and the public is encouraged to avoid accidentally releasing or purposely stocking this popular aquarium fish. The Goldfish periodically shows up in mountain ponds, but harsh winters usually prevent it from living more than a couple of years. One large Goldfish in the foothills of the Rockies grew to 2 pounds (1 kilogram) and was found in the Julia Davis Lagoon near Boise, Idaho.

ID: rounded body; large caudal fin; golden or bronzed orange in color, though escaped varieties take on a brassy green tinge.

SIZE: *Average length:* 2–3 in (5–7.6 cm). *Maximum length:* 8 in (20 cm).

GRASS CARP *Ctenopharyngodon idella*

Originally from East Asia, the Grass Carp or "White Amur" was introduced to North American lakes and ponds to serve as a biological control for aquatic weeds. While limiting unwanted aquatic vegetation is important in irrigation canals and benefits anglers casting from shore, the Grass Carp's appetite can threaten critical spawning and feeding areas for many native fishes and waterfowl. Even though governments stock sterile Grass Carp in controlled (closed) water bodies, escapees and illegal introductions have allowed this species to spread widely. Once introduced, this voracious vegetarian grows rapidly, often reaching 10 pounds (4.5 kilograms) in the first two years.

ID: wide head, flattened between eyes; upper lip thickened in front; large scales; short anal fin is placed far back; forked caudal fin; pale silver or white overall.

SIZE: *Maximum length:* 3¼ ft (1 m) or more. *Maximum weight:* 20 lb (9 kg) or more.

ROUNDNOSE MINNOW *Dionda episcopa*

A native species of the Pecos drainage in New Mexico, the Roundnose Minnow occurs only in the southernmost areas of the Rockies. Historically one of the most abundant fishes in the lower Pecos drainage, this inconspicuous herbivore is rare or uncommon in New Mexico today. Both habitat alteration and loss have restricted the Roundnose Minnow's range to headwater streams between Santa Rosa and Carlsbad, including the Black River.

ID: slender body; rounded snout; subterminal mouth; yellow green above; silver white below.

SIZE: *Maximum length:* 3 in (7.6 cm).

COMMON SHINER *Luxilus cornutus*

Until the late 1970s, the Common Shiner was well distributed throughout Front Range streams in Colorado. Habitat loss and deterioration has subsequently caused the species to decline. Common Shiners are intolerant of silt and require clean, cool water, gravel substrate and overhanging riparian vegetation to provide shade. These silvery fish are on the edge of their range in the Colorado Rockies and occur only in the upper South Platte and St. Vrain drainages. The Common Shiner is considered a threatened species in the state, and conservation goals include expanding the distribution into protected habitats within their native range.

ID: stout body; dark stripe on upper back; two fainter, parallel stripes on upper sides; dark crescent-shaped spots on sides; deeply forked caudal fin; olive above; bright silver or bronze sides. *Spawning male:* nuptial tubercles on head, back and fin rays; pink sides; blue head.

SIZE: *Maximum length:* 7 in (18 cm).

STURGEON CHUB *Macrhybopsis gelida*

Native to the Missouri River basin of Montana, Wyoming and eastward, the Sturgeon Chub frequents shallow sand and gravel runs of turbid rivers. In the mountains, this fish occurs in Wyoming's Bighorn River. In most areas throughout its range it is extremely rare and habitat appears to be decreasing. Population densities are extremely low, so the Sturgeon Chub may become extirpated from Wyoming in the future. Distinctly ridged scales distinguish the Sturgeon Chub from similar minnows such as the Flathead Chub or Longnose Dace.

ID: rounded snout projects beyond upper lip; papillae on ventral side of head; barbel at each side of mouth; straight-edged fins; scales above lateral line have bony keel (or ridge); light brown or olive above; large brown spots on back; silver sides.

SIZE: *Average length:* 3 in (7.6 cm). *Maximum length:* 4 in (10 cm).

PEARL DACE *Margariscus margarita*

The foothills of the Rockies mark the western edge of the Pearl Dace's range. This little fish is native to the Alberta Rockies near Grande Cache and may occasionally venture up the Athabasca River to Jasper. In Montana, it is sometimes found in the Marias River headwaters in Glacier National Park. The Pearl Dace is very similar to the Lake Chub but lacks a noticeable barbel. Sometimes an observer can see a small, flat barbel on each side of the Pearl Dace's mouth when the mouth is held open, but it is barely visible and not always present. Hybrids with mixed characters also occur, making positive identification very tricky (fish biologists often refer to this pretty little fish as "the dreaded Pearl Dace").

ID: body rounded in cross-section; slightly mottled dorsally; silver to white on sides; white belly; terminal mouth; barbel in groove of upper jaw (sometimes missing). *Males (from fall to spring):* orange red band below lateral band; pectoral fins with nuptial tubercles; males in general have larger and longer pectoral fins.

SIZE: *Average length:* 2¾–4 in (7–10 cm). *Maximum length:* 6 in (15 cm). Females are usually larger than males.

GOLDEN SHINER *Notemigonus crysoleucas*

As one of the three most cultured bait species in the United States, it comes as no surprise that illegal bait bucket releases of the Golden Shiner have been made throughout the Rocky Mountains states. In some areas Golden Shiners are introduced as forage for sport fish, but this practice does not occur in the Rockies, because Golden Shiners can outcompete native fish, especially in high alpine lakes. The Golden Shiner occurs in weedy ponds, lakes and slow-moving rivers, including areas of the Missouri River in Montana or the Upper Pecos in New Mexico. This fish was probably introduced into the mountainous areas of Wyoming through the Tongue River in the Bighorn National Forest. When Golden Shiners are the most abundant species at a site, they are an indicator of pollution or habitat change.

ID: extremely compressed body; pointed snout with upturned mouth; downcurved lateral line; scaleless keel along belly; bright silver to yellow green or yellow brown overall.

SIZE: *Average length:* 4–6 in (10–15 cm). *Maximum length:* 12 in (30 cm).

EMERALD SHINER *Notropis atherinoides*

The Emerald Shiner is a very common minnow, found mainly in large rivers, reservoirs and lakes in many parts of North America, east of the Continental Divide. The occasional Emerald Shiner may show up on the fringes of the Rockies in southern and central Alberta or in the Missouri or Teton rivers just west of Great Falls, Montana. This minnow is important to many predators, both aquatic and avian, including pelicans, mergansers, Lake Trout and Burbot. Populations of Emerald Shiners fluctuate greatly, influencing the populations of many other fishes in the process. When numbers of Emerald Shiners are low, predators are forced to focus on other prey, including the fishes that may feed on Emerald Shiners.

ID: shallow, laterally compressed body; silvery overall with greenish iridescence on back and along lateral line; large scales; cone-shaped head; terminal mouth; transparent fins; forked caudal fin; origin of pelvic fins in front of origin of dorsal fin; long anal fin base with numerous rays (usually 11). *Breeding male:* small nuptial tubercles on pelvic fins. *Juvenile:* somewhat transparent.

SIZE: *Average length:* 2–3 in (5–7.6 cm). *Maximum length:* 4 in (10 cm).

BIGMOUTH SHINER *Notropis dorsalis*

The Bigmouth Shiner occurs in the North Platte and South Platte river systems in Wyoming and Colorado. Although it is only found in a small portion of the Rockies, it is widespread and abundant where it does occur. It is typically found in sand-bottomed streams and forages along the bottom of water bodies, consuming aquatic insects and plants and detritus. It is often preyed upon by larger fish and is an important bait species.

ID: very arched body; flattened head; long snout; subterminal mouth; light brown or olive above; dark stripe on back; silver sides.

SIZE: *Maximum length:* 3 in (7.6 cm).

SPOTTAIL SHINER *Notropis hudsonius*

The Spottail Shiner gets its name from the distinct black spot on its caudal peduncle. In the early 1980s, Fish and Game officials introduced the Spottail Shiner to Montana and Wyoming as forage for sport fish. In Montana it is found in several mountain lakes, typically water bodies with firm bottoms and little vegetation. The Spottail Shiner also occurs in the Bighorn River of Wyoming, where it avoids strong currents. This minnow is native along the eastern foothills of the Rockies in Alberta, where it is the main minnow-like prey fish for many predators. It is also native to much of Canada and the east-central United States.

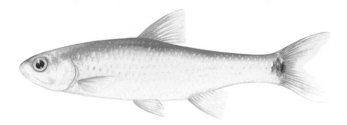

ID: slender, flat-sided body; rounded snout; large eyes; front of dorsal fin is slightly ahead or even with front of pelvic fin; distinct black caudal spot, may fade in older fish; dark, wavy lines are often present above lateral line; silvery overall; olive or light green back.

SIZE: *Average length:* 3 in (7.6 cm). *Maximum length:* 5 in (13 cm).

SAND SHINER *Notropis stramineus*

The Sand Shiner is widely distributed throughout the plains of central and southern North America and into the foothills of the Rocky Mountains from Montana southward. The range of this species has expanded west of the Continental Divide because of illegal bait bucket introductions. This fish is now common to abundant in the upper Colorado and Green rivers of Wyoming, Colorado and Utah, where its impacts on native fishes are still undetermined. Sand Shiners are easy to transport because they tolerate low oxygen levels and will take dry food. However, these small fish are intolerant of cold, turbid streams and heavy pollution.

ID: blunt snout; small mouth; large eyes; oblique, terminal mouth; downcurved lateral line with paired black dashes on scales; black scale edges give the appearance of a diamond pattern on body; light olive back; silver sides, occasionally with purple sheen.

SIZE: *Average length:* 2 in (5 cm). *Maximum length:* 3 in (7.6 cm).

NORTHERN REDBELLY DACE *Phoxinus eos*

Like the ranges of so many other minnows native to the northcentral plains, the Northern Redbelly Dace's range ends at the foothills west of the Continental Divide. In Colorado today, this minnow is found in the South Platte River but historically occurred in the St. Vrain River,

Boulder Creek and West Plum Creek. Though considered endangered in Colorado, recovery goals are modest, owing to the limited historic distribution. North of Colorado, this species is scattered in water bodies along the fringes of the Rockies. The Northern Redbelly Dace frequently hybridizes with the Finescale Dace. In Montana, these hybrids are considered species of special concern. In Upper Pierre Grays Lake, a montane lake in northern Alberta, the female offspring of hybrids were able to create clones of themselves by using male sperm only to stimulate development of their fully formed eggs. Eventually, this strategy will collapse on itself, and there will be a pool of lonely females left!

ID: rounded body, in cross-section; rounded snout; oblique mouth; small scales; two dark lateral lines; fins yellowish; origin of dorsal fin behind origin of pelvic fins; forked caudal fin; dark brown olive dorsally; cream yellowish underparts. *Breeding males:* bright red bellies; 4–5 rows of nuptial tubercles in pectoral area.

SIZE: *Average length:* 1–2 in (4–5 cm). *Maximum length:* 2 in (5 cm).

SOUTHERN REDBELLY DACE *Phoxinus erythrogaster*

The Southern Redbelly Dace is a member of the genus *Phoxinus,* the only genus of minnows native to both Europe and North America. Found throughout the central United States, the western edge of this species' range extends to the headwaters of the Mora River in New Mexico and the Colorado foothills near Pueblo. It requires cool, clear streams, ponds with abundant vegetation and plenty of riparian shade. Of all minnows, the Southern Redbelly Dace is the most brightly colored and sports striking red undersides during spawning season. In captivity, this fish loses its brilliant hues.

ID: snout is somewhat pointed; dark stripe along back; two black stripes along side, lower stripe thicker than upper; black spot on caudal fin; olive above with black spots on upper back; yellowish sides. *Breeding males:* bright red sides and bellies.

SIZE: *Average length:* 2 in (5 cm). *Maximum length:* 3 in (7.6 cm).

ORIENTAL WEATHERFISH *Misgurnus anguillicaudatus*

The Oriental Weatherfish is a member of the loach family, native to Eurasia, Morocco and Ethiopia. This popular aquarium fish was illegally introduced to Idaho, and now occurs on the fringes of the Rockies in the lower Boise River, the lower Payette, and the Weiser area of the Snake River drainage. This unique fish commonly burrows into bottom mud or debris and can survive in waters with little oxygen. In Idaho, the Oriental Weatherfish is successfully reproducing and rapidly expanding its range via irrigation ditches.

ID: long, cylindrical body; 10–12 barbels surround mouth; prominent spine on pectoral fin; small scales; light olive or yellow brown sides with darker mottles; dark spots on dorsal and caudal fins; small caudal spot.

SIZE: *Maximum length:* 10 in (25 cm).

JUNE SUCKER Chamistes liorus

The June Sucker spends most of its life in Utah Lake, Utah, but migrates into the mountains via the Provo River to spawn. This native, endemic fish was once abundant in Utah Lake, but is now extremely rare and listed as endangered by both federal and state agencies. Its decline began in the 1930s, when overfishing combined with drought caused the *liorus* subspecies to nearly become extirpated. In subsequent years, pollution, changes in flow, competition from introduced species and hybridization with non-native suckers caused numbers to decline further. Unlike other suckers, the June Sucker is not a bottom feeder but instead eats zooplankton and tiny invertebrates found in the middle of the water column. The spawning run occurs in June, with fish spawning over gravel and rock substrate in riffles. The eggs sink to the bottom and hatch in about four days.

ID: large, oblique, terminal mouth; plicate or smooth lips; gray or copper back and sides; white-gray fins.

SIZE: *Maximum length:* 24 in (61 cm). *Maximum weight:* 6 lb (2.7 kg).

SMALLMOUTH BUFFALO Ictiobus bubalus

The Smallmouth Buffalo's range is similar to that of the Bigmouth Buffalo, with a few isolated populations occurring in Montana's Rocky Mountains. This fish has been confirmed in Canyon Ferry Lake, Hauser Lake, Lake Helena and Holter Lake. Smallmouth Buffalo are members of the sucker family, and native to the lower Missouri and lower Yellowstone drainage basins in Montana, and the Mississippi drainage basin of the central United States.

ID: deep body; humped back; small head; horizontal, subterminal mouth; thick, grooved upper lip; snout much longer than upper jaw length; large eyes; long, sickle-shaped dorsal fin; slate gray, olive or bronze overall; pale below; dark fins.

SIZE: *Average length:* 23 in (58 cm). *Maximum length:* 3½ ft (1.1 m). *Maximum weight:* 82 lb (37 kg).

BIGMOUTH BUFFALO Ictiobus cyprinellus

Native to Montana, the Bigmouth Buffalo commonly occurs in the middle reaches of the Missouri and Yellowstone rivers. However, small populations are also found in a few mountain lakes near Helena. The Bigmouth Buffalo occurs together with the similar-looking Smallmouth Buffalo, but it can be distinguished by its darker body color and thinner, smoother lips. This fish is a member of the sucker family but young may easily be confused with minnows. Adults also appear similar to the Common Carp.

ID: robust body; large head; oblique, terminal mouth; faintly grooved lips; snout length is almost equal to upper jaw length; long, sickle-shaped dorsal fin; thin upper lip; brown or black overall with a copper sheen; pale underside; dark fins.

SIZE: *Average length:* 10–18 in (25–46 cm). *Maximum length:* 3½ ft (1.1 m). *Maximum weight:* 25 lb (11 kg).

SHORTHEAD REDHORSE *Moxostoma macrolepidotum*

The Shorthead Redhorse is native to central and eastern North America and is locally common to uncommon along the fringes of the central Rockies. The western edge of its range extends just upstream of Great Falls, Montana, in the Missouri River and throughout the Yellowstone drainage, including Clarks Forks. It occasionally ranges up into the Rocky Mountain foothills in the Saskatchewan River systems in southern and central Alberta, but seems to prefer the warmer, silty rivers of the plains. A red tail fin distinguishes the Shorthead Redhorse from other sucker species found in the foothills.

ID: stout body; short head; plicate lips; rear edge of lower lip is nearly straight; somewhat concave dorsal fin; red caudal fin; olive overall; silver or copper sheen on sides.

SIZE: *Average length:* 12 in (30 cm). *Maximum length:* 29 in (75 cm).

YELLOW BULLHEAD *Ictalurus natalis*

Found only in the middle and lower elevation streams of the Rockies, the Yellow Bullhead has a very restricted range in the Rockies. Scattered throughout the East Slopes in locations such as Nine Pines Reservoir, Montana, the Tongue River, Wyoming, and the upper Canadian River in New Mexico, the Yellow Bullhead is an introduced species from eastern North America. This fish thrives in streams but does poorly in ponds or lakes. To anglers, the Yellow Bullhead is one of the most important game fishes in the catfish family.

ID: light-colored barbels; sawlike teeth on rear edge of pectoral spine; anal fin fairly long; overall yellowish brown.

SIZE: *Average length:* 7 in (18 cm). *Maximum length:* 18 in (47 cm). *Maximum weight:* 4 lb (2.4 kg).

BROWN BULLHEAD *Ameiurus nebulosus*

The Brown Bullhead has been introduced into numerous water bodies in Idaho, including American Falls Reservoir, Cascade Reservoir and other lakes in the northern part of the state. Idaho enjoyed a large commercial harvest of bullheads in the 1940s, which were sold to markets in the Western States. Shortly afterward, pressure from anglers led to the discontinuation of the fishery. Today the Brown Bullhead is not a popular game fish, although it is occasionally taken in the spring when schools move into the shallows to spawn. The native range of the Brown Bullhead includes central and eastern North America, from the Canadian border to Mexico. This fish tolerates aquatic pollutants, low oxygen levels and high carbon dioxide levels.

ID: stocky catfish with a slightly notched caudal fin; chin barbells blackish; jagged spine on leading edge of pectoral fin; typically 22-23 (occasionally 21-24) anal fins; tail not deeply forked; olive to dark brown back and sides, sometimes with brown mottling; white or creamy underside; lacks light-colored band near tail fin.

SIZE: *Average length:* 8–14 in (20–35 cm). *Average weight:* 2 lb (0.9 kg)

CENTRAL MUDMINNOW *Umbra limi*

The Central Mudminnow is a hardy species that can withstand extremes in water temperature, high acidity and low dissolved oxygen levels. It has a remarkable ability to use atmospheric oxygen by gulping air at the surface when there is not enough oxygen in the water. A few unauthorized introductions led to populations of Central Mudminnows in the Montana Rockies. These fish were first discovered in Blacktail Creek within the Butte city limits in 1990. Other records include small lakes in the Lola National Forest, northeast of Missoula.

ID: dorsal fin base positioned far back on body but in front of anal fin base; black vertical band on caudal peduncle; rounded caudal fin; dark brown-black overall; mottling or vertical bars on sides.

SIZE: *Average length:* 2 in (5 cm). *Maximum length:* 5 in (13 cm).

CISCO *Coregonus artedi*

Introduced into several lakes and reservoirs near Banff, Alberta, Ciscoes are richly connected in the ecological web of a lake. They form an important food source for Lake Trout, Northern Pike, Yellow Perch, Walleye and Burbot. During the occasional midsummer mass mortalities, they form a key food item for fledgling ospreys and bald eagles. This species is also the major host for the tapeworm *Triaenophorus crassus*, which is sometimes ingested by eating small crustaceans. The parasite does not affect humans but can infect other whitefishes. Transfers of walleye fry from northern Alberta to southern reservoirs for sport fishermen unwittingly also introduced Cisco beyond their natural range, raising the unwelcome possibility of moving this economically disastrous parasite as well.

ID: slender and laterally compressed body; large scales; small head and jaws; terminal mouth, occasionally the lower jaw will protrude farther than the upper jaw; operculum with large scaled pattern; gill rakers are long and numerous (up to 48); base of adipose fin is narrow; bluish to olive dorsally; silvery on sides and belly.

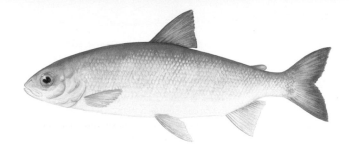

SIZE: *Average length:* 8–12 in (20–30 cm). *Maximum length:* 16 in (41 cm). *Average weight:* less than ½ lb (300 g). *Maximum weight:* 2¼ lb (1 kg).

OHRID TROUT *Salmo letnica*

Ohrid Trout, also known as Yugoslavian Brown Trout, was introduced to Montana, Wyoming and Colorado in the late 1960s from Eastern Europe. They are endemic to Lake Ohrid, an ancient, deep lake in the former Yugoslavian Republic of Macedonia. This fish is endangered within its native range, where overfishing, habitat loss and introduced species pose serious threats. Though introductions in the United States have failed, this long-lived species still exists in Wyoming's Bighorn and Tongue rivers, but it is probably not reproducing. If you are fishing in one of these rivers and happen to catch a strange-looking fish that resembles a Brown Trout, you may have actually landed an Ohrid Trout.

ID: robust body; squared caudal fin; golden brown overall; sides covered with dark brown and black dots.

SIZE: *Maximum weight:* 14 lb (6.3 kg).

ARCTIC CHAR *Salvelinus alpinus*

The circumpolar Arctic Char was once stocked for sport fishing in a few locations in the Rocky Mountains, including the Blue River of Colorado and the high mountain lakes near Challis, Idaho. Though these fish remain in the Blue River, the Idaho stocks are likely extinct. In Alberta, Arctic Char from a fish farm escaped into the Bow River, where they currently survive between Canmore and Calgary. Though some Arctic Char are anadromous, populations in the Rocky Mountains remain in freshwater lakes all their lives. Landlocked populations are generally much drabber in color than their ocean-going relatives. The Arctic Char is native to northern Canada and Alaska, and it has the most northern distribution of any freshwater fish in North America.

ID: elongated body; short head; large eyes; somewhat rounded snout; terminal mouth; teeth on jaws and tongue; silvery overall with cream spots on sides. *Spawning male:* develops kype on lower jaw; overall color is brilliant but variable, steel or silvery blue sides with orange-red sides or spots.

SIZE: *Average length:* 15–18 in (38–46 cm). *Maximum length:* 38 in (96 cm). *Average weight:* 2–8 lb (0.9–3.6 kg). *Maximum weight:* 27 lb (12 kg).

DOLLY VARDEN *Salvelnus malma*

These trout are native to western North America and eastern Asia, with mostly anadromous but also some freshwater populations. In 1974, a university researcher obtained a government permit to release his research subjects into Chester Lake, in Kananaskis, Alberta. The unfortunate researcher had unknowingly received Dolly Varden from a river in the Yukon that was thought to contain Arctic Char. It was an honest mistake, as the northern Dolly Varden can be quite similar to its char relative. The Dolly Varden has been caught in the surrounding tributaries, which indicates its dispersal ability. Fishers may be able to catch a glimpse of this fish along the shores of this lovely alpine lake in the autumn, when the biting bugs have died down but the snow has not begun to fly.

ID: dark body with pinkish belly; red or pink spots; white leading edges to lower fins; dark caudal fin and dorsal fin. *Spawning male:* develops a kype.

SIZE: *Average length:* 8–12 in (20–30 cm). *Average weight:* 1–3 lb (0.5–1.5 kg).

TROUT-PERCH *Percopsis omiscomaycus*

Common in lakes and streams throughout much of Canada and less abundant in the north-eastern United States, the Trout-perch is rarely found in mountain waters. In fact, this native fish is a species of special concern in Montana, because the only known records are from Lower Saint Mary Lake and the Saint Mary Canal, just outside of Glacier National Park. In Canada, Trout-perch may occasionally venture up any of the East Slope drainages as far as the foothills, but these fish prefer the deep lakes and slow rivers east of the mountains.

ID: large, triangular head; large eyes; slightly subterminal mouth; dorsal fin with soft rays, only a few weak spines in both dorsal and anal fins; adipose fin; deeply forked caudal fin; five lines of spots run horizontally along body; one line along midline of back; two lines on each side, the lowest is most conspicuous; olive to brown back, lighter belly.

SIZE: *Average length:* 3–4 in (7.6–10 cm). *Maximum length:* 7 in (18 cm).

PLAINS KILLIFISH *Fundulus zebrinus*

Plains Killifish occur naturally east of the Rocky Mountains and range into the middle and lower East Slope drainages from Big Horn River in Montana south to the Pecos headwaters in New Mexico. These small fish have been introduced west of the Continental Divide, mainly in lower elevation water bodies, where they may negatively affect native fishes, such as the Least Chub. To protect themselves from predators or intense sunlight, Plains Killifish bury themselves in sand, with only their eyes and mouths showing. Their tolerance of high salinity and alkalinity allows them to exist in some areas where other fish cannot survive.

ID: head and back flattened; rounded snout; large eyes; deep caudal peduncle; square caudal fin; 12–26 gray-green vertical stripes on shiny white sides; clear, dark fins; yellow pectoral fins; dorsal, anal and paired fins on spawning male are bright red or orange.

SIZE: *Average length:* less than 3 in (7.6 cm). *Maximum length:* 4 in (10 cm).

SAILFIN MOLLY *Poecilia latipinna*

Sailfin Molly are native to the southeastern states and the Gulf of Mexico. Several populations of illegally released aquarium fish have become established in a few warm springs and ponds in the Rockies. Despite the unfortunate effects these fish have had on the natural systems, they have provided an interesting look at both genetics and Darwin's theory of natural selection. For instance, in the 1960s, several pairs of black Sailfin Molly were illegally introduced into the Cave and Basin Marsh in Banff National Park, Alberta. By 1988, a large proportion of the population had reverted back to its "wild" appearance, a mottled white-and-black pattern. The larger numbers of this morph seem to indicate that it is better adapted to the environment of the brackish marsh.

ID: small; deep-bodied; mouth supraterminal; rounded caudal fin; population may be all black or covered with dark mottling. *Female:* sharp rise to dorsal fin, dorsal fin origin behind pelvic fin origin. *Male:* smaller than female; slight rise to dorsal fin; longer dorsal fin; origin of dorsal fin even with origin of pelvic fins.

SIZE: *Average length:* 2 in (5 cm). *Maximum length:* 6 in (15 cm). Females are larger than males.

SHORTFIN MOLLY *Poecilia mexicana*

Localized introductions of these tropical pet fish, native to Central America, have been made to several warm, spring-fed ponds and streams in the Rocky Mountains. These fish are livebearers—fertilization is internal and females gives birth to live young instead of laying eggs.

ID: dorsal fin behind pelvic fin origin; dark olive to black overall; some have heavy black mottling; 5–6 rows or orange spots on sides; orange edge on caudal fin occasionally.

SIZE: *Average length:* 2 in (5 cm). *Maximum length:* 4 in (10 cm).

GUPPY *Poecilia reticulata*

Guppies are temperature-sensitive fish that are found only in warm, spring-fed streams and ponds in the mountains. In some states, Guppies were introduced for mosquito control (though they have little or no effect), while in other areas populations began from the illegal release of pet fish. These neotropical fish are native to northern South America and the West Indies. Males vary greatly in color, with brighter males having a mating advantage. The pigments of red, orange or yellow come from carotenes in the Guppies' diet and will fade if the fish eats carotene-free food. Iridescent blue and bronze are structural colors, produced from light reflecting off the fish's scales, while black spots are partially under nervous control. Color also varies in response to the type and number of predators, with male Guppies becoming duller in streams where predators are abundant.

ID: highly variable body shape; small head; upturned lower jaw projects beyond upper jaw; female is grayish-greenish brown with shiny blue scales; males are highly variable in color, ranging from green to blue to red.

SIZE: *Average length (male):* 1 in (2.5 cm). *Average length (female):* 2 in (5 cm).

GREEN SWORDTAIL *Xiphophorus helleri*

Like other livebearers in the Rocky Mountains, the Green Swordtail is an illegally released aquarium fish originally from Central America. Local introductions exist in a few warm, spring-fed streams and ponds in Beaverhead, Granite and Madison counties in Montana. When the two occur together, Green Swordtails commonly hybridize with Variable Platyfish and the hybrids have a shorter sword. Crossbreeding also creates new color combinations and varieties that are difficult to identify.

ID: long, swordlike extension from lower edge of tail fin, usually with black edges; green above; red or orange sides; black stripe along sides; may have black fins or black mottling; the classic red variety with yellow stripes is rare in MT.

SIZE: *Average length:* 3 in (7.6 cm). *Maximum length:* 5 in (13 cm).

VARIABLE PLATYFISH *Xiphophorus variatus*

Endemic to Mexico, these tropical aquarium fish are usually only found in North American homes and pet stores. Several populations of illegally introduced Variable Platyfish have become established in warm springs in the Montana Rockies, where they are considered potential pests. Males are most easily identified by their orange-red caudal fin and shimmering, golden dorsal fin, though color variation and hybridization is common. Females of different livebearer species are hard to tell apart because they have similar body shapes and dull coloration.

ID: distinct orange-red caudal fin; golden dorsal fin; body is usually moss green, but color is highly variable; black spots on caudal peduncle; green edge on caudal fin.

SIZE: *Maximum length:* 2 in (5 cm).

WHITE BASS *Morone chrysops*

The White Bass is stocked for sport fishing in warm, foothill waters from Montana southward. It has been introduced to a few lakes and streams on the edges of the mountains, including the Big Thompson and upper Arkansas rivers in Colorado, and the McCelmo River that flows from Colorado to Utah. White Bass are native to the Great Lakes and Mississippi River drainages, and they prefer deep pools in rivers or open waters in large lakes and reservoirs. The White Bass is an active fish that uses its many teeth and strong jaws to devour smaller prey.

ID: deep body; prominent arch behind head; yellow eye; first dorsal fin spiny, second soft; third anal spine distinctly longer than second anal spine; clear or gray caudal and dorsal fins; silver white overall; up to seven dark gray-brown horizontal stripes run along sides.

SIZE: *Average length:* 10 in (25 cm). *Maximum length:* 18 in (46 cm). *Average weight:* ½ lb (300 g). *Maximum weight:* 5¼ lb (2.4 kg).

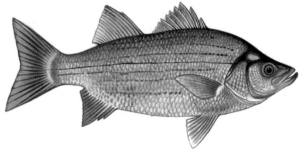

ROCK BASS *Ambloplites rupestris*

The Wyoming Fish and Game Department introduced Rock Bass into the Bighorn and Tongue drainages, in the north-central part of the state. This sport fish prefers clear, rocky streams and medium-sized rivers and is often found around submerged trees, tangled roots or rocky ledges. The Latin name *Ambloplites* means "blunt armature" and refers to the anal spines characteristic of the genus, while *rupestris* means "living among the rocks."

ID: thick body; large mouth; scarlet red eye; short, rounded pectoral fin; 5–6 anal spines; brown black spots in rows along sides; five large saddles on back; dark brown spots or wavy lines on most fins; pale green ventrally; brassy iridescence on side; pale back.

SIZE: *Average length:* 10 in (25 cm). *Maximum length:* 17 in (43 cm). *Maximum weight:* 3 lb (1.4 kg).

PUMPKINSEED *Lepomis gibbosus*

The Pumpkinseed is a schooling fish that may be seen swimming through the sunny shallows in large numbers. Its gold-flecked body reflects the sunlight and this fish appears to shimmer as it moves. Native to the Atlantic drainages of east-central North America, the Pumpkinseed has been widely introduced elsewhere, including small ponds and lakes west of the Continental Divide. This fish has been incidentally stocked on the East Slopes when the Department of Fish and Wildlife stocked other warmwater fishes. Currently it may be found in weedy areas on the fringes of the mountains, including the upper South Platte River and Cache La Poudre, St. Vrain and Big Thompson tributaries near Fort Collins, Colorado or in the Wyoming's Tongue River. Since the Pumpkinseed is a small fish, it is ideal forage food for other predatory fishes such as basses, Walleye or Yellow Perch.

ID: deep, flattened body; rounded back; long, pointed pectoral fin extends past eye when pointed forward; small mouth; bright orange or red spot on ear flap; wavy blue lines on "cheek"; posterior and caudal fins have many dark brown lines or orange spots; olive overall with gold or yellow speckles; bright yellow belly.

SIZE: *Average length:* 6 in (15 cm). *Maximum length:* 10 in (25 cm). *Average weight:* ½ lb (300 g). *Maximum weight:* 1¼ lb (600 g).

LONGEAR SUNFISH *Lepomis megalotis*

The southern Rockies of New Mexico mark the edge of the Longear Sunfish's range. These fish are native to the headwaters of the Pecos and Canadian rivers but were introduced to the Rio Grande. They may be found in weedy areas of clear, low-gradient streams, rivers, irrigation canals or reservoirs.

ID: blue line borders long, horizontal ear flap; wavy blue lines on "cheek"; small, rounded pectoral fin; dark red above; orange sides spotted with blue.

SIZE: *Maximum length:* 9 in (23 cm). *Maximum weight:* 1 lb (0.5 kg).

BLUEGILL *Lepomis macrochirus*

Bluegill were first introduced to the southern Rockies in the early 1900s. Stocked largely in ponds and larger impoundments as both a sport fish and a forage food for Largemouth Bass, Bluegill are also prey for an assortment of furry, feathered and scaly creatures. To combat the high mortality rate, Bluegill produce large numbers of young. However, mountain waters are too cold to support good growth and reproduction—populations are not self-sustaining, so stocking continues today, though not in Montana.

ID: olive back and sides flecked with green and yellow; white or yellow belly; blue sheen overall; bold, vertical bars on sides (bars not apparent in turbid water); black ear flap; rear of operculum is flexible; large, black spot on rear of dorsal fin; deep, extremely laterally compressed body; small mouth; 10 or more dorsal spines; three anal spines; long, pointed pectoral fin. *Spawning male:* blue head; bright orange belly; black pelvic fins.

SIZE: *Average length:* 6–8 in (15–20 cm). *Maximum length:* 16 in (40 cm). *Average weight:* 1 lb (0.5 kg). *Maximum weight:* 4½ lb (2 kg).

SMALLMOUTH BASS *Micropterus dolomieu*

The Smallmouth Bass is native to east-central North America and has been introduced to the streams and lakes of the southern Rocky Mountains in waters too warm for trout but too cool for warm-water fish. Its tolerance of cool waters allows it to be stocked in mid-elevation waters for sport fishing. The Smallmouth Bass gets its unusual scientific name from 18th-century French geologist Dieudonné de Dolomieu, the same man that the mineral dolomite was named after.

ID: light brown overall with bronze mottling; vertical stripes often present along sides; robust, elongate body; three lateral stripes on head; upper jaw extends to eye; more than 55 scales in lateral line; spines on first dorsal fins are relatively even in height; second dorsal fin is soft; shallow notch between spiny and soft dorsal fins.

SIZE: *Average length:* 8–12 in (20–30 cm). *Maximum length:* 27 in (69 cm). *Average weight:* 2–4 lb (0.9–1.8 kg). *Maximum weight:* 11 lb (5 kg).

LARGEMOUTH BASS *Micropterus salmoides*

Native to east-central North America, this fish was introduced to the southern Rockies as a sport fish more than a century ago. In some areas of the mountains, fisheries managers must balance the now well-established stocking policy with the needs of endangered and threatened native fishes. In areas such as the upper Colorado River basin, stocking continues only in waters where there will be little conflict between introduced and native fishes. For example, in Highline Lake Reservoir near Grand Junction, Colorado, a unique barrier net system over the outlet pipe and spillway prevents bass from escaping into the Colorado River, where they might prey upon several endangered species. Even in the cold waters of Banff, early 20th-century fish managers tried to introduce this popular sport fish, likely hoping to entice more tourists familiar with bass from eastern Canada and the U.S. Luckily for the native trouts, this competitor never got a toehold in the mountain waters of Canada. Because Largemouth Bass must consume 4 lb (1.8 kg) of food to gain 1 lb (0.5 kg) of weight, they are often stocked with forage fishes such as Bluegill.

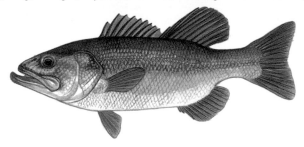

ID: brassy or silver overall; white ventrally; dark stripe or broken blotches often along sides; dark mottling; black flecks on lower sides; somewhat compressed, elongated body; upper jaw extends beyond eye; first dorsal fin is spiny and highest in middle; second dorsal fin is soft and almost separate from first fin; deep notch separates dorsal fins.

SIZE: *Average length:* 10–13 in (25–33 cm). *Maximum length:* 38 in (97 cm). *Average weight:* 2–3 lb (0.9–1.4 kg). *Maximum weight:* 10 lb (4.5 kg).

WHITE CRAPPIE *Pomoxis annularis*

Despite the weather, January may be the best time to discover White Crappie habitat. When you see piles of Christmas trees scattered across a frozen lake, it may be that White Crappies are swimming about under the ice. To enhance habitat, fisheries biologists leave the Christmas trees to sink when the ice melts. The sunken trees are meant to imitate the flooded woodlands that "Timber Crappies" favor, especially for spawning. Native to the warmer waters of the eastern United States, these fish were introduced to the southern Rockies in the early 1880s as sport fish. Although they are no longer stocked in most mountain lakes, a few scattered populations have survived in some areas, including Corn Lake and Fruta State Park in the Colorado Rockies.

ID: green to olive body and head; lighter, iridescent green sides; silver or cream belly; 5–10 vague vertical bands on side; deep, laterally compressed body; mouth reaches to under eye; back arches sharply between eye and dorsal fin.

SIZE: *Average length:* 9 in (23 cm). *Maximum length:* 17 in (43 cm). *Average weight:* less than 1 lb (0.5 kg). *Maximum weight:* 5 lb (2.3 kg).

BLACK CRAPPIE *Poxomis nigromaculatus*

Black Crappies are native to the central and eastern United States and Canada, excluding the northeastern seaboard. While frenzied schools of Black Crappies are sometimes seen feeding in the shallows within their native range, viewing opportunities in the mountains are rare. From a taxonomist's point of view, sunfishes are some of the more highly evolved fish species. Their pelvic fins are farther forward than on more primitive fishes, and their dorsal, pelvic and anal fins have protective spines. Black Crappies are built to dart out and ambush minnows: they depend on their maneuverable bodies to surprise prey, and the spiny dorsal fins protect them from predation by basses, Walleye and Northern Pike. Sunfishes also evolved in warmer waters, among a richer diversity of species than the soft-rayed, coldwater fishes such as trouts.

ID: gray-green back; dark mottling or blotches on body; silver blue sides flecked with green; white belly; black spot on edge of ear flap; bold pattern on fins; deep, laterally compressed body arches sharply from head to dorsal fin; large mouth; 7–8 spines on dorsal fin; 6–7 anal spines.

SIZE: *Average length:* 7–10 in (18–25 cm). *Maximum length:* 19 in (48 cm). *Average weight:* 1–2 lb (500–900 g). *Maximum weight:* 4½ lb (2 kg).

IOWA DARTER *Etheostoma exile*

Like tiny, colorful jewels, Iowa Darters dash about the clear waters of the Great Lakes, Hudson Bay and Mississippi River basins west to the Rockies including the North Platte headwaters and upper Laramie River, in Colorado and Wyoming, as well as the tributaries of the upper South Platte River in Colorado. These small members of the perch family are indicators of healthy waters, disappearing quickly when the water quality decreases. The Iowa Darter's quick movements and habit of hiding under rocks or vegetation makes it difficult for predators to catch this species. When one is caught, its torn scales will release "Scheckstoff," an alarm substance that is usually associated with the minnow family. When other Iowa Darters sense this substance, they know that danger is near and react accordingly.

ID: olive green or brown dorsally and ventrally; small, slender body; squared caudal fin; two dorsal fins, the first red, black and spiny, the second fleshy and transparent with black markings; other fins are transparent with black markings. *Spawning males:* dark red and black markings on sides.

SIZE: *Average length:* 2 in (5 cm). *Maximum length:* 2½ in (6.4 cm). Females are usually larger than males.

JOHNNY DARTER *Etheostoma nigrum*

The Johnny Darter's native range covers the Mississippi River basin and central United States and extends west to the fringes of the Rockies in North Platte River, Wyoming. It has also been introduced to the Bighorn River in Wyoming and west of the Continental Divide to the Colorado River drainage. Though many species of darters are federally listed as threatened, the Johnny Darter is common and secure, and in Wyoming its range appears to be expanding. This coolwater fish prefers sandy and muddy headwater pools of streams and small rivers.

ID: slender body; blunt snout; two dorsal fins; large fan-shaped pectoral fin; black eye stripe; dark brown "X"s and "W"s on sides; dark, wavy lines on upper sides; light brown above; six dark saddles. *Spawning male:* black head; black lower fins.

SIZE: *Maximum length:* 2¾ in (7.2 cm).

SAUGER *Sander canadense*

Sauger are rare in Wyoming and Montana, where they occur at the fringes of their North American range. Population densities are extremely low or physically isolated from each other, and concern is mounting over this sensitive species. In Montana this fish is native to the large, turbid rivers of the plains, including the Milk River, the Missouri drainage near Helena and downstream and the Yellowstone River below Billings. In Wyoming, the Sauger is native to the Bighorn and Tongue rivers. This fish has also been stocked in several lakes and reservoirs in the Montana Rockies for sport fishing. In Alberta, Sauger are residents of the large prairie rivers of the Saskatchewan River system, and rarely swim far enough upstream to see foothills, let alone real mountains.

ID: long body, rounded in cross section; scaled "cheek"; large teeth on jaws and roof of mouth; first dorsal fin is spiny with rows of spots; second dorsal fin is soft; two spines on anal fin; lower edge of caudal fin is white; grayish body with darker blotches.

SIZE: *Average length:* 13 in (33 cm). *Maximum length:* 28 in (71 cm). *Maximum weight:* 8¾ lb (4 kg).

CONVICT CICHLID *Cichlasoma nigrofasciatum*

A popular aquarium fish, the Convict Cichlid is found in Barney Hot Springs, Idaho. Introduced from an illegal aquarium release, the Convict Cichlid is an unwanted addition to the geothermal waters. Because this fish requires high temperatures to maintain itself, there is little danger of it spreading outside the springs. The Convict Cichlid is native to Central America, from Guatemala to Costa Rica along the Pacific Ocean, and Honduras to Panama along the Atlantic.

ID: compressed body; one nare on each side of head; 7–9 dark side bands; first band is Y-shaped; anal fin has four or more spines; black spot on gill cover; black caudal spot; blue-gray body.

SIZE: *Maximum length:* 4½ in (12 cm).

AFRICAN JEWELFISH *Hemichromis bimaculatus*

A popular aquarium fish, the African Jewelfish is an unwanted but beautiful addition to the Cave and Basin Marsh in Banff National Park. Introduced from an illegal aquarium release, the African Jewelfish is a highly territorial species from central and northern Africa. This introduction allowed biologists to examine the consequences of introducing such an exotic species to the area. The native resident fish in the marsh, the Banff subspecies of the Longnose Dace, is now extinct.

ID: rounded body with thick caudal peduncle; rounded caudal fin; large eyes; terminal mouth; long dorsal fin; body is green and red with mostly blue spots along entire body including head and fins; three black spots, one on the operculum, one on the middle of the body and one at the end of the caudal peduncle. *Spawning:* both sexes turn bright red, all spots remain.

SIZE: *Average length:* 2–3 in (5–7.6 cm).

MOZAMBIQUE TILAPIA *Oreochromis mossambicus*

The Mozambique Tilapia is an illegal introduction to Barney Hot Springs, Idaho. This fish is probably the product of an aquarium release. Though it is confined to one location in Idaho, the Mozambique Tilapia is a potential pest. This fish can reproduce and spread through irrigation ditches, causing adverse ecological impacts. Like the name suggests, it is native to Africa.

ID: compressed body; one nare on each side; black spot on operculum; long dorsal fin ends in a point; three spines on anal fin. *Male:* underside of head is white; black fins with red edges.

SIZE: *Maximum length:* 15¼ in (39 cm). *Maximum weight:* 9½ lb (4.3 kg).

REDBELLY TILAPIA *Tilapia zilli*

Like the Mozambique Tilapia, the Redbelly Tilapia is an illegally released aquarium fish that is found only in the warm waters of Barney Hot Springs, Idaho. Native to north-central Africa and Eurasia, this colorful fish prefers shallow, vegetated areas and warm waters. The Redbelly Tilapia can potentially interfere with the natural ecological balance when introduced to new environments.

ID: compressed body; wide head; one nare on each side; large, horizontal mouth; bright green lips; black spot surrounded by yellow on second dorsal fin; dark head with wavy blue lines; 6–8 faint bars on light olive sides; sides may have iridescent blue, green or red sheen; pink to bright red underside.

SIZE: *Maximum length:* 15½ in (40 cm).

FISHING IN THE ROCKY MOUNTAINS

Eight states and provinces have parts of the Rocky Mountains within their boundaries, and each jurisdiction has its own laws, regulations, guidelines, restrictions and instructions with respect to fishing. All jurisdictions distribute an annually updated guide to fishing regulations available from tourist centers, outdoor recreation retail stores, registry offices and wherever else fishing licenses may be sold. And of course, they are all available online:

Alberta
http://www.albertaregulations.ca/Fishing-Regs-2008.pdf

British Columbia
http://www.env.gov.bc.ca/fw/fish/regulations/ and click on the cover of the regulations booklet featured

Parks Canada Fishing Regulations Summary
http://www.pc.gc.ca/pn-np/ab/jasper/visit/visit14a_E.asp

Colorado
http://wildlife.state.co.us/Rules/Regs/ and look in the Attention Anglers paragraph for the link to the current guidebook in use

Idaho
http://fishandgame.idaho.gov/fish/fish_guide

Montana
http://fwp.mt.gov/fishing/regulations/default.html and click on the cover of the guide shown on the website

New Mexico
http://www.wildlife.state.nm.us/recreation/fishing/index.htm and click on Publications

Utah
http://wildlife.utah.gov/guidebooks/2009_fishing/

Wyoming
http://gf.state.wy.us/fish/fishing/fishregs.pdf

These guides all stress the importance of ethical fishing, fun, safety and conservation. Most have maps and detailed information on type of fish to be caught, access and fishing seasons, and include opportunities for additional recreational activities such as camping and boating. Information on specific programs are included, such as Free Fishing Days, Annual Trophy Contests and Master Angler Programs.

Licenses and permits, available through a variety of outlets, online and by telephone, are required unless specified otherwise for certain events. The guides specify which species of fish may be caught where and when, and what kinds of lures and baits may be used. They specify the number and size of fish that may be caught. There is usually detailed information for every species of fish and every stream, river, lake and other waterbody of significance. Definitions of terms and descriptions of the different methods of fishing (e.g., fly fishing and ice fishing) are provided, as well as the hazards and precautions associated with each.

Access to fishing sites through private property or native land is forbidden unless express permission is obtained. Some fishing sites have additional restrictions such as not allowing dogs or campfires.

Advisories are posted from time to time on emergency stream closures caused by overfishing concerns and habitat disruptions, among other reasons. The guides note that contaminants such as dioxin, furan and mercury might be present in some species of fish and in some waterbodies, and they include information on how often certain people should consume fish from these waters. In some cases, emergency closures can affect certain parts of waterbodies but not others.

Fish health and habitat health are important issues in all jurisdictions. The guides emphasize catch and release and provide instructions to improve the chances of the released fish surviving the ordeal. They identify diseases (such as whirling disease) or nasty plants (European milfoil) or animals (zebra mussels) that may be transported into mountain waters accidentally. Ways of preventing the spread of these harmful threats to fish stocks and habitat including proper draining and cleaning your boat. In addition, regulations such as no illegal fish stocking are meant to help reduce the disruption to existing species and habitat. Some waterbodies are stocked with species of fish for recreational purposes, and note is made of those places.

Overfished species are protected—in Alberta for example, if you catch a bull trout, which is the provincial fish, you have to release it back into the water. "No black—put it back" is what the provincial fish regulations specify.

Every year, conservation officers and biologists are on the alert for violators. The public is encouraged to report poachers or violators, and to contact certain people if they notice spills or catch tagged fish.

These broad regulations appear in each of the guides; we encourage you to obtain the specific guide for your province or state and become aware of both the regulations and the efforts to manage fish stocks and habitats in a sustainable manner.

The following pages feature maps of each of the Rocky Mountain states and provinces, with the lists of the best fishing sites and species of fish you will likely encounter. Fish may vary with stocking or season. These sites were chosen because they are generally well known, easy to access and on main routes. We have consulted many sources for the lists of sites, but your favorite location may not be included.

Please check fishing regulations, restrictions and guidelines for each location.

BRITISH COLUMBIA —Best Fishing Sites
Please check fishing regulations, restrictions and guidelines for each location.

1. **Liard River**
   Arctic Grayling, Bull Trout, Mountain Whitefish, Northern Pike
2. **Muncho Lake Provincial Park**
   Arctic Grayling, Bull Trout, Lake Trout
3. **Charlie Lake**
   Northern Pike, Walleye
4. **Williston Lake**
   Bull Trout, Rainbow Trout, Mountain Whitefish
5. **Moberly Lake**
   Arctic Grayling, Bull Trout, Northern Pike
6. **Gwillim Lake Provincial Park**
   Arctic Grayling, Bull Trout, Lake Trout, Mountain Whitefish, Northern Pike
7. **Kakwa Provincial Park (access by horseback, hiking or aircraft only)**
   Rainbow Trout, Bull Trout
8. **Fraser River**
   Bull Trout, Rainbow Trout, Mountain Whitefish
9. **Kinbasket Lake (especially near small stream mouths)**
   Bull Trout, Kokanee, Rainbow Trout
10. **Yoho National Park**
    Brook Trout, Cutthroat Trout, Lake Trout, Mountain Whitefish, Rainbow Trout
11. **Columbia Lake**
    Bull Trout, Kokanee, Rainbow Trout
12. **Kootenai River**
    Bull Trout, Cutthroat Trout, Rainbow Trout
13. **Elk River**
    Cutthroat Trout, Bull Trout
14. **St. Mary River**
    Cutthroat Trout, Rainbow Trout, Brook Trout, Bull Trout
15. **Lake Koocanusa**
    Bull Trout, Kokanee, Rainbow Trout

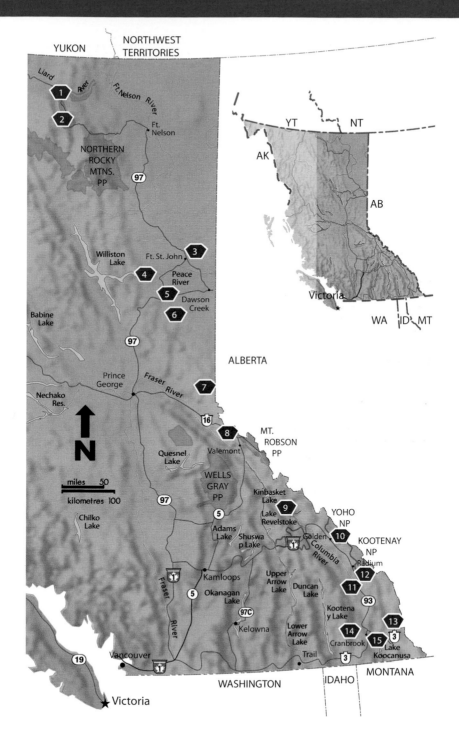

YUKON

NORTHWEST
TERRITORIES

Liard

Ft. Nelson River

Ft. Nelson

NORTHERN
ROCKY
MTNS.
PP

97

Williston
Lake

Ft. St. John

Peace
River

Dawson
Creek

Babine
Lake

97

Nechako
Res.

Prince
George

Fraser River

ALBERTA

N

miles 50

kilometres 100

97

Quesnel
Lake

Valemont

MT.
ROBSON
PP

16

WELLS
GRAY
PP

Kinbasket
Lake

YOHO
NP

Chilko
Lake

Lake
Revelstoke

KOOTENAY
NP

Adams
Lake

Shuswa
p Lake

Golden

Columbia River

Radium

Kamloops

Upper
Arrow
Lake

Duncan
Lake

Kootena
y Lake

93

Fraser River

Okanagan
Lake

97C

Kelowna

Lower
Arrow
Lake

Cranbrook

Lake
Koocanusa

Trail

MONTANA

19

Vancouver

WASHINGTON

IDAHO

★ Victoria

YT   NT

AK

AB

Victoria

WA ID MT

ALBERTA — Best Fishing Sites
Please check fishing regulations, restrictions and guidelines for each location.

1. **Grande Cache Area (Smoky River South, Sulphur Gates, Sheep Creek and Kakwa Provincial Recreation Areas)**
   Arctic Grayling, Bull Trout, Mountain Whitefish; catch and release of all species on Kakwa River
2. **Willmore Wilderness Park (horseback or hiking access only; no motorized vehicles)**
   Bull Trout, Mountain Whitefish
3. **Berland River**
   Bull Trout, Rainbow Trout, Mountain Whitefish
4. **Rock Lake**
   Lake Trout, Mountain Whitefish
5. **William A. Switzer Provincial Park**
   Brown Trout, Rainbow Trout
6. **Athabasca River in Jasper Park**
   Brook Trout, Bull Trout, Mountain Whitefish, Rainbow Trout
7. **Talbot Lake**
   Northern Pike
8. **Pyramid Lake**
   Rainbow Trout, Lake Trout
9. **Beaver Lake (walk in)**
   Brook Trout
10. **Medicine Lake**
    Rainbow Trout
11. **Maligne Lake/Maligne River**
    Brook Trout, Rainbow Trout
12. **Sunwapta River**
    Brook Trout
13. **Hector Lake**
    Rainbow Trout, Brook Trout, Mountain Whitefish

14. **Cascade River and associated lakes**
    Brook Trout, Bull Trout, Cutthroat Trout, Rainbow Trout
15. **Lake Minnewanka**
    Lake Trout, Mountain Whitefish
16. **Vermillion Lakes**
    Rainbow Trout, Brook Trout
17. **Bow River**
    Brook Trout, Brown Trout, Bull Trout, Cutthroat Trout, Rainbow Trout
18. **Kananaskis Lakes, Kananaskis River and associated tributaries**
    Brook Trout, Bull Trout, Cutthroat Trout, Mountain Whitefish, Rainbow Trout
19. **Chain Lakes Provincial Park**
    Rainbow Trout
20. **Oldman River System**
    Bull Trout, Brown Trout, Rainbow Trout, Mountain Whitefish
21. **Crowsnest River and Lundbreck Falls**
    Brook Trout, Bull Trout, Cutthroat Trout, Rainbow Trout, Brown Trout
22. **Beauvais Lake Provincial Park**
    Brown Trout, Rainbow Trout
23. **Castle River**
    Bull Trout, Cutthroat Trout, Rainbow Trout, Mountain Whitefish
24. **Waterton Lakes National Park**
    Brook Trout, Bull Trout, Burbot, Cutthroat Trout, Lake Trout, Mountain Whitefish, Northern Pike, Rainbow Trout

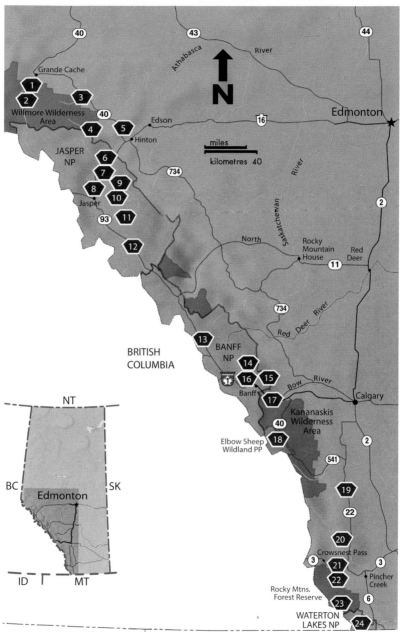

MONTANA —Best Fishing Sites
Please check fishing regulations, restrictions and guidelines for each location.

1. **Lake Koocanusa, Kootenai River and adjacent lakes**
   Bluegill, Bull Trout, Kokanee, Largemouth Bass, Northern Pike, Rainbow Trout, Smallmouth Bass, Westslope Cutthroat Trout, Yellow Perch
2. **Stillwater River and adjacent lakes**
   Black Crappie, Largemouth Bass, Kokanee, Northern Pike, Rainbow Trout, Westslope Cutthroat Trout, Yellow Perch
3. **Thompson Chain-of-Lakes**
   Black Crappie, Brook Trout, Lake Trout, Kokanee, Lake Whitefish, Mountain Whitefish, Northern Pike, Largemouth Bass, Rainbow Trout, Smallmouth Bass, Westslope Cutthroat Trout, Yellow Perch
4. **Flathead River**
   Bull Trout, Lake Trout, Mountain Whitefish, Northern Pike Rainbow Trout, Westslope Cutthroat Trout, Lake Whitefish
5. **Flathead Lake**
   Lake Trout, Lake Whitefish, Westslope Cutthroat Trout, Yellow Perch
6. **Swan River and Adjacent Lakes**
   Brook Trout, Largemouth Bass, Mountain Whitefish, Northern Pike, Pumpkinseed, Rainbow Trout, Smallmouth Bass, Westslope Cutthroat Trout; Yellow Perch
7. **Hungry Horse Reservoir**
   Bull Trout, Cutthroat Trout, Whitefish
8. **Rocky Mountain Front Fishing Access Site (FAS) Reservoir Sites**
   Largemouth Bass, Rainbow Trout, Northern Pike, Walleye, Yellow Perch
9. **Clark Fork (Lower) and adjacent areas**
   Brown Trout, Largemouth Bass, Mountain Whitefish, Northern Pike, Rainbow Trout, Smallmouth Bass, Westslope Cutthroat Trout, Yellow Perch
10. **Blackfoot River**
    Brook Trout, Brown Trout, Mountain Whitefish, Rainbow Trout, Westslope Cutthroat Trout
11. **Clark Fork (Upper) and adjacent areas**
    Brook Trout, Brown Trout, Mountain Whitefish, Northern Pike, Rainbow Trout, Smallmouth Bass, Westslope Cutthroat Trout, Yellow Perch
12. **Bitterroot River and adjacent areas**
    Brook Trout, Brown Trout, Rainbow Trout, Mountain Whitefish, Westslope Cutthroat Trout
13. **Rock Creek**
    Brook Trout, Brown Trout, Mountain Whitefish, Rainbow Trout, Yellowstone Cutthroat Trout
14. **Georgetown Lake**
    Brook Trout, Kokanee, Rainbow Trout
15. **Missouri River**
    Brown Trout, Black Crappie, Burbot, Channel Catfish, Northern Pike, Rainbow Trout, Paddlefish, Sauger, Shovelnose Sturgeon, Smallmouth Bass, Walleye, Yellow Perch
16. **Canyon Ferry Lake**
    Brook Trout, Brown Trout, Burbot, Common Carp, Largemouth Bass, Northern Pike, Rainbow Trout, Smallmouth Bass, Walleye, Yellow Perch
17. **Big Hole River**
    Arctic Grayling, Brook Trout, Brown Trout, Burbot, Mountain Whitefish, Rainbow Trout
18. **Jefferson River and adjacent areas**
    Brown Trout, Mountain Whitefish, Rainbow Trout
19. **Beaverhead River**
    Brown Trout, Mountain Whitefish, Rainbow Trout
20. **Ruby River**
    Brown Trout, Mountain Whitefish, Rainbow Trout
21. **Madison River**
    Brown Trout, Mountain Whitefish
22. **Gallatin River and adjacent areas**
    Brown Trout, Rainbow Trout, Mountain Whitefish

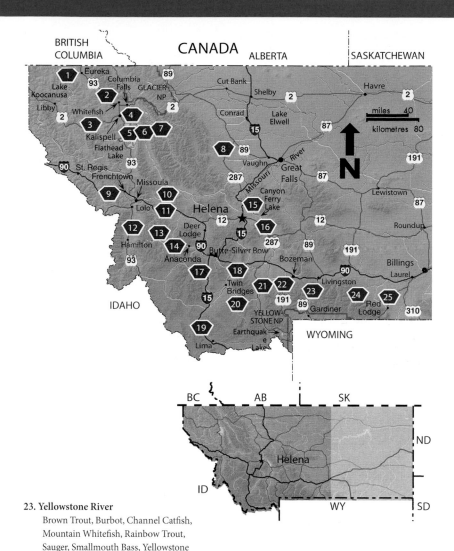

23. **Yellowstone River**
    Brown Trout, Burbot, Channel Catfish, Mountain Whitefish, Rainbow Trout, Sauger, Smallmouth Bass, Yellowstone Cutthroat Trout
24. **Stillwater River**
    Brook Trout, Brown Trout, Mountain Whitefish, Rainbow Trout, Yellowstone Cutthroat Trout
25. **East Rosebud Creek**
    Brook Trout, Brown Trout, Mountain Whitefish, Rainbow Trout, Yellowstone Cutthroat Trout

IDAHO —Best Fishing Sites

Please check fishing regulations, restrictions and guidelines for each location.

1. **Kootenai River**
   Brook Trout, Brown Bullhead, Cutthroat Trout, Kokanee, Mountain Whitefish, Pumpkinseed, Yellow Perch
2. **Priest Lake**
   Brook Trout, Cutthroat Trout, Lake Trout, Mountain Whitefish
3. **Lake Pend Oreille**
   Bull Trout (world record), Kokanee, Lake Trout, Largemouth Bass, Rainbow Trout, Smallmouth Bass, Whitefish, Yellow Perch
4. **Spirit Lake and Twin Lakes**
   Kokanee, Rainbow Trout
5. **Hayden Lake**
   Largemouth Bass, Northern Pike, Rainbow Trout, Smallmouth Bass
6. **Lake Coeur d'Alene**
   Black Crappie, Chinook Salmon, Cutthroat Trout, Largemouth Bass, Northern Pike, Smallmouth Bass, Yellow Perch
7. **Dworshak Reservoir**
   Bull Trout, Cutthroat Trout, Kokanee, Largemouth Bass, Rainbow Trout, Smallmouth Bass, Mountain Whitefish
8. **Clearwater River**
   Chinook Salmon, Cutthroat Trout, Rainbow Trout, Steelhead Trout, Whitefish
9. **Salmon River**
   Brook Trout, Chinook Salmon, Channel Catfish, Crappie, Cutthroat Trout, Rainbow Trout, Steelhead, Sturgeon, Smallmouth Bass, Whitefish
10. **Snake River to Hells Canyon Dam**
    Bluegill, Bullhead Catfish, Bull Trout, Channel Catfish, Chinook Salmon, Crappie, Cutthroat Trout, Largemouth Bass, Pumpkinseed, Rainbow Trout, Steelhead, Sturgeon, Smallmouth Bass, Whitefish, Yellow Perch
11. **Hells Canyon Dam Reservoirs (Brownlee, Oxbow, Hells Canyon)**
    Bluegill, Bullhead Catfish, Channel Catfish, Largemouth Bass, Lake Sturgeon, Pumpkinseed, Rainbow Trout, Smallmouth Bass, Whitefish, Yellow Perch
12. **Payette Lake and Upper Payette Lake**
    Kokanee, Lake Trout, Rainbow Trout

13. **Cascade Dam Reservoir**
    Brown Bullhead, Channel Catfish, Coho Salmon, Rainbow Trout, Smallmouth Bass, Whitefish, Yellow Perch
14. **Paddock Valley Reservoir**
    Bluegill, Bullhead Catfish, Crappie, Largemouth Bass
15. **Deadwood Reservoir**
    Bull Trout, Chinook Salmon, Cutthroat Trout, Kokanee, Mountain Whitefish, Rainbow Trout
16. **Redfish Lake and adjacent areas**
    Bull Tout, Cutthroat Trout, Kokanee, Rainbow Trout
17. **Lake Lowell**
    Bluegill, Bullhead Catfish, Channel Catfish, Crappie, Largemouth Bass, Pumpkinseed, Smallmouth Bass, Yellow Perch
18. **Lucky Peak Reservoir**
    Bluegill, Bull Trout, Chinook Salmon, Kokanee, Lake Sturgeon, Pumpkinseed, Rainbow Trout, Whitefish
19. **Arrowrock Reservoir**
    Bull Trout, Kokanee, Mountain Whitefish, Rainbow Trout, Smallmouth Bass, Yellow Perch
20. **Anderson Ranch Reservoir**
    Bull Trout, Kokanee, Mountain Whitefish, Rainbow Trout, Smallmouth Bass, Yellow Perch
21. **C.J. Strike Reservoir**
    Bluegill, Brown Bullhead, Channel Catfish, Largemouth Bass, Pumpkinseed, Rainbow Trout, Smallmouth Bass, White Sturgeon, Yellow Perch
22. **Twin Lakes Reservoir**
    Bluegill, Largemouth Bass, Rainbow Trout
23. **Salmon Falls Creek Reservoir**
    Kokanee, Rainbow Trout, Smallmouth Bass, Walleye, Yellow Perch
24. **Magic Reservoir**
    Brown Trout, Rainbow Trout, Yellow Perch
25. **Mud Lake and Camas Creek**
    Bullhead Catfish, Channel Catfish, Cutthroat Trout, Largemouth Bass, Yellow Perch
26. **Island Park Reservoir**
    Brook Trout, Kokanee, Mountain Whitefish (world record: 5 lbs, 14 oz), Rainbow Trout

BRITISH COLUMBIA

Priest Lake **1**
95
2 Pend Oreille Lake
Sandpoint
3
4 **5**
Coeur d'Alene
6
WASHINGTON
95
Dworshak Res. **7**
• Orofino
Lewiston **8**
12
9 • Grangeville
HELLS CANYON NRA **10**
11
12
Cascade Dam Res. **13**
SAWTOOTH NRA **75**
16
95
14 **15**
84
Boise
17 **18** **19**
Ketchum
Hailey
20
95
Mountain Home AFB
Mountain Home
20 **22** **24**
23
Gooding
84
21
93
30
Twin Falls
30
26
MONTANA
Salmon
93
SNAKE RIVER

27
26
15 **20**
St. Anthony
25
26 **20** **26**
91 Idaho Falls
32
Blackfoot **30**
American Falls Res. **29** **15**
Pocatello **31**
American Falls
28 **86**
30
Soda Springs
Montpelier
15 **91** **89**
Preston **33**
84
WYOMING
OREGON

0 miles 40
0 kilometres 80

NEVADA | UTAH

27. Henry's Lake
Brook Trout, Cutthroat Trout, Cutthroat Trout–Rainbow Trout hybrids

28. Lake Walcott Reservoir
Rainbow Trout, Smallmouth Bass

29. American Falls Reservoir
Brown Trout, Cutthroat Trout, Largemouth Bass, Rainbow Trout, Yellow Perch

30. Blackfoot River
Yellowstone Cutthroat Trout, Whitefish

31. Blackfoot Reservoir
Cutthroat Trout, Rainbow Trout, Yellow Perch

32. Palisades Reservoir
Brown Trout, Cutthroat Trout

33. Bear Lake
Bear Lake Whitefish, Bonneville Cisco, Bonneville Cutthroat Trout, Bonneville Whitefish, Lake Trout

WYOMING —Best Fishing Sites

Please check fishing regulations, restrictions and guidelines for each location.

1. **Yellowstone National Park**
   Arctic Grayling, Brook Trout, Brown Trout, Lake Trout, Mountain Whitefish, Rainbow Trout, Yellowstone Cutthroat Trout
2. **Beartooth Lakes**
   Arctic Grayling, Brook Trout, Lake Trout, Rainbow Trout, Yellowstone Cutthroat Trout
3. **Yellowstone River: Clarks Fork**
   Brown Trout, Rainbow Trout, Yellowstone Cutthroat Trout
4. **Bighorn Lake**
   Black Crappie, Brown Trout, Burbot, Channel Catfish, Lake Trout, Largemouth Bass, Mountain Whitefish, Sauger, Walleye, Yellow Perch
5. **Newton Lakes**
   Brook Trout, Brown Trout, Burbot, Splake, Yellowstone Cutthroat Trout
6. **Buffalo Bill Reservoir and Shoshone River**
   Brown Trout, Cutthroat Trout, Lake Trout, Rainbow Trout
7. **Greybull River**
   Brown Trout, Cutthroat Trout
8. **Bighorn River Drainage**
   Brown Trout, Burbot, Channel Catfish, Rainbow Trout, Sauger, Walleye
9. **Grand Teton National Park and Jackson Lake**
   Arctic Grayling, Brook Trout, Cutthroat Trout, Lake Trout, Mountain Whitefish
10. **Snake River to Palisades Reservoir**
    Cutthroat Trout, Mountain Whitefish
11. **Wind River**
    Brook Trout, Brown Trout, Mountain Whitefish, Rainbow Trout, Sauger, Yellowstone Cutthroat Trout, Walleye
12. **Boysen Reservoir**
    Black Crappie, Brown Trout, Burbot, Channel Catfish, Cutthroat Trout, Lake Trout, Largemouth Bass, Rainbow Trout, Walleye, Yellow Perch

13. **Bull Lake**
    Brook Trout, Golden Trout, Lake Trout, Rainbow Trout, Snake River Cutthroat Trout, Yellowstone Cutthroat Trout
14. **Ocean Lake**
    Black Crappie, Burbot, Walleye, Yellow Perch
15. **Lake Cameahwait**
    Largemouth Bass, Rainbow Trout, Yellow Perch
16. **Wind River Lakes**
    Rainbow Trout
17. **Popo Agie River**
    Brook Trout, Burbot, Rainbow Trout
18. **Sweetwater River**
    Brook Trout, Brown Trout, Cutthroat Trout, Rainbow Trout
19. **Hams Fork**
    Brook Trout, Brown Trout, Cutthroat Trout, Rainbow Trout, Mountain Whitefish
20. **Fontenelle Reservoir**
    Brown Trout, Kokanee, Rainbow Trout
21. **Big Sandy Reservoir**
    Brown Trout, Channel Catfish, Cutthroat Trout, Rainbow Trout
22. **Bear River**
    Cutthroat Trout
23. **Meeks Cabin Reservoir**
    Colorado River Cutthroat Trout
24. **Green River**
    Brook Trout, Brown Trout, Channel Catfish, Cutthroat Trout, Lake Trout, Mountain Whitefish, Rainbow Trout, Smallmouth Bass
25. **Flaming Gorge Reservoir**
    Brown Trout, Channel Catfish, Kokanee, Lake Trout, Rainbow Trout, Smallmouth Bass
26. **Gray Reef Reservoir (N. Platte)**
    Brown Trout, Cutthroat Trout, Rainbow Trout, Walleye

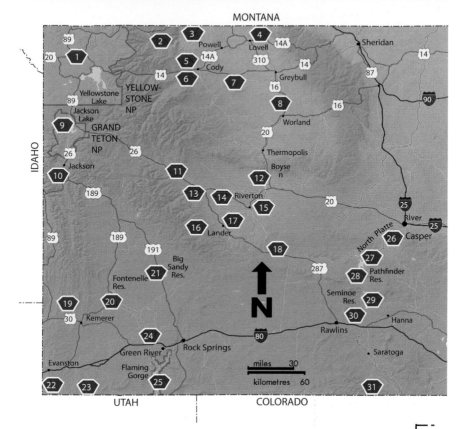

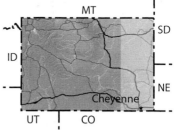

27. **Alcova Reservoir (N. Platte)**
    Brown Trout, Rainbow Trout, Walleye
28. **Pathfinder Reservoir (N. Platte)**
    Brown Trout, Cutthroat Trout, Rainbow
    Trout, Walleye
29. **Seminoe Reservoir (N. Platte)**
    Brown Trout, Cutthroat Trout, Rainbow
    Trout, Walleye
30. **North Platte River**
    Brown Trout, Channel Catfish, Cutthroat
    Trout, Rainbow Trout, Walleye
31. **Encampment River**
    Brown Trout, Rainbow Trout

UTAH —BEST FISHING SITES
Please check fishing regulations, restrictions and guidelines for each location.

1. **Bear Lake**
   Bear Lake Whitefish, Bonneville Cisco, Brown Trout, Cutthroat Trout, Lake Trout (Mackinaw), Rainbow Trout, Yellow Perch

2. **Hyrum Reservoir**
   Bluegill, Brown Trout, Channel Catfish, Largemouth Bass, Rainbow Trout, Tiger Trout, Yellow Perch

3. **Willard Bay**
   Black Crappie, Bluegill, Bullhead Catfish, Channel Catfish, Smallmouth Bass, Walleye, Wiper (Bass and Striped Bass hybrid)

4. **Mantua Reservoir**
   Bluegill, Green Sunfish, Largemouth Bass, Rainbow Trout, Yellow Perch

5. **Pineview Reservoir**
   Common Carp, Largemouth Bass, Rainbow Trout, Smallmouth Bass, Tiger Muskellunge, Yellow Perch

6. **Jordan River**
   Black Bullhead, Black Crappie, Bluegill, Channel Catfish, Common Carp, Rainbow Trout, Walleye, White Bass

7. **Little Dell Reservoir**
   Brook Trout, Brown Trout, Cutthroat Trout

8. **East Canyon Reservoir**
   Brown Trout, Cutthroat Trout, Rainbow Trout

9. **Echo Reservoir**
   Brown Trout, Yellow Perch, Rainbow Trout, Smallmouth Bass

10. **Rockport Reservoir**
    Yellow Perch, Rainbow Trout, Smallmouth Bass

11. **Jordanelle Reservoir**
    Brown Trout, Cutthroat Trout, Largemouth Bass, Rainbow Trout, Smallmouth Bass, Walleye, Yellow Perch

12. **Provo River**
    Brown Trout, Common Carp, Cutthroat Trout, Rainbow Trout, Mountain Whitefish, Walleye, White Bass

13. **Deer Creek Reservoir**
    Bluegill, Brown Trout, Common Carp, Green Sunfish, Largemouth Bass, Rainbow Trout, Smallmouth Bass, Walleye, Yellow Perch

14. **Utah Lake**
    Bullhead Catfish, Common Carp, Channel Catfish, Black Crappie, Largemouth Bass, Walleye, White Bass

15. **Uinta Lakes - Low elevation**
    Brook Trout, Brown Trout, Cutthroat Trout, Rainbow Trout, Tiger Trout

16. **Moon Lake**
    Brook Trout, Brown Trout, Cutthroat Trout, Rainbow Trout, Tiger Trout

17. **Uinta Lakes - High Elevation**
    Arctic Grayling, Brook Trout, Cutthroat Trout, Rainbow Trout

18. **Flaming Gorge Reservoir**
    Brook Trout, Brown Trout, Burbot, Cutthroat Trout, Channel Catfish, Kokanee, Lake Trout, Largemouth Bass, Mountain Whitefish, Rainbow Trout, Smallmouth Bass, Tiger Trout

19. **Strawberry Reservoir**
    Cutthroat Trout, Kokanee, Rainbow Trout

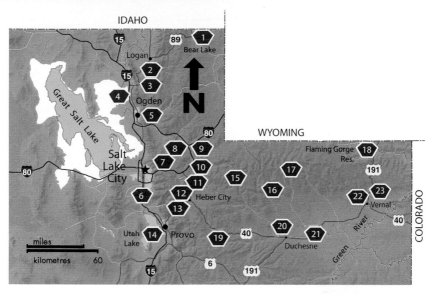

20. **Starvation Reservoir**
    Brown Trout, Cutthroat Trout, Rainbow
    Trout, Smallmouth Bass, Walleye,
    Yellow Perch
21. **Duchesne River, West Fork, North Fork**
    Brown Trout, Cutthroat Trout, Mountain
    Whitefish, Rainbow Trout
22. **Steinaker Reservoir**
    Brown Trout, Bluegill, Largemouth Bass,
    Rainbow Trout
23. **Red Fleet Reservoir**
    Brown Trout, Bluegill, Green Sunfish,
    Largemouth Bass, Rainbow Trout

COLORADO —Best Fishing Sites
Please check fishing regulations, restrictions and guidelines for each location.

1. **Yampa River**
Black Crappie, Bluegill, Channel Catfish, Green Sunfish, Largemouth Bass, Northern Pike, Smallmouth Bass

2. **Steamboat Lake**
Cuttthroat Trout (Snake River), Rainbow Trout

3. **North Park/North Delaney Butte Lakes**
Brook Trout, Brown Trout, Rainbow Trout, Snake River Cutthroat Trout

4. **North Platte River**
Brown Trout, Rainbow Trout, Snake River Cutthroat Trout

5. **Laramie River**
Brown Trout, Cutthroat Trout, Rainbow Trout

6. **Cache la Poudre Lake**
Brown Trout, Cuttbow Trout, Cutthroat Trout, Kokanee, Rainbow Trout

7. **Rocky Mountain National Park (including Colorado River)**
Brook Trout, Brown Trout, Greenback Cutthroat Trout, Mackinaw Trout, Rainbow Trout

8. **Thompson River**
Brown Trout, Rainbow Trout

9. **St. Vrain Creek, Brainard, Red Rock and associated lakes**
Brown Trout, Cutthroat Trout, Rainbow Trout

10. **Fraser River**
Brown Trout, Cutthroat Trout, Rainbow Trout

11. **Williams Fork Reservoir**
Brown Trout, Colorado River Cutthroats, Kokanee, Lake Trout, Northern Pike, Rainbow Trout

12. **Blue River**
Brown Trout, Rainbow Trout

13. **Flat Tops Wilderness Area/Trappers Lake**
Brook Trout, Colorado River Cutthroat (the largest concentration in the world!)

14. **Gore Creek**
Brown Trout, Rainbow Trout

15. **Eagle River**
Brown Trout, Rainbow Trout

16. **Roaring Fork**
Brook Trout, Brown Trout, Cutthroat Trout, Mountain Whitefish, Rainbow Trout

17. **Frypan Creek**
Brook Trout, Brown Trout, Cutthroat Trout, Rainbow Trout

18. **Dillion Reservoir**
Arctic Char (stocked some years), Brown Trout, Kokanee (uncommon), Rainbow Trout

19. **Clear Creek**
Brook Trout, Brown Trout

20. **South Boulder Creek**
Brook Trout

21. **Chatfield Reservoir**
Black Crappie, Bluegill, Channel Catfish, Largemouth Bass, Rainbow Trout, Smallmouth Bass, Tiger Muskellunge, Walleye, Yellow Perch

22. **South Platte River drainage and reservoirs**
Brook Trout, Brown Trout, Cutthroat Trout, Kokanee, Northern Pike, Rainbow Trout

23. **Arkansas River**
Brown Trout, Rainbow Trout

24. **Taylor River/ Taylor Reservoir**
Brown Trout, Cutthroat Trout, Rainbow Trout

25. **Blue Mesa Reservoir (Gunnison River)**
Brown Trout, Cutthroat Trout, Lake Trout, Northern Pike, Rainbow Trout

26. **Gunnison River/ Morrow Point Reservoir**
Brown Trout, Cutthroat Trout, Rainbow Trout

27. **Uncompahgre River**
Brown Trout, Cutthroat Trout, Rainbow Trout

28. **Dolores River**
Brown Trout, Cutthroat Trout, Rainbow Trout

29. **Animas River**
Brown Trout, Cutthroat Trout, Rainbow Trout

30. **Piedra River and Williams Creek**
Brown Trout, Cutthroat Trout, Rainbow Trout

31. **San Juan River**
Brown Trout, Cutthroat Trout, Rainbow Trout

32. **Conejos River**
Brown Trout, Cutthroat Trout, Rainbow Trout

33. **Rio Grande**
Brown Trout, Cutthroat Trout, Rainbow Trout

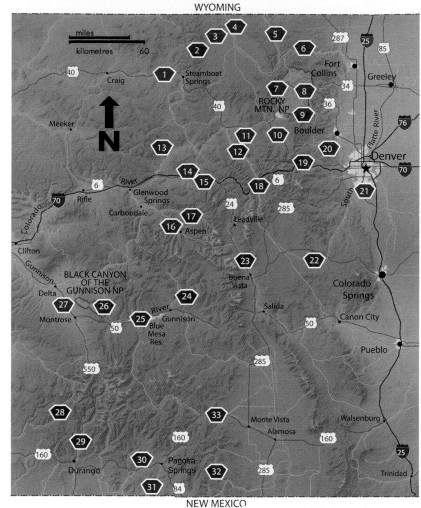

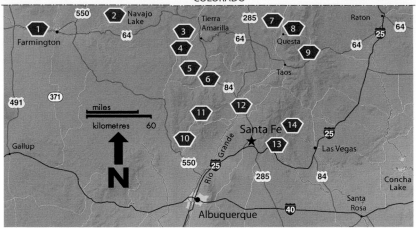

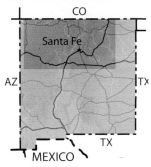

NEW MEXICO
—Best Fishing Sites

Please check fishing regulations, restrictions and guidelines for each location.

1. **San Juan River**
   Brown Trout, Rainbow Trout
2. **Navajo Lake**
   Brown Trout, Rainbow Trout, Kokanee,
   Largemouth Bass, Northern Pike, Rainbow
   Trout, Smallmouth Bass
3. **Heron Reservoir**
   Kokanee, Lake Trout, Rainbow Trout
4. **El Vado Reservoir**
   Kokanee, Rainbow Trout
5. **Rio Chama**
   Brown Trout, Rainbow Trout
6. **Abiquiu Reservoir**
   Channel Catfish, Kokanee, Largemouth
   Bass, Walleye
7. **Rio Costilla**
   Rainbow Trout, Rio Grande
   Cutthroat Trout

8. **Red River**
   Rainbow Trout
9. **Eagle Nest Lake**
   Kokanee, Rainbow Trout, Yellow Perch
10. **Jemez River**
    Rainbow Trout
11. **San Pedro Parks Wilderness lakes &
    streams**
    Rainbow Trout, Rio Grande
    Cutthroat Trout
12. **Rio Grande**
    Brown Trout, Cutthroat Trout,
    Rainbow Trout
13. **Pecos River**
    Brown Trout, Cutthroat Trout,
    Rainbow Trout
14. **Pecos Wilderness Streams**
    Brown Trout, Rainbow Trout, Rio Grande
    Cutthroat Trout

GLOSSARY

alevin: a juvenile fish that is still attached to its yolk sac.

anadromous: a fish that hatches in fresh water, lives its adult life in salt water and returns to fresh water to spawn.

barbel: fleshy "whiskers" near the mouth of some fish that have sensory and chemical receptors; barbels help fish to find food and to navigate in murky waters.

basibranchial teeth: teeth inside the mouth at the base of the tongue that may be present in some trout species.

benthic: pertaining to the bottom of a lake or river.

caudal peduncle: the narrowing of the body, just ahead of the caudal fin (tail fin).

cloaca: the opening at the base of the tail, which the reproductive, urinary and digestive systems open into; also called "vent."

detritus: dead and decaying organic matter.

endemic: exclusive to a particular region and native to that region.

endorheic: a basin in which there are no rivers or streams (above or below ground) to carry water out to the ocean: water only leaves by evaporation or seepage, and consequently the water in these basins is often saline and more vulnerable to environmental pollution.

fin rays: cartilaginous rods that support the fins; fin rays may be soft and branched ("soft rays") or they may be stiff and unbranched ("spines").

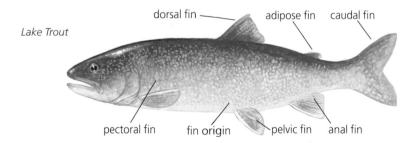

Lake Trout

dorsal fin — adipose fin caudal fin

pectoral fin fin origin pelvic fin anal fin

fluvial: pertaining to flowing water, as in rivers and streams.

gill rakers: thin, fleshy projections located over a fish's gills that help to protect the delicate gills from being harmed by particles in the water; some species may also use their gill rakers for filter feeding.

gonopodium: elongated rays of anal fin modified into a long rod-like projection for transfer of sperm into female cloaca.

gravid: a female fish that is full of eggs.

gular folds: skin fold on the "chin" of a fish.

icthyophiles: fish-lovers.

lateral line: a line of specialized scales with sensory pores that runs lengthwise along the central axis of a fish; the lateral line is a sensory organ that can detect vibrations and pressure changes in the water.

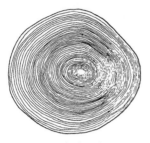
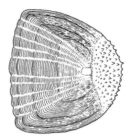

Cycloid scale   *Ctenoid scale*

nares: a fish's nostrils.

natal stream: the stream where a fish was born.

nuptial tubercles: small bumps that can develop on a fish's head and body during spawning.

operculum: the bony flap that covers the gills.

opercle: one of the bones, typically the largest, that makes up the operculum.

palatine teeth: small teeth found on the roof of the mouth in some fishes.

papillae: small bumps found around the mouths of some fish that function similar to barbels, with sensory and chemical receptors that help a fish find food and navigate.

parr marks: dark blotches located along the lateral line of some juvenile trout species.

pharyngeal teeth: teeth located at the back of a fish's throat.

piscivorous: fish-eating.

preopercular spines: spiny projections arising from the "cheek" of a fish.

redd: a nest of fish eggs dug into a riverbed (usually gravel or sand).

thoracic: relating to the chest.

truncate: shorten.

tubercle: a small lump or projection.

tuberculate: covered with tubercles.

zooplankton: very small, often microscopic organisms drifting in the water column that feed on phytoplankton (very small, often microscopic plant organisms) or decaying matter in the water.

REFERENCES

Behnke, Robert J. 2002. *Trout & Salmon of North America.* The Free Press, New York, NY.

Carey, Kip. 2002. *Kip Carey's Official Wyoming Fishing Guide.* Kip Carey Publications, Littleton, CO.

Coad, Brian W., Henry Waszczuk and Italo Labignan. 1995. *Encyclopedia of Canadian Fishes.* Canadian Museum of Nature, Ottawa, ON.

Gilbert, C.R. and J.D. Williams. 2002. *National Audubon Society Field Guide to Fishes.* Rev. ed. Random House of Canada, Ltd., Toronto, ON.

Holton, G.D. and H.E. Johnson. 1996. *A Field Guide to Montana Fishes.* 2nd ed. Montana Fish, Wildlife and Parks, Helena, MT.

Johnson, Dan. 2007. *Fish of Colorado Field Guide.* Adventure Publications, Inc., Cambridge, MN.

Joynt, Amanda and Michael G. Sullivan. 2003. *Fish of Alberta.* Lone Pine Publishing, Edmonton, AB.

Lee, David S., et al. 1980. *Atlas of North American Freshwater Fishes.* North Carolina State Museum of Natural History, Raleigh, NC.

McPhail, J.D. and R. Carveth. 1992. *A Foundation for Conservation: The Nature & Origin of Freshwater Fish Fauna of British Columbia.* Queen's Printer for British Columbia, Victoria, BC.

Nelson, J.S. and M.J. Paetz. 1992. *The Fishes of Alberta.* 2nd ed. University of Alberta Press, Edmonton, AB.

Page, Lawrence and Brooks Burr. 1991. *A Field Guide to Freshwater Fishes.* Houghton Mifflin Co., New York, NY.

Piper, Ti. 1989. *Fishing in New Mexico.* University of New Mexico Press, Albuquerque, NM.

Scott, W.B. and E.J. Crossman. 1998. *Freshwater Fishes of Canada.* Galt House Publications, Ltd., Oakville, ON.

Sigler, W.F. and John Sigler. 1996. *Fishes of Utah:* A Natural History. University of Utah Press, Salt Lake City, UT.

Simpson, James and Richard Wallace. 1982. *Fishes of Idaho.* University of Idaho Press, Moscow, ID.

Tomelleri, J.R. and Mark E. Eberle. 1990. *Fishes of the Central United States.* University Press of Kansas, Wichita, KS.

Varley, John D. and Paul Schullery. 1998. *Yellowstone Fishes: Ecology, History & Angling in the Park.* Stackpole Books, Mechanicsburg, PA.

Wooding, Frederick H. 1997. *Lake, River & Sea-Run Fishes of Canada.* Harbour Publishing, Madeira Park, BC.

INDEX

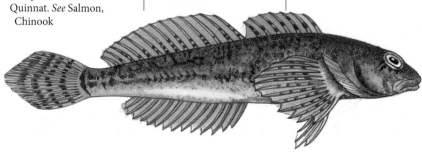

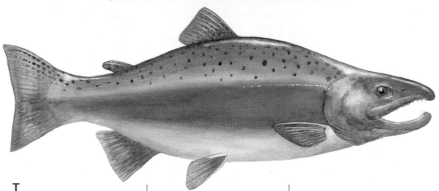

ABOUT THE AUTHORS

MICHAEL SULLIVAN

Michael Sullivan lives in, works in, plays in and loves the wild spaces of boreal and montane Alberta. As a 3rd-generation western Canadian, Dr. Sullivan has heard the family stories and seen the monumental changes (both good and bad) brought about by Alberta's amazing economic development. Passions for wildlife lead him through three academic degrees at the University of Alberta and 25 years of fisheries, wildlife and land-use management with the Alberta Fish and Wildlife Division. Through close working relationships with other landscape management and research agencies (e.g., Parks Canada, the Alberta Conservation Association and the Alberta Cooperative Conservation Research Unit at the University of Alberta), Michael has built a network of strategic learning around the complex interplay between ecological and social systems. This has led to much more appreciation for the sensitive nature of our precious (and totally cool!) mountain fishes. When not being a stolid academic in his position as Provincial Fisheries Scientist at Alberta Fish and Wildlife, he can often be spotted hiking along a stream bank, or skiing up into some remote mountain valley, searching for new stories to tell about the fascinating ecology of our wild spaces.

DAVID PROPST

Since receiving his Ph.D. from Colorado State University, David L. Propst has spent most of his professional career working with native fishes and their habitats in the southwestern United States. As the New Mexico Department of Game & Fish non-game native fishes project leader, he has attempted to balance research and management while ensuring bureaucratic sensitivities are accommodated. His responsibilities in New Mexico have been interrupted occasionally to work with Mexican and American colleagues in the Sierra Madre Occidental searching for "undiscovered" native trout populations.

WILLIAM GOULD

William R. Gould, Professor Emeritus of Fisheries at Montana State University, specialized in ichthyology and freshwater invertebrates. During his distinguished career, he developed the Key to Fishes of Montana, was curator of the fisheries museum at MSU and was assistant leader of the Montana Co-op Fishery Unit. Active in the graduate studies program with over 33 students, he is most proud of the contribution his students have made toward conserving fisheries, wildlife and natural resources. He holds a Ph.D. from Oklahoma State and a Post-doctoral Fellowship from the Marine Lab in Miami. Bill "brought his son up right" (as an avid fisherman), and together they enjoy fishing Montana's Blue Ribbon trout streams and sport fishing in the Florida Keys.